R. C. SHARMA

Mounted Warriors

Other Books by Gene Smith

Until the Last Trumpet Sounds: The Life of General of the Armies John J. Pershing

The Ends of Greatness: Haig, Pétain, Rathenau, and Eden: Victims of History

The Dark Summer: An Intimate History of the Events That Led to World War II

Lee and Grant: A Dual Biography

High Crimes and Misdemeanors: The Impeachment and Trial of Andrew Johnson

The Shattered Dream: Herbert Hoover and the Great Depression

When the Cheering Stopped: The Last Years of Woodrow Wilson

Mounted Warriors

From Alexander the Great and Cromwell to Stuart, Sheridan, and Custer

Gene Smith

John Wiley & Sons, Inc.

Published by John Wiley & Sons, Inc., Hoboken, New Jersey
Published simultaneously in Canada

Photo Credits: Library of Congress: pages 76, 120, 167, 169, 200, 224, 279; National Archives: page 306; New York Public Library: pages 9, 18, 27, 42, 52, 68, 92, 216, 242, 263.

For general information about our other products and services, please contact our Customer Care Department within the United States at (800) 762-2974, outside the United States at (317) 572-3993 or fax (317) 572-4002.

Wiley also publishes its books in a variety of electronic formats. Some content that appears in print may not be available in electronic books. For more information about Wiley products, visit our web site at www.wiley.com.

Library of Congress Cataloging-in-Publication Data:

Smith, Gene.
 Mounted warriors : from Alexander the Great and Cromwell to Stuart, Sheridan, and Custer / Gene Smith.
  p. cm.
 Includes bibliographical references and index.
 ISBN 978-0-471-78332-9 (cloth)
   1. Cavalry—History. I. Title.
UE15.S64 2009
357'.109—dc22

2008047043

Printed in the United States of America
10 9 8 7 6 5 4 3 2 1

Contents

Acknowledgments

The majority of the research for this book was done in the library of the United States Military Academy at West Point. I am indebted to all who so generously helped me there: Alan Aimone, Suzanne Christhoff, Susan Lintelmann, Alicia Maudlin-Ware, Deborah McKeon-Pogue, and Laura Mosher.

Dr. Richard Sommers of the U.S. Army Military History Institute, Carlisle Barracks, was very kind, as was Jeff Flannery of the Manuscript Division of the Library of Congress. It has always been my experience that librarians and archivists are the most forthcoming of people and deserve a place not only in heaven but also in the happy memories of any author they assist.

Finally, I express my thanks to my kind and patient editor, Hana U. Lane, and her extremely industrious associates at John Wiley & Sons.

Introduction

To ride a horse, "This is one of the most important things in the world," wrote the ex–hussars subaltern Winston Churchill. But how many feel that way now? A century and a quarter ago Manhattan had 750 livery stables. In time they became garages or warehouses, and for many years only one gave lessons and rented out mounts that you could take along Central Park's bridle paths. Then the Claremont Riding Academy closed its doors. The building, and more important, the land it stands on are worth $10 or $15 million.

Certainly you can find riding centers all over the country with pampered and cosseted steeds, and people preparing for dressage and three-day-event competitions, and even here and there a hunt club with hounds, yet we speak now but of hobbies. Mounted warfare? "During my presidency," said Ronald Reagan, accepting the 1989 Thayer Award of the United States Military Academy at West Point, "I had a goal I could never fulfill. I wanted to reinstate the horse cavalry." The long in the tooth will recall that Reagan always loved to have his joke. He would have known that West Point's equestrian training for cadets was ended in 1947, its vast riding hall—said to have been at one time the world's largest building—now given over to endless corridors of offices and classrooms. (Yet a colonel once told me that when years earlier as a cadet he had been detailed to escort an ancient returning grad around, the old gentleman halted for a moment, sniffed the air,

1

and said, "I can still smell the horses." The same is said on warm days after it has rained of Buffalo Soldiers Field, just inside the academy's main gate—named for our post–Civil War black cavalry regiments, their men termed by Indians the Buffalo Soldiers for the texture of their hair. The Point's stables stood where now are a great parking lot and athletic fields.)

So what is left today is an expensive pastime for a tiny percentage of the population, racing as a minor sport when compared to football or baseball, mounted policemen in selected cities. And for some a dim image, and in places a scent, perhaps imaginary, of what once, indeed for four thousand years, had to do with brilliance, magnificence, jingle and clatter, glory, snapping guidons, panoply, bugles, the lance and the glittering sabre, and the sabretache and pelisse and dolman and elaborate headgear, the knight, the hidalgo, the chevalier, the Reitritter, the cavaliere, the caballero, the charge like a thunderbolt and whirlwind that shook the earth, the crested shields and feathers and plumes, the smartness and dash and instantly distinguishable sound of tinkling spurs when the horseman was afoot, the "spectacular" and "vivid and majestic splendor" that was possessed only by the cavalry, as Churchill wrote. They wept who saw the final march-past of Fort Riley's horses, this just before World War II, when in the wake of the departing and doomed squadrons there followed in line a smoky and clanging group of little tin-can tanks—the armored cavalry, as it was and is titled. The last horse to die at Riley was interred on his feet, standing erect under the great parade ground.

Now it is gone, all that, and with it the concept that there is that of war which is romance. Who among us today dreams so? Your friends and mine? Were one of them to offer such an opinion—with U.S. troops in Iraq and Afghanistan—we would inquire if prescribed medication usage was being adhered to, or head for the nearest exit. So why this book on war so measurelessly antiquated and distant, so Saturday afternoon visit-with-the-kids to the museum with the armored knight-at-arms or European tour stop at Waterloo and guidebook description of Marshal Ney's disastrously misperceived charge? Have the old black-and-white movies on late-night TV with their depictions of the cavalry coming to the rescue; and tales of Mongol hordes and Assyrians who minus saddle or stirrups got off ten aimed arrows a minute; and Oliver Cromwell screaming and laughing as he and his Parliamentarians rode home; and Alexander, a horse lover in a culture that saw the horse as unworthy of love, lost their appeal? And the last mounted charge of United States history, which found a Japanese waterborne landing party seemingly encountering phantoms from the past from which they recoiled, running back through waves? Who can care?

It is all so unimaginable, so out of time. We can try to believe ourselves when on vacation-time rented steeds not all that removed from Lancelot or Parzifal—never mind the improbability that the next day they suffered such stiffness—but can we really take it all in? I have to reach beyond myself to try to see in my mind's eye the doings that I have attempted to chronicle in this book, to hear the sounds. And I have had to omit multitudes of events, for a book can only be so long. Accepting that my choices as to what I should describe are very much open to argument, I yet offer a work that I hope has two unifying themes.

One is that there is no human activity that over eons has changed less than war. Harold of Hastings's housecarls with their great axes decapitating with a stroke the horses bearing William the Conqueror's archers, Her Britannic Majesty's men riding off in upland punitive expeditions, the horsed Goths' destruction of the footmen Roman legions at Adrianople—it is all of a piece, the objective the same, and also the result.

The other is that horses haven't changed, not fundamentally. We shall in succeeding pages study something of horse furniture— such is the long-outdated phrase—and learn a bit about their conformation, size, and training, but at the last nothing I nor anyone else can say about the horse in war comes anywhere near what is found in the Old Testament, Job, 39: 19–25:

> Hast thou given the horse strength? Hast thou clothed his neck with thunder?
> Canst thou make him afraid as a grasshopper? The glory of his nostrils is terrible.
> He paweth in the valley, and rejoiceth in his strength: he goeth on to meet the armed men.

He mocketh at fear, and is not affrighted; neither turneth
he back from the sword.

The quiver rattleth against him, the glittering spear and
the shield.

He swalloweth the ground with fierceness and rage: neither
believeth he that it is the sound of the trumpet.

He saith among the trumpets, Ha, ha; and he smelleth
the battle afar off, the thunder of the captains, and the
shouting.

I

Beginnings

The creature began as a fox-size and somewhat rabbit-looking entrant into the world departed by dinosaurs less than ten million years before. This was in what we call the Americas, fifty million years gone. Little *Eohippus*, the "dawn horse," lived in moist and spongy primeval forests and went about on spread-out toes. His head, fossils show, was recognizably horselike.

From climatic changes, tropical foliage was replaced by grass, the eating of which required large and strong teeth, the walking or running upon a foot with few and small toes. Limbs were long to provide greater speed to escape pursuers' fang and claw. About twenty million years passed, and by fifty million years ago there was a trimmer body, a longer head, longer hind legs, and teeth of greater grinding ability, and *Eohippus* morphed into *Orohippus*, who became, some twenty-five million years ago, *Mesohippus*. He was all over North America, two feet high at the shoulder, the toes shrinking, the teeth powerful. There followed *Miohippus* and divided branches whose toes were gone in favor of a hoof and whose size reached that of the pony of today, some to be ancestor of the zebra and the donkey, but all of whom vanished from the lands where their common progenitor, *Eohippus*, had arisen.

There is no definitive explanation for their disappearance. There might have been a deadly epidemic, perhaps climatic change, perhaps hunting to extinction by humans, whose appearance in the area coincided with the annihilation of many large mammals, including what we call the horse. He was gone from the Western Hemisphere, the Pleistocene era seeing his finish. When he returned, epochs later, he conquered the land of his ancestors, the inhabitants of which, the Aztecs, beheld in fearful astonishment what appeared to be a new species of being. It went about at great speed on four long legs joined to a monstrous body, topped by a specter glittering with metal and wielding Toledo steel to cut people down in fearsome number and manner. Second only to God, Hernando Cortes wrote his king, "we owe our successes to our horses."

But all that was in the unimaginable future when the ancestors of Cortes's horses, of all horses, migrated from what today we call Alaska to what we now call Siberia. Who knows why some went while others remained behind to perish. Those who left traveled over what was then land and is now water, the Bering Strait, arriving in their new home to play an inglorious role there in the prairie grasslands that reached from Mongolia to Hungary: for millennia, Stone Age Asians saw horses as useful only for their meat and hide. In time, the value of animal power was recognized, and people took to riding donkeys and onagers—wild asses—or having them carry loads. But the horse was no good for that. The anatomy was all wrong. Little weight could be loaded on between the withers and the rear, as carrying capacity had not yet developed. For a rider to sit far back, almost on the croup, as was done with other beasts of burden, was impossible; the animal was uncontrollable and the hindquarters collapsed.

The yoked bullock—the ox—placid, slow, strong, was useful for the transport of heavy goods, and even more so when ingenuity produced rollers that eventually became wheels. Again the horse fell short. The ox could be made to plod along drawing a wagon by being led, or prodded with a stick or flicked with a tree branch, but the horse was unable to do much for being jumpy or flighty and by physical makeup. It was the matter of the collar of the times. It fitted the ox of broad shoulders, but could not be effectively utilized by the horse of slim ones. We can only with great imagination put ourselves in the place of these people so remote from our times, and therefore it seems to us truly incredible that for hundreds of years no one realized that a harness gripping the neck squeezed the windpipe of the horse. It effectively half strangled him. The harder he pulled, the less he achieved.

Archeology does not deal in exact dates and moments, and so it cannot be said precisely when someone, or some ones, came to the realization that the horse was so constructed that in order to pull with any great effect he must push, and that the way to get him to do that was to outfit him with a breast band or a padded collar encircling the whole neck. Then he could get his body up against such and so gain traction. Horses were put to pulling carts.

The herdsmen of times now very long gone knew the merits of selective breeding for their goats, sheep, and cows; in time they applied themselves to improving their horses. It is believed that the domestication of the horse began something like six thousand years ago, perhaps as many as ten thousand, in the East. Some feel the inaugural location was on the Central Russian steppe near where the Dnieper and the Don flow into the Black Sea in what is now Ukraine; others say it was in China or Kazakhstan. It is the teeth of disinterred horse skeletons of prehistoric times that tell the story. Their teeth were worn down by primitive bits. The horse had become man's servant, or perhaps his ally.

There followed what the military historian Sir John Keegan has called "one of the most extraordinary episodes in world history": the amazingly swift exploitation of the horse's drawing capacity in the creation and use of the war chariot.

It is of course no less lamentable than accurate to say that man has always made war. The methodology remained unchanged for thousands of years. Opponents used close-range weapons, the caveman's club, the Iron Age's crude slashing or stabbing device, or at-range missiles—the slung stone, the flung spear, the arrow shot from the bow. The horse-drawn war chariot added entirely new dimensions to armed disputes: mobility and maneuverability of a speed previously undreamed of, and for those facing it a terror hitherto unapproached. Within the space of three hundred years, warfare was revolutionized. Of a sudden there coursed about men battling on foot a vehicle moving at great speed. It carried a driver and an archer, the latter filling the air with arrows fired from his platform. The perfected chariot weighed some seventy-five pounds and sat atop spoked wheels far lighter than the solid ones of transport wagons. When the archer exhausted his stock of arrows, he could be taken back to a resupply point at a speed better than twenty miles an hour. Sometimes a twirling sharp scythe extended from the chariot axle, to devastating effect upon the legs of enemy footmen.

Against this machine no infantry could stand. A line of charging chariots, most drawn by two horses, some by four, the rumble of wheels mixing with the pounding of hooves, the skies darkened with showers of arrows—for more than a thousand years, from around 1700 B.C., chariotry ruled the battlefield. Charioteers were warrior-aristocrats, the foot soldiers they slaughtered almost an incidental by-product of battle. As it is in the nature of war that no weapon remains uncopied for long, all the suzerainties along the eastern shores of the Mediterranean soon maintained fleets of chariots; and soon they competed in improving the product. But there was a limit to how much could be done. The addition of armor for men and vehicle meant a reduction in speed, as did adding another passenger carrying a shield to protect the driver and the archer, whose bow reached a level of development beyond which it could not advance. (The simple bow formed of a single sapling had given way to the composite one utilizing several layers of wood, bone, sinew, and leather to offer far greater hitting power to the arrow it sent on its way.)

There remained room only for the improvement of another chariot component—the horse. War and battle being endemic and constant, dynasties, and the fate of their nations and peoples, depended upon him. The most ancient document we have for his use and care comes from the master to the horses of the king of Mitanni, a vanished domain that existed in present-day Iraq and Syria. The trainer, Kikkuli, wrote his exacting and precise treatise in 1400 B.C., in Hittite, and it was translated into several other languages of the time. He prescribed a seven-month period of training before one of his charges could be put into service. Several types of grasses were named for feed to build up young animals; on the seventy-first day of training a harness was put on for a brief stint of

Armed conflict was terrifyingly revolutionized when horses were taught to draw chariots. *Hittite frieze, circa fourteenth century* B.C.

chariot work, after which, back at the stables, horses were watered and fed. Following the evening distribution of grain, they were again harnessed and galloped over "ten fields." After a time, training was extended to the hours of darkness when the blazing sun was down: "When midnight comes the charioteer harnesses them for a gallop exceeding seven fields." After this they were rubbed dry in the stables and fed two handfuls of hay, one of wheat, and four of barley. They ate hay all night. At dawn the gallop was repeated, and the feeding. If warm after work, they were given salt dissolved in a fire and added to a bucket of wholemeal barley.

The horses must gradually be worked up to gallops of ten, twenty, ninety fields, Kikkuli decreed, and sometimes for a period their feed was drastically curtailed, for they must be accustomed to restricted rations when on campaign. During training they were washed with warm water five times daily, with the routine sometimes replaced by four river baths followed by feed of a scoop of flour preceding the grain offering.

In time Mitanni vanished from history, smashed and then integrated into other states, with little left to tell of its existence and with the location of its buried-under-the-shifting-sands capital,

Washukanni, now unknown. But the words of the master to the king's horses lasted, to be taken to heart by the pharaohs of a succeeding dynasty, and it was a daring use of chariotry trained to Kikkuli's dictates that won for Thutmose II the first battle in history for which there is a detailed record. Some fifteen centuries before Christ's birth, the Egyptian monarch marched ten days through Gaza seeking a combination of enemies, Palestinian and Syrian, concentrated near modern-day Haifa, Israel. He had three possible routes and chose the most dangerous. It is an undying military truism that no move is more hazardous than to snake a force through a thin defile, a pass. Only a small number of men, or in this case chariots, can come through to debouch upon the spot where they will mass for combat, and their issuing forth in dribs and drabs presents an enemy the opportunity to pick them off at his leisure.

But the pharaoh chanced all on getting unexpected and undetected through the Aruna Pass, a mountain notch so slim as to allow but two chariots at a time to go forward side by side. Records say the pharaoh had one thousand. His was bedecked in silver and gold. The move was never anticipated by the enemy. Thutmose swooped down upon them, his chariot in the center of a great line, the assemblage so terrifying a surprise that the Palestinians and the Syrians instantly fled, allowing Egypt to dispatch of but a tiny number of them—eighty-three. The remainder took refuge in a nearby fortress, from which they shortly emerged for complete surrender. The battle—really an utter rout—took its name from the fortress town near where it was fought: Megiddo. "A place called in the Hebrew tongue," says the book of Revelations 16:16, "Ar-ma-ged'don." We shall, much later in this book, again visit the Aruna Pass and Megiddo to take note of, three thousand and more years on, what was if not the final battle of Biblical depiction, then the world's last great use of horses in war, a victorious cavalry general in a time of the internal combustion engine and airplane using Thutmose as a guide to what he should do and did.

Our culture bequeaths to us a concept of what it is to sit a horse, and of those who through history have done so. "There is the indefinable superiority of the man on horseback," wrote the last U.S.

Army chief of cavalry, Major General John Herr, and we know what he meant. The European plaza with bronzed hero-king atop rearing charger, the American square, roundabout, or boulevard adorned with mounted general—we've all seen it. Even Adolf Hitler, who loved machinery and hated horses to the extent that he was enraged when the Berlin crowds at a Third Reich march-past before the war reserved their most fervent applause not for the clanking tanks and half-tracks and tractor-towed artillery pieces but for the two leftover horsed regiments dating back to the Great King, Prussia's Frederick II—even he, Hitler, authorized and permitted the dissemination through postcard and poster a representation of himself in gleaming white armor holding a lance and seated on a charger.

So it is perhaps a matter of some surprise that there was a time, the time of chariots set upon fleeing foes, and before, and after, when to sit upon a horse was the last thing from a mark of distinction. "My lord should honor his position as a king, and not ride," recommends a letter written around 1789 B.C. and sent by a protocol chief to King Zimrilim of the city-state of Mari on the Euphrates River. Only barbarians from uncivilized tribes went about mounted on horses; people of advanced cultures did not. Militarily, the ridden horse was of secondary or even lesser importance, transporting a messenger to the real warriors, the charioteers, or used for a scouting trip seeking water sources. There were no saddles and no stirrups—they would not be seen for two thousand years. Ancient Fertile Crescent monument and temple pictorial and incised-stone representations show riders sitting on a pad placed far back over the horse's haunches, legs dangling. Sporadic attempts to use mounted riders in a more meaningful manner included two men riding side by side, one to hold the reins of both mounts, the other to fire arrows. It was a clumsy business, a duplicate of chariot warfare minus the chariot, and minus the relatively stable platform the vehicle offered as opposed to the jolting of a moving steed.

The great chariot battle of the epoch, of all epochs, took place some two hundred years after Thutmose went through the Aruna Pass, in about 1275 B.C., when Egypt's New Kingdom's Ramses II, with two thousand chariots, met the Hittites' king, Muwatalli, who had thirty-five hundred. It was at Kedesh along the Orontes River, in western

Syria. The Hittite vehicles were heavier than those of the Egyptians, and transported besides driver and archer a man carrying a shield for protection of the other two. The fighting swirled across a battlefield some eight by four miles. We can almost see the clouds of dust and hear the rumbling wheels and the sounds of wounded men and horses, the latter emitting when mortally stricken a scream very much like that of a woman in agony before falling with lips drawn back in ghastly parody of a grin. Some thirty-five thousand men on foot supported the chariots, swinging and thrusting bronze axes and swords.

The affair was considered something of a draw, although perhaps the Egyptians had a bit the better of it, and afterward the contestants agreed on what is seen as the world's first peace treaty, a signal novelty when battles were fought to merciless annihilation by one side or the other. ("The commander-in-chief of the king of Elam, together with his nobles, I cut their throats like sheep," a warrior-monarch of the day had his court historiographer record. "My prancing steeds, trained to harness, plunged into their welling blood as into a river; the wheels of my chariots were besplattered with blood and filth. As for the sheiks of the Chaldaeans, panic from my onslaught overwhelmed them like a demon. They passed scalding urine and voided their excrement in their chariots.") For miles along the lines of retreat, bodies turned rotten and then skeletal, the few of the defeated who survived taken for lifetime slavery, the irrigation systems of their lands destroyed, fruit trees cut down, granaries burned. The times knew no idealistic rationalization for the making of war, nor ideological cant; fighting was for new acquisitions: water sources, provinces with subjects for the king, and glorious depictions of his exploits on monuments and temples (Ramses II was portrayed as personally cutting down thousands from his chariot). For the underlings, a measure of acclaim, gold, jewels, spices, silks, exotic foods, slaves, land, position, was a reason to participate.

And to expand its area and destroy its foes in such manner and for such reasons there arose the first realm to use the horse in war in a way that we find familiar. (The story of the Trojan Horse holding concealed soldiers is of most doubtful historical accuracy; it is fanciful myth, really, as is Homer's allegation that the chariot was used solely to transport men and not as a firing platform. But then,

Homer wrote four hundred years after the siege of Troy—Hissarlik in modern Turkey—and was, after all, a poet, not a war correspondent.) That realm was Assyria, and its business was war. Its army was "an instrument of terror, using torture, massacre and mass deportation." Its King Sennacherib's description of his chariot-borne destruction of Elam and the Chaldaeans struck the right tone when telling of the 691 B.C. doings. The Assyrian Empire, eventually encompassing parts of what are today Arabia, Iran, Iraq, Turkey, Syria, and Israel, and reaching its peak around 1000 B.C., had the first army to possess the serious logistic arrangements of supply depot, transport force, and water-bridging equipment. It had battering rams and siege engines. Its professional soldiers were paid regularly and issued mass-produced and standardized weapons.

The Assyrians were the first peoples to realize that a horse could be ridden in organized battle, not simply used to draw a chariot. By the eighth century B.C., selective breeding had developed a horse smallish by modern standards, never reaching more than fourteen hands, but of sufficient carrying capacity to bear a man in a forward seat position, weight over the animal's shoulders. It was for the Assyrians to grasp that a group of mounted men would be able to operate in mountain terrain or over uneven ground impossible for chariots. Cavalry was born. The men were archers, for to spear an enemy while holding on to the weapon in a world that did not yet know of the saddle or stirrups meant a danger of being propelled backward over the horse's haunches, landing on the ground and effectively at footmen's mercy. (One could safely fling a spear, but then one was disarmed.) Striking with a sword raised the possibility of falling sideways off the horse when the target was hit. But as to reach into their quivers for an arrow, fit it into the bow, and send it on its way meant giving up the use of their hands for controlling the horse, the Assyrian archers had to perfect a degree of horsemanship unapproached by organized forces in succeeding eons. In their era, it is true, archers of tribal steppe peoples in the East did in individual cases equal Assyrian performance, but not in formed, disciplined, trained units—what we would call the troop, squadron, regiment. It is said that only the Plains Indians of the American West exactly duplicated the equestrian bow-and-arrow capabilities shown in

Assyrian bas-relief and clay tablet portrayal; but the Indians, brilliant as their riding was, did not, as we shall see much later, perform in military order under a hierarchy of what we would call officers.

The Assyrian bridle connected to a loose rope with a tassel that lay atop the horse's neck where it met the withers. A rider could use it in an emergency for turning or halting. But the primary riding aids were knees and legs pressing movement directions upon highly trained horses, each of whose value was listed as equal to that of thirty slaves or five hundred sheep. The savage and brutal state whose interests rider and mount served—the Assyrian empire has been compared to Nazi Germany—was able to project power hundreds of miles from base and move at speeds of advance not equaled until the arrival of the motor age.

But empires fall, particularly empires whose borders have been extended too far, whose ruling class contends too much for personal treasure and too little for the country, and whose subject peoples hate their overlords. A conglomeration of enemies pressed upon Assyria, and its great city of Nineveh was taken; and in 605 B.C. its last king was defeated and its power passed to Babylon, and then in time to Persia. The leadership of Persia was secured to who later was referred to as Darius the Great by: his horse. We have it from Herodotus, acclaimed through the ages as the Father of History. With five other men, Darius was in contention to be named king of Persia. It was 521 B.C The group agreed that they would ride in darkness to a particular place, there to await the dawn. "He whose horse neighed first after the sun was up should have the kingdom," Herodotus related.

This high gamble involving horses is perhaps to our manner of thinking a curious fashion of selecting a leader. We also cannot but be aware that not every horse race, of any type, is uniformly contested with complete purity. Darius went to his groom. "Oebares, if then you have any cleverness," Herodotus tells us the aspirant to the throne said, "contrive a plan whereby the prize may fall to us."

"Truly, master, if it depends on this whether thou shalt be king or no, set thy heart at ease and fear nothing: I have a charm which is sure not to fail."

"Hasten to get it ready."

That night Oebares took a mare in heat to the place where the six riders would convene to await the sunrise. He tethered her there and returned with his master's stallion to lead him round and round the mare, eventually letting them couple.

The next day, as the sky began to lighten, the six riders came to the appointed spot, where unknown to the others, Darius's horse had mounted the mare and where now he sprang forward and neighed. "Just at the same time there was a flash of lightning, followed by a thunder-clap. It seemed as if the heavens conspired with Darius, and hereby inaugurated the king; so the five other nobles leaped with one accord from their steeds, and bowed down before him and owned him for their king." This is the account that some of the Persians gave of the contrivance of Oebares; but there are others who relate the matter differently.

"They say"—this of Oebares—"that in the morning he stroked the mare with his hand, which he then hid in his trousers until the sun rose, when he suddenly drew his hand forth and put it in the nostrils of his master's horse, which immediately snorted and neighed."

There was never any equivocation about the manner in which Darius gained his throne, for after making advantageous marriages, Herodotus says four in number "according to the notions of the Persians," with two of his brides sisters, and "with his power established firmly throughout the kingdom, the first thing he did was to set up a carving in stone, which showed a man mounted upon a horse, with an inscription in these words following: 'Darius, son of Hystaspes, by aid of his good horse and his good groom Oebares, got himself the kingdom of the Persians.'" Proving an enterprising and dominant ruler, he was nevertheless, said Herodotus, regarded by some as a huckster. From his population he soon extracted a donation of 360 horses along with 500 talents of silver, a talent in roughest estimation about the value of one or two thousand dollars today. "Of this sum one hundred and forty talents went to pay the cavalry which guarded the country, while the remaining three hundred and sixty were received by Darius." We can infer from this the position that cavalry, as opposed to the more favored chariotry, occupied in his mind, for 140 was a pretty paltry amount when compared with other incomes and donations amounting to 9,540 talents in addition to 100 boys and as many maidens, 500 eunuchs, and 1,000 talents' worth of frankincense, ebony logs, elephant tusks, corn, and fish.

The Persian Empire came to dominate the heartland of civilization and beyond, its forces deploying war elephants and ships in addition to infantry and cavalry and the dominant chariotry. It fell afoul of, and was destroyed by, one whose destined road was, as with Darius, pointed to by: a horse.

2

Xenophon and Alexander

Philip of Macedonia was king of a country backward, crude, and barbarous, its cultural level far below that of the sophisticated Greek city-states to its south. The king had a son. The boy was twelve when Philip took delivery of a highly touted and expensive horse, Bucephalus, the purchase price being thirteen talents, $20,000 to $25,000 today. The animal upon first viewing appeared a poor investment; he cavorted about and permitted no one to mount. The king told a groom to take him away.

But the king's son asked for a chance to get on board. There was, both the historians Pliny and Plutarch tell us, a general laugh from King Philip's retainers, the monarch joining in. "Boy," he asked, "do you boast of greater knowledge than your elders and betters? Do you think you are more skilled in horsemanship?" The youth persisted with his request, and his father told him to go ahead and give it a try.

Alexander—for so was named he who has gone down in history with "the Great" affixed—

> immediately ran to the horse, and taking hold of the bridle, turned him directly towards the sun, having, it seems, observed that he was disturbed at and afraid of the motion of his own shadow; and then letting him go forward a little, still keeping the reins in his hand, and stroking him gently when he found him begin to grow eager and fiery, he let fall

his upper garment softly, and with one nimble leap securely mounted him, and when he was seated, by little and little drew in the bridle, and curbed him without either striking or spurring him. . . . Presently when he found him free of all rebelliousness and only impatient for the course, he let him go at full speed, inciting him now with a commanding voice, and urging him also with his heels.

Horse and rider circled a courtyard and then raced out into a field. When they returned to King Philip and the others, the king said, "My son, you must seek out a kingdom worthy of you; Macedonia is not broad enough for you."

Six years later, at eighteen, riding Bucephalus, Alexander commanded his father's cavalry against a combined force of Athenians and Thebans. Far outnumbered, he feigned a retreat, which drew his enemies forward; then his horsemen came in from the side to shatter them, and Macedonia ruled all Greece. Two years later, his father assassinated, Alexander was king. His first attention was to his army. He divided his cavalry into light and heavy units, the first to flit

Greek history knows no parallel to the love a king felt for his war horse. *Alexander the Great on Bucephalus, Pompeii mosaic.*

about, the second to charge en masse, and added what became known as dragoons—men trained to fight on foot as well as atop a horse. (Debate over such soldiers has lasted more than twenty-five hundred years, opponents terming dragoons an assault to logic: either a man believed that aboard his oncoming steed he could overrun a footman, or he believed that by standing fast he could unseat and then dispatch a rider coming at him. To hold both concepts in mind simultaneously was impossibly self-contradictory, critics said, and say.)

Alexander outfitted his heavy cavalry in mail armor hanging from the shoulders and issued them long spears despite the danger that use of the same might unseat them; his light cavalry had no mail, and flung javelins or shot arrows. Both carried short swords for slashing, without sharpened points. There were a variety of cuirasses of breast and back piece made of metal, ox hide, or stuffed linen, and a selection of helmets, some with protective visors for the eyes and cheeks or a neck protector, the crest done up with plumes of feathers or horsehair, a horsetail streaming from the lower section. Riders carried small round shields brilliantly colored and emblazoned with varied devices. King Philip had favored a wedge-shaped formation for his charging heavy cavalry, but his son saw that as unwieldy, bulky and slow, and too much a massed target for enemy arrows, and substituted a shallow and extended order. "Alexander ranks the first of cavalry generals," says the historian J. Roemer in his important 1863 work, *Cavalry: Its History, Management, and Uses in War.* (The author is identified on the title page as "Late an Officer of Cavalry in the Service of the Netherlands.") The young king's personal attitude toward horses, or at least one horse, was at odds with that of all other men of his times. For Greeks had no love for horses, the concept of riding for pleasure not existing, and the sole example in all Greek literature of love between horse and man is that of Alexander and Bucephalus. The horse permitted besides his master only a particular groom to mount him, disdaining all others, and when arrayed for battle in protective armor forbade even that groom a seat on his back.

Bucephalus knelt for Alexander to get on him—other riders vaulted aboard or used a bent-over slave as mounting block—and to get off. On campaign in the Caspian, "in the land of the Uxians," the chronicler Arian tells us, "this horse vanished from

Alexander"—stolen by bandits—"who thereupon sent a proclamation throughout the country that he would kill all the inhabitants unless they brought the horse back to him. As a result of this proclamation it was immediately brought back. So great was Alexander's attachment to the horse. Let so much honor be paid by me to this Bucephalus for the sake of his master."

Even though Alexander was alone among Greeks in personal devotion to a horse, the area's horsemen of the period mastered riding, as the frieze of the Parthenon shows in representing men of flawless seat and perfect form. The riders had for written advice the words of Xenophon the Athenian, who authored his *About Horsemanship* in around 365 B.C. Unlike Kikkuli, who directed his attention to horses destined to draw chariots, Xenophon concerned himself exclusively with riding them. The hoof, Xenophon wrote, was the first thing to be considered when estimating a horse. "For just as no part of a building would be serviceable even it should have wholly fair upper parts if it lacks the right sort of underlying foundations; so also no part of a warrior's horse would be serviceable, even if it should have all the other parts good, but should be unsound of foot, for in no way could it use its good parts." He discussed bone structure in great detail:

> They must not be excessively straight like those of a goat, for then they are too stiff, and jolt the rider and chafe his legs too much; neither, indeed, must the bones be excessively low, for the fetlocks would be skinned and made sore should the horse be ridden on clods or stones.
>
> The veins and the flesh should not be coarse, otherwise when ridden on hard ground perforce they are filled with blood and become bigger and the legs are thickened and the skin is made to stand out. And if this goes slack the cannon bone also often gives way and makes the horse lame. If the colt bends its knees supply when walking, you should expect it will have supple legs for riding too, for as time goes on they will all bend in the knees more supply. And suppleness is justly esteemed, for it makes the horse with stiff legs less apt to stumble and less wearying.

Antiquity's premier equestrian authority, his words studied for millennia and still taken into account today, Xenophon wrote that the horse's neck should grow out from the chest and not droop forward "like that of a boar," but should be erect like that of a rooster, "and should be pliant at the poll, and the head should be bony and have a small jaw." He discussed the withers, ribs, loins, head, eyes, ears—all of the conformation going to make a warhorse. He spoke of gentleness in breaking and training the animal "so that men shall be not only liked but longed for by colts." He had advice about stabling, feed, exercise, grooming, attentive washing. ("You must wet the forelock, too, for when long hair hinders the horse from seeing but it does ward off irritating things from the eyes. And you must know, too, that the gods gave this hair to a horse as a defense for the eyes, instead of the big ears they gave to donkeys and mules.")

He then followed with instructions for bitting and bridling, mounting, riding with the legs straight and body upright (thus "able to throw more vigorously"), and finally with his most important decree: "A warrior's horse must be tried out in every which way war also will try it out. They are these: jumping ditches, jumping over walls, jumping upon banks, jumping off of banks, going uphill and going downhill, and running obliquely—these are to be tried out, for all these things prove whether its heart is steadfast and its body sound." Xenophon prescribed that only stallions should be used in war, and utilized with as little whipping and spurring as possible, for such could "frighten them into confusion. This is the way horses behave that are fretted into ugly and ungraceful action. But if you teach your horse to go with a light hand on the bit, you will make him do exactly what he himself delights in." Xenophon's tips stand up today: it is said that our greatest jockeys could almost ride with reins of delicate silk instead of strong leather, and in the show ring, the acclaimed dressage rider uses motions almost undetectable.

Of the brilliant horse, Xenophon wrote, "gods and heroes take note, and men who ride them appear superb. Such is the horse that rears up beautifully, or admirably, or wonderfully, so that no one, therefore, either goes away or gives up gazing as long as it exhibits its brilliance." Such concepts and such views occupied the mind of Alexander the Great. His Companion Cavalry unit was formed of the elite of the nation, young nobles educated not only militarily but in a manner to ready them for eventual duty as statesmen and diplomats of the empire he would establish, that greater realm for which his father said he was destined the day he first mounted Bucephalus. For a thousand years liege men on horseback looked back to the Companion Cavalry for precedence and example. It represented fealty, rank, class, the superiority of the horseman to the man on foot, the serf and peasant plodding along the ground.

Its members surrounding him at all times, Alexander in battle performed alike the duties of the junior officer and those of the commander in chief. A cavalry leader must. Always in the thick of things, he possessed a sense of timing unexcelled in history, knowing through instinct exactly when to launch an attack. Timing is the essence of success in war—Napoléon said that a single moment can decide a battle, that the smallest thing sometimes decides the argument—and with cavalry there can never be hesitation. Sometimes it came to Alexander that he must strike early, as in the Battle of the Granicus in western Anatolia, when before most of his troops were up and ready he splashed through waters with the Companions, white plumes on his helmet identifying him to friend and foe, and up a bank to where Persian horsemen were, the son-in-law of Darius III commanding. He put his spear through the man's face. A second Persian leader swung a battle-ax and sheared off a portion of the king's helmet, along with one of the plumes, but Alexander hurled him off his horse and drove a weapon through his cuirass and into his breast. Another enemy raised a weapon, but one of the Companions severed his arm from his body. The battle was effectively over, for after such a display of speed, determination, and ruthlessness the thirty-five thousand Persians and their twenty thousand Greek auxiliaries broke and ran. Alexander sped his horsemen after them. No victory was held complete without a cavalry pursuit, the purpose of which in Alexander's time and for centuries afterward was to cut down the fleeing enemy, to kill as many soldiers as possible or at least incapacitate them and leave their final slaughter to the infantry coming up behind. Fifteen thousand of Alexander's opponents died at the Granicus.

One year later, in 333 B.C., he again faced Darius III, at Issus, on the Gulf of Iskenderun in present-day Turkey. He was outnumbered by three to one, but his cavalry swung left and came driving into the Persian flank to scatter them. The slaughter of the enemy is estimated at fifty thousand. Alexander turned south, conquered Egypt, and met the Persians again at Gaugamela in northern Iraq. They had two hundred chariots, for the charge of which they had leveled and smoothed an area eight miles square. There they stood in place. And waited for four days. While at the Granicus Alexander had been precipitous, attacking with the Companions with almost no support from the rest of his army, at Issus he hung back. Then he moved on masse across the face of the Persian line.

Darius unleashed his chariots, only to find them charging into air. There is a time when to be nimble is to win all; and Alexander had drilled his men in sidestepping away. As the chariots came on, they were met from two sides by flung javelins. Then, with the Companions, Alexander rode into the gap that the Persians, with their useless advance, had themselves created. He had split their army. Darius had come to the battle with fifteen chariots carrying his children and their governesses and governors, with his mother and wife and two hundred relatives, with squads of eunuchs and concubines, with mules pulling wagons loaded with valuables. All turned and ran for it, Alexander on Bucephalus galloping after. He was in golden ceremonial armor. As at Issus, the slaughter is estimated at fifty thousand men. The battle marked the end of the chariot age.

Self-anointed now as pharaoh of Egypt and king of Babylon, Alexander styled himself also as king of Asia, where at northwest India's Hydaspes River, now the Jhelum, he met a host marshaled against him by King Porus, the leading rajah of the Punjab. Porus had one hundred elephants, against which even Alexander could not make his horses stand. (Time would prove, as Hannibal of Carthage showed centuries later, that horses could come to take elephants in stride, even as, yet more centuries on, they could learn not to rear at the sight and sound of an automobile. But it took long training in the case of the elephants, and exposure from birth to cars in later days.)

Alexander of course was aware of the menace the elephants presented, even if they potentially presented no less a menace to the archers and spearmen carried in howdahs atop them. For if wounded or panicked they could run amok, trampling friend and foe indiscriminately. (It was a common practice to outfit each mahout, the man who directed an elephant, with a metal spike to hammer into his charge's brain if it became unmanageable.) Alexander divided his forces, taking his horsemen in a circular route to attack from the rear while having javelin throwers assault the elephants from the front. King Porus's army wavered. The Companion Cavalry came in with a rush. The battle was won.

But it came with a price for Alexander the Great. It was not the inconsequential wound he suffered, but the ones to his horse. An enemy javelin protruding from Bucephalus's neck and one from his flank, Plutarch tells us, "almost drained of blood, he turned, carried his master from the very midst of the foe and then and there fell down, breathing his last tranquilly now that his master was safe." Alexander buried him with full military honors and said that even as he had named cities for himself, he would alike do so for Bucephalus one day. The horse was more than twenty-five years of age. Three years later, not yet thirty-three, the king was gone. He left no heirs. His subordinates took to divisive and destructive quarreling among themselves, and in short order his great empire, which included much of Asia and parts of India, North Africa, and Europe, became, as did many that preceded and succeeded it, a memory only. From a place insignificant in his time, a village along an Italian riverbank, arose an empire that dwarfed his.

3
Barbarians and the Age of Chivalry

The Roman attitude toward horses in war is difficult to get into focus. After Darius III's chariot disaster at Issus, the use of that once-dominant weapon largely vanished. Rome employed not a one in combat, and it was a surprise to Julius Caesar when in 55 B.C., landing on the Kentish beaches, he found a few harassing his force. Although the revolt against Roman rule a century later led by Queen Boudicca is commemorated in London by a heroic sculpture showing her in a scythed chariot, her fight was entirely unsuccessful, the losses of the two Roman legions putting down the rebellion amounting to four hundred men as opposed to the Britons' tens of thousands, one source saying eighty thousand. Yet the greatest reward Imperial Rome offered to anyone not of the emperor's rank involved a chariot. The honor was called a Triumph. It had to be voted on by the senate. By its terms, a general winning a great victory with a stipulated number of enemy casualties was permitted to lead his troops into the city, an act otherwise expressly forbidden. Behind them, in chains, marched or were dragged captives to be ritualistically strangled. For three days Rome celebrated the Triumph. Bedecked in victor's wreath of laurel and other adornments, the general rode throughout in a four-horse chariot.

Racing the vehicles was an immensely popular Roman sport; the Circus Maximus, where contests were held, was several times larger than the Colosseum. Chariot racing was a team sport, one group against another. In one celebrated competition, adherents of the losing team displayed disappointment so intense that the authorities ordered a mass turnout of troops to halt rioting that resulted in thousands of fan deaths, and doubtless deaths of folk innocent of affiliation but caught up in the chaos.

Race riding over the jumps or on the flat never came close to chariot competition popularity, and in fact the Romans were indifferent horsemen. Mountainous Italy was not horse country, and the city become ruler of the world never developed leaders above mediocre in handling cavalry. Its horsed soldiers were almost never of Italian origin, and equally rarely citizens, but recruited from outlying lands integrated or conquered. Rome's military supremacy was based upon such discipline as saw a legion of infantry advance upon an enemy in eerie silence, forests of spears showing, the men protected by shields so close one to the other as to present an impenetrable turtlelike shell. A legion of Augustus's time had 5,300 footmen and but 120 cavalrymen. After the long, slow, cadenced, infinitely menacing advance, the legion broke into a sudden disciplined rush, the men screaming. Few could stand against this. On the outskirts, the trifling cavalry's contribution was as much moral as physical, a vague background threat. At least the uniforms and the armor were impressive, the horsemen frequently wearing metal masks, the horses also, both terrifying in an otherworldly, ghostly fashion to an enemy usually a mass of barbarians as ill equipped as they were trained. The stirrup as yet uninvented, Roman cavalrymen used a four-horned saddle that offered substantial support for the legs and the seat.

Yet the long-held belief that riding was for barbarians and not the civilized lived on. For a time there was a unit that went by the name of the Order of Equestrian Knights, which like the Companion Cavalry recruited only the high born, but eventually it petered out. It was the infantry that counted in Rome, and the engineering troops constructing catapults to fling great rocks—plus dead horses and dead enemy soldiers, or sometimes their cut-off heads—into besieged points. The cavalry of disciplined foes usually ran rings around the Romans. Hannibal habitually turned legions' flanks with his horsemen and unleashed cavalry ambushes. On occasion he won battles using no infantry at all, remarking that Romans performed as though they and their horses were tied up hand and foot. "The Carthaginians owe not only their victory at Cannae," wrote the chronicler Polybius, "but all their victories to the preponderance of their cavalry." At the battle of Carrhae in Syria, in 53 B.C., seven thousand Parthians, entirely cavalry, annihilated a Roman force of thirty-nine thousand, killing twenty-four thousand and making captives of the rest. Often Roman generals took positions in hills rather than risk a plains encounter during which enemy horsemen might well overwhelm them. An indication of lack of faith in their cavalry was that sometimes they used horses to carry an infantryman behind the rider, the foot soldier leaping down to get into action when the enemy formation was reached.

Barbarians—the horse peoples of the East.

Rome in time tried to amend its cavalry delinquencies, and eventually fielded a force of two hundred thousand horses. Their riders were overwhelmingly of barbarian origin and from the East, of uncertain loyalty to Rome. It was their mounted kinsmen who in the end so ravaged the empire that the city for which it was named became a broken relic of a mere twelve thousand inhabitants living in the ruins of past glory, the fallen statues and arches, the shattered obelisks and columns. The empire divided itself, with the capital of its eastern segment at what is now Istanbul, then Constantinople, abutting the very edge of civilization. Beyond was the vast steppe country three thousand miles across, where dwelt nomadic horse peoples. One group was the Huns, warlike, fearsome, brutal and brutish. The horse had come into his own in their midst, and they literally lived on their mounts, eating, sleeping, and attending to natural functions without getting off. It is said that their women conceived babies on horseback, and gave birth to them there. If a Hun had to travel a hundred yards on an errand, he did not walk, but vaulted onto a horse. At birth an infant boy was plunged into freezing water to harden him; afterward he may never have washed again, and it is said one could smell an approaching Hun force at a distance of twenty miles. Boys' faces were slashed to produce scars likely to inspire fear in a foe.

The Huns' hardy little mounts knew no grain, for their owners were anything but farmers. Warriors mostly rode mares, milking them five times a day for sustenance and sometimes fermenting the liquid into an alcoholic drink. (The Hun choice of gender in a mount is strikingly opposed to the views of another horsed people, the Arabs, who held that a battlefield was no place for women— mares and fillies. Arabs also felt it would be an intolerable affront to a warhorse to geld him.) If out of water and on the move, Huns sliced a vein in a horse's neck, drank, then sewed up the wound. (They also ate horses, steak tartare having its origins in the Hun custom of tenderizing the meat beneath a rider's saddle.) Warrior bands traveled great distances without stopping, one raid covering 180 miles across the Carpathian Mountains in deep snow without a bite of food for man or animal. Behind riders came replacements for fagged horses, the mass trained to follow along. A man might have ten horses available to him, Marco Polo noted.

These raiders usually began a movement in early winter, when frozen waters permitted passage over them and agrarian societies along the way could be counted on to have stored grain available for plunder. In addition to feed for their horses, Huns regularly demanded and received bribes to keep the peace; the eastern segment of the Roman Empire, Byzantium, paid out thousands of pounds of gold. In the fourth century A.D. their masses moved in unstoppable force against members of the Ostrogoth and Visigoth tribes, who seeing themselves likely to be annihilated, asked Byzantium for permission to cross its borders to escape.

The request was reluctantly agreed to, and the Goths came over, weapons surrendered as a condition of entry. Then word spread that the supplicants were actually in collusion with the Huns. There was panic at what may have been only a false rumor, but it hardly evaporated when Goths, outfitted with newly created weapons, went on a Grecian rampage. Valens, emperor in the east, moved to restrain them. He fell upon them at their camp outside Adrianople, now Edirne, in western Turkey. The Goths were perhaps inferior to the Huns as mounted warriors, but it was they who now put paid to what was left of the glory of Rome. It was 378 A.D. Byzantine infantry legions whose predecessors had conquered the world and marched their eagle emblems to the edge of civilization and beyond were now found wanting. When Valens attacked, the Goth cavalry was away on a raid. They returned "descending from the mountains like a thunderbolt," recorded the historian Ammianus Marcellinus. The horsemen poured on the foot soldiers and folded them in upon themselves, mashed them together to form an unmissable target for arrows, spears, and swords. So tightly packed that their dead were unable to fall to the ground, they suffered losses from the suffocation of men crushed by their fellows. All around swirled the barbarian horsemen, alternately crashing in. Forty thousand soldiers died, their emperor also. "Such was the battle of Adrianople," wrote the historian Sir Charles Oman, "the first great victory won by that cavalry which had now shown its ability to supplant the infantry of Rome as the ruling power of war.

"The Goth found that his stout lance and his good steed would carry him through the serried ranks of the Imperial infantry. He had become the arbiter of war, the lineal ancestor of all the knights of the Middle Ages, the inaugurator of that ascendancy of the horseman which was to endure for a thousand years."

Thirty-two years later the Goths rode upon Rome to do with it and its remaining inhabitants as they would: "sack" is the word customarily used. Such would occur again as the Lombards and the Vandals came, the "horse people," as they are always termed.

Then came the horse people whom the others feared, who terrified the others, before whose relentless mounted warriors the world quailed and whom the world has not forgotten. Attila's horses, "the innocent agents of the harm they were to do, the little rough-coated ponies," wrote Sir John Keegan. But their master? He had no political impulse to build an empire, no affiliation with nor desire to unite under his rule other tribes. He was no conqueror of new lands. He and his reveled in the slaughter—the loot was welcome but incidental. "The horse and human ruthlessness," Keegan said, "together thus transformed war, making it for the first time 'a thing in itself.'"

The Hun force was entirely a cavalry one; it had no infantry, no engineering, no commissary, no capacity to lay siege to a fortified town. But departing from modern-day Hungary, it swept across Europe as what was called the Scourge of God, leaving where it went blood, columns of smoke from burned settlements, mountains of bodies. Attila was in 451 A.D. within an ace of watering his horses or at least bathing them in the English Channel when a patched-together force of Franks, Burgundians, Saxons, displaced Visigoths, Alans, and remnants of the Romans fought him to a draw at Chalons, in northeastern France. He went back to the Rhine, to come again the following year, this time to Italy. (Word of his coming so terrified people along the Po River that they raced for safety to the islands that became in time the city of Venice.) Two years later he died. That both his sons soon followed, Keegan remarked, "is the last news we have of the Huns." They were, say the members of a five-person team that studied their times and tactics, the historians Simon Anglim, Phyllis Jestice, Rob Rice, Scott Rusch, and John Serrati, "ugly men who spent their lives on the backs of their ugly horses, hooked-nose animals with long bodies, narrow faces, bent backs, long manes, scrawny muscles, skinny haunches and wide hooves." But the animals "were also even-tempered, bore wounds well, were trainable and willing to work and capable of withstanding cold and hunger." Before the terrible flaming star they had brought went out, they confirmed what Adrianople had shown: the horseman was now master of the field.

The Huns left in their wake a Europe torn, disordered, impoverished, with the Romans' largely depopulated cities in ruins and the outlying settlements piles of ashes whose fields were given over to thorns and brambles and saplings as they turned into empty forest. The cowed and cowering peasantry lived in habitations akin to animals' dens, with what passed for the local gentry in hardly a better situation. There were no national states and no national armies, but in their stead the marauding brigand who knew no law and no restraint. Upon a world that had known classical Greece and great Rome there descended desolation, anarchy, brutishness. The Dark Ages.

But even in squalor and deprivation and insecurity, people seek or produce structure, and so rulers of a sort came into being. Men of a commanding disposition claimed from the traditions of Roman days the designation of a noble, assembled bands of retainers, and built themselves strongholds. Their retainers were coarse strong-arm men, the strongholds no more than a crude wooden fort. In this morass of a Europe so unrecognizable to the modern eye, this "slum," as H. G. Wells called it, war was the recognized order of things. But not what we now think of as war. Rather there was perpetual brawling after the fashion of today's urban street gang contending with perceived enemies from down the block over petty spoils and "turf" and "respect." The thuggish leader attacked his neighbor the other noble, who struck back. (Their descendants sit today in the House of Lords as the 18th Earl of This, His Grace the Duke of That.)

Then this distasteful violent squabbling suddenly became a far more efficient and disciplined business. For at last the stirrup came into existence, and that made all the difference. The man atop a horse could brace himself to impale a foe with a spear knowing that there was little likelihood of being rammed back over his mount's rear at the moment of contact. He could swing a sword sideways and down without fear of ending up on the ground.

Soon this revolutionary invention became commonplace, investing a horsed combatant with not only a physical but a moral advantage. He could wreak enormous havoc while glaring down from a great height at his lessers. He was a horseman, the heir to the vaguely remembered Companion Cavalry of Alexander the Great and Rome's Order of Equestrian Knights. The stirrup banished instantly and forever the notion that it was for vulgar barbarians to ride. Replacing that view was the concept that it was given to a higher class of man to make war atop horses. How did the stirrup find its birth? That cannot be said from this range in time. Its earliest representation is found in an Italian church sculpture dating from the late eighth century, although it may have been seen in China earlier. Also unknown is when the saddle with a very high pommel in front and cantle in back arrived to make the mounted man even more formidable, his seat as secured in place as his stirruped feet.

There had from earliest times been armor made of metal or thick leather; now, with not all the craftsmanship of antiquity forgotten, warriors went at their work draped in a robe of chain mail capable of stopping even the best-aimed arrow. But the hauberk, as it was called, hung heavily on the shoulders, swung about awkwardly, and impeded movement. Those who could afford the expense commissioned artisans to create plate armor painstakingly hinged to allow pliancy of the rider's limbs and joints, and so shaped that an enemy arrow or spear would slide away upon contact. Face-covering headgear was adorned with plumes, feathers, and horsehair after the manner of Alexander and the Romans. You will know from childhood storybooks and have seen in museums or on a European castle tour the prime figure, the supreme representation of what the historian J. Roemer termed "the ten centuries which intervened between the fifth and fifteenth, a night of misty darkness only occasionally lit by sparks from the knightly sword." Yes. The sword of the knight in shining armor, from whose pointed tip his boy child was offered the first bite of food, was his symbol of honor, identity, meaning, self. Then there was his horse.

"The scope of *Parzival*"—Percival in English—"is greater," the authorities Helen Mustard and Charles Passage have said, "than

that of any other medieval work except Dante's *Divine Comedy*."
We meet at the outset a boy adept at flinging a javelot, the short
version of the javelin, which he uses to bring down game for his
mother to cook. He meets King Arthur, who tells him, "the simple lad" in Wolfram von Eschenbach's romantic-poetry epic written early in the thirteenth century, that perhaps one day he may
become a knight. In a meadow, Parzival speaks with the Red
Knight, whose "armor was so red that it made your eyes red to look
at it. His swift horse was red, all red was his horse's hood piece, red
samite [rich silk fabric] were its trappings, his shield was redder
than a flame, all red was his gambeson [tunic worn under armor]
red was his spear shaft, red was his spear point, his sword had been
dyed red."

Parzival says, "Now give me what you're riding on there, and all
your armor too; I have to be made a knight in it." He grabs the red
horse's bridle and is answered by a blow from the butt end of the
red rider's spear. Blood flowing, he flings his javelot. "Just where
the helmet visor had holes, there the javelot went" to penetrate an
eye. The knight dies, and Parzival dons his array, and in full armor
leaps upon the horse. "People still talk about his swiftness." He gets
the horse going and they are away. "There were certain qualities in
his horse: it took great exertion as nothing; cold weather or hot, over
rocks or tree trunks it never sweated from travel; there was no need
to tighten its girth by a single notch even if he rode for two days. In
his armor that simple man rode further that day than a sensible man
without armor would have ridden in two. He rode at a gallop, rarely
at a trot, because he did not know how to check the speed."

Parzival comes to a castle whose pinnacles and towers he takes
to be growing from the ground. Perhaps the great King Arthur has
planted them, he reasons—his mother's garden crops never grew so
tall. He is made welcome by castle inhabitants. "At one spot in the
courtyard they all begged him to dismount." And here is the point.
He refuses to do so. "*A king bade me to be a knight, and I don't care
what happens, I'm not going to get off this horse.*" Dismounted, he
knows, he is nothing, armor or no, and when finally he gets off and
removes the armor the people are shocked to see that his clothing
is that of a peasant. They make to throw him out, but one prince

sees beyond, saying, "Bring him his horse, and me mine, and every knight his."

They go to a meadow and "there some practice was had at riding." Parzival's benefactor displays how to use spurs, how to apply pressure from the thighs, to lower a lance and bring up the shield to ward off an opponent's thrust. "Be so good as to do the same," he says. Parzival proves a wondrous learner: "He knocked a stout rider, who was no slight fellow, back off his horse. A second jouster had come up, and Parzival had taken a fresh strong spear. He rode at full career head on and his host's knight did not keep his seat but measured the field in a fall. Little bits of splintered lance were all around. In this manner he struck down five of them. All who saw him ride and who understood these matters said that he had skill and courage." The prince instructs him in the knightly virtues of honor, compassion, humility, and mercy mingled with daring, manliness, generosity, and cheerfulness, and takes him as sent to be his son. Parzival goes on to great things.

This improbable story is jammed with anachronisms. King Arthur lived in the sixth century, long before elaborate armor, stirrups, a castle of the type depicted, jousting, and, most telling of all, any slightest concept of that knight's code Eschenbach details. But the dreamy, fanciful tone was precisely correct for when the author wrote his saga, the days, we are told, When Knighthood Was in Flower. And what the knight-errant was meant to be lives on yet. Once, Manhattan's Claremont Riding Academy received a call from a man wishing to rent a horse for a couple of hours. He arrived bearing a suitcase from which he extracted a plastic costume replicating the armor of a knight, casque and all. Putting it on, he rode to a Central Park destination where a group that included his lady friend had gathered for a picnic. Dismounting to kneel in his finery before her, he asked her hand in marriage. That she consented goes without saying. Friends in on his plan produced bottles of champagne. She was his lady fair, he her knight-at-arms. The horse was central to the matter. Without the trusty steed—getting out of a cab, say—he would have looked at best eccentric. With the horse he was Prince Charming.

To be a knight in the Middle Ages called for a professed devotion to Christianity, the display of correct manners, adherence to ritual, a talent for speaking well and in a light fashion—*persiflage* is the word that comes to mind—and the ability to proffer elaborately polite remarks to an enemy. A knight was expected to demonstrate extreme gallantry to women of his own class, to dance well, and to appreciate music and art. His word of honor was absolutely unquestioned (as contrasted with those below him, who might say anything and to whom nobody of import listened in any case). It was required that he show lordly largesse so that all would know he was generous. (Yet we may quail at what sometimes that involved: both Raimond de Venous and Raimond de Saint-Gilles, Count of Toulouse, on separate occasions ordered the burning to death of thirty horses for the comfort of guests gathered in cold weather.) Perhaps it was precisely the value of the incinerated offerings that made for such rich and noble display of largesse, for it was the horse above all that defined the knight, as even the simple Parzival knew. "To be a skilled rider was before all things necessary for a knight," we are told by Maurice Keen, who wrote on chivalry, the word deriving from the French *cheval*—horse. "His own peculiar place was on horseback."

Training for youths of correct birth began when at age seven they were sent to serve as page to some noble lord. They would have learned at home to display perfect manners and to sing, walk on stilts, fly kites, play shuttlecock, and shoot marbles. And ride. From very earliest childhood it was drilled into them that this constituted the highest ability and calling and that its mastery would typify their future existence. Even as toddlers taking lessons on a pony, they were lifted aboard their fathers' warhorses and put to going around the courtyard.

It would have been a long way down should a child fall off. (But to accept injury with disdain was part of the code.) For by the High Middle Ages, selective breeding had produced a colossal horse. The destrier, a word instantly comprehended then while generally unknown even to knowledgeable horse people now, stood eighteen hands high. Other horses of the period were twelve or thirteen hands. But the destrier was bred to carry, in addition to his rider, armor draped over his entire body save for the lowest part of his

legs. The animal was always male, for it was considered a degradation for a knight to ride a mare or a filly. With the rider seated in a
high-cantle-and-pommel saddle, completely encased in metal, and
equipped with lance, sword, dagger, and perhaps a mace, the total
weight assignment approached four hundred pounds. The mount's
ears and tail were docked. His most highly prized color was white.
His name derives from the Latin for *right*, the hand with which the
knight's squire led him.

It was to becoming a squire that the page's path led. At fourteen he left off service in his master the lord's kitchen, where he cut
up and handed out the food, and in the stables, where he groomed
and washed the horses, picked out their hooves, and poured out
their grain, work aimed at teaching obedience and humility. After
solemn consecration services the page became the squire, his duties
to care for a knight's accoutrements, the armor, weapons, and stable of horses: the destrier, of course, plus palfreys for his attendants
and his lady, perhaps a draft horse to pull a wagon with gear, and
for his younger children, a hobby or two, it being a miniature animal from which we derive the word *hobbyhorse*. One thousand five
hundred productive acres were required to supply adequate income
for a knight's activities, work done under the supervision of his
steward or bailiff. It was proper form that he never pay attention
to the source of his funds. It was beneath his dignity. Similarly, he
could never think of involving himself in any kind of commerce, or
trade, or indeed do for the most part anything but prepare for war.
(It was considered by his associates a matter worth remarking that
the emperor Charlemagne attempted to learn to read. His instructor was a monk who had taken the tonsure instead of the helmet,
the only choices available for those of gentle birth. That the emper-
or's attempts met with indifferent success is hardly surprising, for he
had more important matters to attend to: in the forty-three years of
his reign there was but one twelve-month period without a military
campaign.)

Knights were constantly at war, one baron against another, or
fighting with the duke. Their endless encounters saw peasants dragooned in to be shoved forward in battle wielding axes or scythes
or pitchforks. They did what they could for a while, seen as coarse

brutes and churls by the mounted knights behind them who then unleashed a charge, not infrequently riding down those wounded or too slow to get out of the way. It was cavalry warfare at its most inelegant, skillful tactics entirely lacking and without central control or discipline, simply a lances-lowered frontal attack. A knight's prime aim was to bring down one of his opposite number. It was of little import if one skewered a screaming swineherd with a couched lance secured under the arm and equipped with a crosspiece six inches from the tip to prevent penetration so deep as to make withdrawal difficult; what was wanted was that an enemy displaced from his saddle be secured by one's squire, attendants, or vassals. Only rarely were knights slain in battle. There were two reasons: first, it was extremely difficult to get a weapon through armor and into a vital point. Second, such an act was undesirable. A knight off his horse but alive was worth far more than one dead: he could be held for ransom.

A captured man was treated well while negotiations regarding a price went on; indeed, sometimes a warrior was permitted to go home upon his pledge to return with money raised by mortgages, loans, or donation from the liege lord above him in the feudal scale. In a lawless world where pillage, rape, arson, and despoilment were the regular potion of knights' social inferiors, the courtesy they meted out to one another can be seen as the beginning, if only in most limited scope, of respect for established rules and the honoring of treaties.

In another, far later, era, a man of knightly demeanor, "the realized King Arthur" and of such heredity as to warrant being called "the son of a hundred earls," said, "It is well that war is so terrible, else men would grow too fond of it." Robert E. Lee's concept would have seemed risible to the knights of the High Middle Ages, including, we may be sure, the Lee ancestors. A friar once told Sir John Hawkwood that he wished him peace. "May the Lord take away your alms," the knight replied. "Do you not know that I live by war and that peace would be my undoing?" War was Sir John Hawkwood's daily bread, in a physical, moral, and spiritual sense, as it was for all who rode great destriers to seek glory and meaning. It was so for the inheritors of their way of thinking, as we shall see, an example—to leap far ahead—being a cavalry commander remembered not for his brilliant achievements but instead for his catastrophe, George Armstrong Custer. He wished there could be a battle every day, he wrote. Or, to go even later into a future of which of course the Middle Ages could know nothing, there was George S. Patton, with his string of a dozen and a half polo ponies for riding in a game that closely replicates horsed combat as he declaimed that he was in fact a reincarnated knight-at-arms sent to do with tanks in World War II what in an earlier life or lives he had done with horses.

How do we not remember them, those of the Age of Chivalry, the drama, the romance, the pageantry, the shade and substance, the *color* of the glittering knight and man-at-arms on his towering armor-clad stallion! And their view of themselves, impossible for us to emulate but which grips us and lives in our thinking. He who with his fellows and liegemen checked the pagan Vikings coming off their raiders' ships and the savage Magyars of braying horns and clashing cymbals to accompany their terrifying wolflike cries of *"Hui, hui!"* as they came on their shaggy ponies from the Hungarian plains saw himself as more than the embodiment of courage, loyalty, honor, grace, courtesy, largesse: he was the designate of a Heaven-appointed task. It was to free the Holy Land from the grip of non-Christians. To go on crusade as defender of the faith also offered opportunities for stupendous garnering of the storied treasures of the East. There was no contradiction. Professed high piety and war for booty characterized the High Middle Ages. (Knights slew by the thousands Jews met along the way to Jerusalem for both reasons.)

The tactics the Crusaders brought to the desert of the Holy Land had not changed for hundreds of years. The low footmen did such work as they could, and then the knights thundered upon the foe, a line of dancing lance tips preceding them. To those defending what they saw as the lands of their Moslem birthright—had not Mohammed ascended to Heaven from here, riding a great white horse?—the Europeans were crude, brutal, rough, coarse in their war-making. The Seljuk Turks adhered to the light cavalry tactics the West had forgotten, or let go. They rode not great destriers but lightly built, nimble little horses. To swerve from the straight course that one learned in jousting and practiced on the battlefield was for a knight to court dishonor, but their Holy Land opponents knew no such code. They did not stand and fight like men, they were not stalwart and honorable warriors, so the Crusaders thought, but instead devious, sneaky villains who came in on an angle, shamelessly ducked away, and then came again. And who could not be defeated. Yet for two hundred years the knights, in their surcoats worn over armor to protect against the blazing sun, persisted in their Crusades, finally to give it up. Sitting his charger just outside Jerusalem, Richard the Lion-Hearted turned his gaze away, unwilling to look upon the city that he and his could never take.

When they got home, the knights returned to what they considered real wars, and when not on campaign, they played at war. Throughout the twelfth century there were weekly tournaments all over Western Europe in tents and pavilions, with great crowds circulating around the grandstand erected for the elite, food offered for sale, singers and musicians, jugglers and acrobats and stilt-walkers, magicians and fortune-tellers, beggars and gamblers, hustlers and prostitutes. Opponents moved their mounts to each end of the straight barrier along which they would ride one against the other, lowered their helmet visors, and went at full tilt. To enter the lists and be the focus of the pageantry so entirely alien to the impoverishment and the wretched short life of poor food, clothing, and shelter of the era's overwhelming majority was to show who and what you were, "with the painted shields," said R. Rudorff, "gaily colored banners, embroidered and richly patterned surcoats, coats of armor and crests, the elaboration and language of the coat of arms, the display of armorial bearings."

Jousters rarely suffered serious injuries, for lighter lances were used than those of the battlefield—hence the splinters that covered the ground when Parzival first displayed his prowess. A victorious knight could expect two rewards for felling his opponent. Parzival had been informed that winners would "be praised before the women," and Rudorff confirms it: "None of these ladies esteemed any knight worthy of her love but such had given proof of his gallantry in three several encounters at tournaments. Thus the valour of the men encouraged chastity in the women and the attention of the women proved an incentive to bravery"—which does not seem illogical.

The second inducement for tournament success: with your opponent supine on the ground, put there by your lance, your squire and attendant took charge of his horse. It was not impossible that the fallen man might find women despite his defeat, but a carefully bred and highly trained destrier was hard to come by. Negotiations for the sale of the steed by victor to loser commenced as moneylenders came forward. The destrier usually went home with his original owner.

The magnificence of the knight cannot be overstated. It was dishonor, infamy, disgrace for him to be overcome by someone socially below him; indeed there was a way such a calamity could be averted: he had the right to anoint others as knights in an emergency. Unhorsed in battle by a mounted enemy, the Earl of Suffolk asked if he dealt with a knight. The answer was no.

"I should like you to be a knight before I surrendered myself," the earl said, and dubbed his conqueror on the spot before going off into captivity. When a knight died, his horses followed his body for last service and interment, riders atop them dressed in the deceased's colors and bearing his weapons. A rider in full armor clattered down the nave of the church to deposit at the choir screen what were called funeral achievements, the dead man's livery, hatchments, banners, and pennons. The other horses stood in the church's rear. It was understood that they belonged there. The dead warrior, after all, had aboard them appealed to the god of battles, the lord of hosts.

It went on, almost to the decade, one thousand years, the reign of the unquestioned supremacy of cavalry, and then it was over.

4
The High Middle Ages

If the Battle of Adrianople in 378 A.D. that saw Byzantium's infantry legions overwhelmed by Goths on horseback marked the beginning of cavalry's dominance, the Battle of Crécy in 1346 can be seen as ending it. The contestants at Crécy, on the French northern coast near Calais, were not the petty brawlers of earlier days but representatives of national rulers, France's Philip VI and England's Edward III. The French knights formed up, impatiently taking the point of honor and not letting foot soldiers precede them. They charged.

The English infantry was equipped with longbows, six-foot weapons of elm, hazel, basil, and yew. They did not shoot the light arrows of the nimble mounted riders met in the East, but three-foot missiles with a range of four hundred yards. A skilled man could get off up to twelve a minute. And England had skilled men. Any sport other than archery had been banned nine years earlier.

The French cavalry took the bowmen as low and base cowards fighting at a distance and did not comprehend the immense hitting power of what flew at them. Even as downed horses and men began to litter the field, the flower of French chivalry launched more than a dozen charges—sixteen, says one account. The number of English arrows flying through the air was such as to remind one chronicler of a snowstorm. Only once were the French able to menace a portion of King Edward's army, the one commanded by his sixteen-year-old son, called the Black Prince for the color of his armor. Word of his predicament was brought to his father. Edward declined to send aid. "Let him win his spurs." He did. It was all very well for England to conquer by virtue of its footmen, but a royal prince's doings must be seen as those of a horseman.

The French kept going down as the arrows penetrated their armor and that of their horses, but they kept coming on in adherence to the medieval belief of their class that one does not count the cost when living up to the code and the canon, but rides at the enemy. Their losses at Crécy approached twenty thousand men and thousands of horses. No less than five thousand lords, nobles, and knights fell from their mounts. The English took casualties of some two hundred dead and wounded.

There were technological innovations in addition to the deadly longbow, psychological and social ones also, with which time and history brought about the end of an era and a way of seeing the world. Among King Edward's forces was a contingent of mercenaries from Switzerland. They rode no horses. They were solid and sturdy countrymen plying their trade for whoever would meet their price, and their workman's tool was a pike sixteen feet long. It was an ancient piece of military knowledge that the way to hold off cavalry was to present a forest of spears with butts securely planted into the ground, but putting that concept into practice was another thing. To hold formation while the first faint drumming of hooves grew greatly louder, the shouts of the approaching riders became more clear, and

Medieval warfare.

the glitter of the weapons shone—that was not so easy. To expect a group of the usual footmen of the High Middle Ages to hold fast before oncoming horsemen was to ask the impossible. They saw the lords and masters born to make war on horses who when off them wore fine furs and silks as beings of another world, who danced with high-bred ladies and then visited the villages they owned to require of a maiden whose marriage would be celebrated the next day the Right of the First Night—her virginity. A neighboring knight might come to a peasant's small holding for slaughter, rapine, and arson knowing no law would restrain him. How could these downtrodden possibly stand against a knight, a noble, a man of war? They broke ranks and ran.

It was quite different for the Swiss. They were professionals, not serfs force-marched into combat from their piddling muddy farm-steads. Their unwavering thicket of pikes made a horse stop short and "prop" with suddenly straightened forelegs, the rider propelled forward out of the saddle to be dealt with when on the ground. Or he found himself assaulted with halberds, pikes with a hook attached to the shaft to yank him off his horse so that a knife could be shoved through a gap in his armor. There were no brother-in-arms courtly negotiations about ransom—he was put down like an animal.

The Swiss did not wear the elaborate and beautifully worked armor of those who represented the Age of Chivalry, and they were innocent of the concepts that went along with its wearing. When they moved forward, in rigorously disciplined fashion, a mass and not a collection of individuals, they did so to the slow cadence of beating drums, keeping their alignment and showing no gaps. Their fighting for hire became practically the national occupation, and they made infantry an element of offensive warfare for the first time since the days of the legions. They were soldiers.

As such they displaced those who for so long had ruled the battlefield. But not entirely. The knightly heavy cavalry lingered. Pride, class consideration, status, and reluctance to use weapons below a knight's dignity—all that was not easy to cede to new times. So the horseman kept a place in the armies of the three hundred years following Crécy, but it was as diminished as the armor that replaced that of the Age of Chivalry: full head-to-toe gave way to just a helmet and a cuirass—a strapped-on breastplate with, some-times, back protection. Soon enough gunpowder came to supplant the bow and arrow. The first cannons were reasonably effective at leveling squads of foes, although they were very slow, requiring some fifteen minutes to get off a shot. But they were a nail in the coffin of what had been. "What is the use any more of the skill at arms of the knights," bemoaned a French chronicler of his times, "their strength, their hardihood, their discipline, when such weapons can be used in war?" The early gunpowder weapon for individual infantrymen, the harquebus, was heavy, cumbersome with its requirement for a sup-porting stand to hold it, inaccurate, unreliable, and although not as slow as a cannon, very measured in its rate of fire. But it gave rise to what gave cavalry new life: the pistol.

Here everything was compressed. There was no muzzle longer than a man was tall, no laborious scrubbing out of great quantities of powder residue, no burning fuse or lanyard, and little concern about long-range accuracy. The pistol was invented so that horsemen could swoop down to within almost arm's length of foes, or at least beyond the reach of a pike, fire a shot into their faces, draw a second pistol, fire again, and be off so that a second wave of riders could come in and repeat the process. Timing and control of the horses was required as riders came on in a line and then wheeled off in a circle, reloading as they went as another part of the circle arrived—an elegant "elephantine ballet," said the historian J. Roemer. Pistoleering resurrected the cavalry, and the pike speedily vanished, the bayonet its heir. But while more readily brought into play, short and easily deployed up or down or in any direction, the bayonet could not bring down a high rider whose aim as member of a cavalry unit was to break an infantry formation. Once in through a gap, the horseman with his sword could wreak havoc on footmen jammed in one upon the other. His horse participated in the action with hooves. Today's visitor to Vienna's Spanish Riding School can visualize when viewing what are termed "airs above the ground" what a kicking warhorse contributed to its master's cause.

But with his organized forces far less dominant than in the past, when individualized showing meant everything, and far more susceptible to disaster, the cavalry commander of the seventeenth century and later was required to perform at a standard much higher than previously known. What he required is difficult to define. Courage, yes, that is a given. The French knights at Crécy had courage. They had nothing else. "It is magnificent, but it is not war," said one of their fellow countrymen centuries later of an equally mindless galloping effort with not a possible chance of success. (We shall study what occasioned the remark in good time.)

Beyond bravery, the leader of horse needed dash, élan, willingness to be at the front, that concern for men that makes them go with you, discipline, the desire to lay the enemy in the dust, and a sense of the tradition of cavalry, the poetry and rhythm of its nature, the theme. Yet possession of all these can be held by the foolish and the deluded. Something more is needed.

"Character is the first thing," said the Prussian military theorist Alfred von Schlieffen. Napoléon once remarked that his subordinates could ask anything of him but time. The two concepts join in at least a partial definition of what made the great cavalry officer for the centuries that followed the independent knight-errant Age of Chivalry, when commanders became as important to their formed, professional armies as Alexander the Great was to his. It is the man, not the men, who wins, Napoléon said.

As regards time, the cavalry officer never has any. The infantry or artillery leader deals with the fact that there is no swift manner of bringing to bear a force necessarily slow-moving and encumbered with a long train of supplies. Arrived on a field, he issues orders for preliminary deployment, arranges lengthy or brief bombardments, maneuvers about seeking the place and the moment for attack. It is an entirely different matter for the officer of both heavy and light cavalry. He is of no use if he lingers about with no role to play, and with horses and men difficult to conceal unless a fortunate sheltering hill or forest is nearby, he is in danger of decimation by missile fire of arrows in the far past and shells more recently. He cannot hug the ground, and so once in view of his target, the heavy cavalry leader must immediately launch his brute-force charge and the light go flitting and darting.

So each must think fast and have the moral strength to make a decision the price for which will be paid by his men and horses and, if wrong, by his reputation and place in the world. And perhaps by his blood. For even at the most elevated levels, an officer of cavalry, like Alexander exchanging sword slash and spear thrust with Persian enemies, must be as one with the most forwardly placed of his riders. To think fast and take immediate and often personally dangerous action is the product of ownership of the highest attribute a great leader of horse knows, what has always been termed the "coup d'oeil." It refers to the capacity to look at the ground upon which you will fight and see in a moment what you will do, how the enemy will likely react, and what your response will then be. Through your mind there must of an instant come speeding the condition of your horses; how recently they were fed, watered, and groomed; the amount of wear endured upon their approach whose possibly debilitating rate of march you must take into account.

The hills before you; the woods and streams and boulders or enemy fortifications; felled trees, trenches, fences; the enemy troop armament and deployment and artillery pieces; their commander whose mind and spirit and determination you must read across the lines; any recent losses perhaps limiting your strength; the capabilities of your subordinates and the state of their morale as influenced by recent events, their personalities, physical condition, and experiences of the recent or remote past—all this must be digested and utilized for ruling what you will do, all to be governed at the last by how you know, and what you know of, yourself: the coup d'oeil. "The moment I see the enemy my dispositions are already made," said Prussia's Hans Joachim von Ziethen, who was called the Dragoon King.

This cannot be taught. Its dispatch and installation in a particular mind, and that mind's character and spirit, are determined by— who knows?—genetics, God, fate, placement in a location and time when it can be used. (The mathematical mind superior to Einstein's may have existed in some prehistoric African tribesman, and the inhabitant of a medieval Romanian ghetto may have owned baseball capability superior to Babe Ruth's, but who would have known or taken note?) What we speak of is, as with the two examples just adduced, genius. Napoléon said that he had fought forty battles and knew no more at the end than he had at the beginning. What he had was not learned, but simply *was*.

It is an act of arrogance to attempt to understand a genius. If we knew why Mozart was Mozart, *our* works would be known in every concert hall. The best posterity can do is chronicle a genius's doings, and those of the near genius, and that, as will be seen in succeeding pages, is the attempt of this book. The men to be discussed almost universally aimed from early days to be soldiers. There is a notable exception. He was middle-aged by our standards before he ever gave a thought to military matters, even oldish by those of his time, but his name is known to anyone who has the tiniest knowledge of world history—for reasons having nothing to do with horses. Yet there is a school of thought holding him to be perhaps the greatest cavalryman who ever lived. We will get to him in a moment. Like that of other men of his brilliance, his ability was wholly innate and inborn, but he learned from a great contemporary.

5
"Terrible as Death, relentless as Doom"

Sweden in the 1600s was weak and backward, with little industry, few exports, and neither great population nor important cities.

It had one asset: the Snow King, the Lion of the North. History remembers him as the father of modern warfare. Gustav II Adolf was seventeen when he came to the throne, a youth who loved music and composed hymns that are still played today; he was fluent in several languages, including Latin and Greek; was notably abstinent when it came to liquor; and had, it is authoritatively recorded, one sexual encounter prior to his marriage, which was a very happy one. He entered his country's army when he was eleven. He loved horses. "A born cavalry leader," says one of his biographers.

That might have been his basic self, but he expanded and built greatly upon it. When he became king, warfare for a thousand years and more had been static. Once there had been the art and method of an Alexander and then a Julius Caesar, but since the end of the Roman Empire only on-and-off brutish barbarian invasions of the West followed by constant petty disorders seeing one lord's pickup, raggedly put together horde ravaging that of another, or thuggish freebooters going around in search of loot. The professedly high ideals of the knight were, as we have seen, the only light shining in the Dark Ages. Charles VII of France had in 1445 constructed something similar to what we recognize as an army, his organized force paid by the state and therefore of a different nature from raiding parties dragooned into service by feudal lords, but it was hardly less brutish. (Drilling his so-called troops, Charles in one day rode to death two horses.)

The domination of cavalry declined as the pike and then gun-powder came to the battlefield, but the tone of soldiers remained what it had been for a millennium. Hundreds of years later, speak-ing of his men at Waterloo, the Duke of Wellington defined them in his haughty way as "the scum of the earth, enlisted for drink and booty." That characterization universally applied elsewhere, but not to the soldiers of Gustav Adolf, for his manner of see-ing them was distant from Lord Wellington's. The king of Sweden provided regular and on-time pay, and rewarded with promotions men who did well while punishing in a fair and just manner those who shirked their duty. He arranged for the best food and medi-cal attention possible, and was the first general since Roman days to outfit soldiers in regulation uniforms. (For a thousand years pre-vious, aggregations of battlers selected before a fight some token to set one group off from the other, a white armband or a green branch or a red cord.) The king toned down the apparel of offi-cers, who in the fashion of the period adorned themselves with flashy scarves and belts, giving a gaudy rakehell appearance, and issued simple light helmets to go with a light cuirass, and some-times just a wide-brimmed felt hat. For his horses were not to be forced to carry one ounce of unnecessary weight, being as they were on average twelve hands high. He did not wish them to draw more than was wise, and used teams of three dozen to pull each of his artillery pieces, which threw shells weighing forty-eight pounds.

Gustav Adolf created a highly organized force, upon whose mem-bers he enforced a regard for other people, civilians and armed ene-mies alike. Before him, war had been conducted by leaders deadly and destructive, likened to wolves, highway robbers, the Huns. They left deserts in their wake. To rape, burn, sack, wantonly destroy, steal, and ravage was common to them and to the marauders serving under them. ("Do you think my men are nuns?" asked Count Tilly, one of the king's greatest opponents.) The Swedish ruler gave his men no license for looting or pointless destruction, but he gave them victory after victory. His little country humbled great Russia and powerful

Poland, and in the Thirty Years' War, armed with money sent by France to stalemate the Hapsburg Empire, saved the Reformation for Protestantism against a host of Catholic enemies.

He did what he did by amalgamating his musketeers with his cavalry, the training and equipment for whose members cost man for man nine times that of an infantryman. Horse and foot slowly moved forward in unison, with the musketeers shooting openings in enemy formations so that the suddenly swift horseman could ride in to fire pistols and lay about with his sword. The quick charge was made from a very short distance away, generally around fifty yards, a complete reversal of the heavy-knight lumbering advance of the past, for Gustav Adolf esteemed horsed maneuver and mobility as far more important than the Middle Ages tactics of brute weight. This concept united with arrangements for a sure base and lines of communications to produce the first modern commander campaigning with well-considered and broad plans.

He was personally reckless in battle, but when his subordinates urged caution he replied, "Believe me, I love a comfortable life as well as any man, and I have no desire to die an early death" while continuing to put himself in danger. At the Battle of Lützen in Saxony, near Leipzig, in 1632, he detected a menace to his forces from a gathered assemblage of enemy riders in dark cuirasses. "We must charge yonder black troopers, or they will do us some serious mischief," said the king, and put his horse through mist and over a ditch and at them (exhibiting "the true cavalry spirit," per one of his biographers). When he arrived, they fired their pistols, striking him in an elbow and through the body. He lost control of his horse and slipped from the saddle, one foot caught in a stirrup with the horse dragging him across the ground. His foot came free, and the people asked his name and situation.

"I am the king of Sweden," he murmured. The days of ransom and of gallantry toward a downed foe were gone; he was shot again and run through with a sword. His charger's caparisons were covered in blood, and when the horse galloped to the Swedish troops, they knew what had happened. Gustav Adolf was taken away amid wailing fifes and muffled drums playing "Adeste Fideles." All that has followed since on every battlefield originated with him, who died in the classic manner of making war, *à cheval, au gallop*. Soon enough there arose the first of the legions of great soldiers to be his student.

In 1599 the Williams family of Huntingdon, England, welcomed a baby boy. The Williamses did not call themselves by that name. Of the lesser country gentry, quite well off, they were a branch of the very rich Cromwell clan, and had changed their name accordingly. In later years, the enemies of their infant Oliver wrote of him as "Cromwell," the quotation marks pointing to the assumed name.

He was a crude sort of boy and young man, loud, overly hearty, superstitious, and with an explosive temper. He suffered from what appears at this range to have been psychosomatic illnesses, or more likely depression, leading him to take to his bed for extended periods of time. At seventeen he traveled fifteen miles to Cambridge University—it was April 23, 1616, the day Shakespeare died—but withdrew from classes after a short while when his father's death brought him home to manage the family's land holdings. His main interests were horses and falconry.

He married, had children, put in some work in local government, and as the squire of his local area stood for and was elected to Parliament. There his rustic ways and rough clothing, which seemed, sniffed a fellow legislator, "to have been made by an ill country tailor," combined with a coarse face marked by warts around the eyes and lower lip to make him notable as lacking the presence and bearing of many in the House. They had the fluent manners and gracious ways of noble and knightly origin, and were of the English aristocracy backing King Charles when the monarch became embroiled with Parliament in such a manner that civil war resulted.

England then, in 1643, was a country of no regular army, with no barracks or garrison town, no recent experience in land war, and few military instruction manuals save those written abroad. There was not a man of the population ignorant of war who was more ignorant than Cromwell. Few seemed less equipped for armed conflict. He was forty-three, a country bumpkin inclined to blurt out whatever came into his mind, harsh and quarrelsome one moment and roaring with laughter the next, a man who appeared entirely too emotionally up-and-down and illogical to dream of playing the role of commander.

Cromwell is largely remembered for other things, but his biographers join in agreement that he was fundamentally and primarily an officer of horse.

But he put himself to studying the career of Gustav Adolf, and then went about raising a company of cavalry to combat the Royalists. His choice of the side in whose forces he would enroll was never in question; he was no aristocrat wearing hair to the shoulders and even below so that it draped down over elaborately done-up uniform jackets. He was of the champions of Parliament who wore their hair close-cropped, the Roundheads warring against the Cavaliers. The word defining the king's supporters came from "chivalry," which came from *cheval*, French for, as noted earlier, horse. Cromwell had no equine term defining his allegiances, but he was certainly not behindhand when it came to the animal. "Horse-flesh he had always loved," says his biographer John Buchan, "and he knew more about it than most Royalist squires"; he was "the best judge of a horse in England."

That he was a knowledgeable horseman served him well as he sought men for his cavalry company. It gained him respect, and he proved, Buchan wrote, "an incomparable recruiting sergeant with his homely humor, his rustic cajoleries and his sudden prophetic raptures." He paid no attention to social class in selecting his under officers: "I would rather have a plain russet-coated captain that knows what he fights for, and loves what he knows, than that which you call a gentleman and is nothing more."

In the first encounters between Parliamentarian and Royalist, Cromwell's riders killed one hundred of the enemy while sustaining losses of only two men. "From the first day he took the field," wrote John Milton, "he was a veteran in arms, consummately practiced in the toils and exigencies of war." But other Roundheads fared poorly. Cromwell thought he knew why. It was a matter of moral strength that made the victorious soldier: virtue. His study of Gustav Adolf had taught him that. He would emulate the Lion of the North, make moral exemplars of his small troop, and perhaps also of the additional men he would someday command—for he seems to have had an ambition slumbering within him in the years before the war that was now flamingly awake. "No man swears but he pays his twelve pence; if he is in drink he is set in the stocks or worse"—by which he meant given a whipping. He saw that whoring and raping Royalist troops would in the midst of a battle desert to seek loot, but had his men comport themselves in such fashion that civilians upon their approach would "leap for joy of them."

Along with the emphasis on proper behavior came endless cavalry drills emphasizing cohesion and unity. His horses were the heavy animals of the Fenlands, who to our eyes would appear underbred, for as yet there was no Arab or barb blood in England. "He bought horses at fairs and markets, requisitioned them, begged and borrowed them, and when necessary stole them. He and his officers became the most shameless horse thieves," wrote Buchan. It was acceptable, he felt, for the struggle against Catholicism's King Charles was that of those he saw as the righteous against those whom he perceived to be the evil limbs of the anti-Christ frequenting tavern and alehouse, inheritors of the kingdom of darkness, companions of the infernal spirits. His own men were pure—Puritans. He would lead "godly, precious men," he said, "such men as has the fear of God before them and made some conscience of what they did," the lieges of whom Thomas Carlyle called "the Armed Soldier, terrible as Death, relentless as Doom, doing God's judgment upon the Enemies of God."

It was a cavalry war, the inexperienced footmen unreliable and the artillery cumbersome. Horsemen were paid three times the wages of the infantry, with their chief, which Cromwell soon rose to be, holding higher rank than any infantry officer. His opposite number was Prince Rupert, the king's cousin. No soldier more embodied what history, and we, esteem to be the cavalry officer. If the word "dashing" did not exist, it would have had to be invented for him. He was glamorous in his dress and romantic in appearance, a gallant, fiery, besworded figure on his charger below his personal standard, which was five yards across. He had fought in the later stages of the Thirty Years' War, and like all that conflict's leaders save Gustav Adolf, was immune to pangs of conscience, or even a concept of such, when it came to pillage, arson, the ravaging of towns, or the slaughter of enemies. Prince Rupert swooped down upon Parliamentarian strongholds and conducted flashing raids around London, devastation following in his wake. His charges were unstoppable. His making of horsed war possessed one flaw, although he never saw it so: his men, once unleashed, were seized by so inspired a fury, their leader its originator and encourager, that after being launched they could never be controlled. The arrow shot from the bow—and kept going. The usage, the very nature of cavalry, he and they felt, was that it wreak havoc untrammeled. To consider maneuver, to stop and regroup and come again, such was the preoccupation of a mathematician or a bookkeeper, not a gentleman and a knight.

Rupert was like the bee who can sting only once before attending to other matters. The enemy displaced and shattered, his men roared on, their scattered rampage proceeding for miles as they sought slaughter and loot. He disdained armor for his riders, and seeing his low opponent—so he viewed Cromwell—put his cavalry in front-and-back cuirasses, he dubbed this base calculator "Ironsides," the term coming to define all the Parliamentarians. When after a fight and an exultant chase, merchants and traders came to offer wine or money for trophies his men had garnered, Prince Rupert did not care. Let the men sell what they took from enemy baggage trains, or jewels, silks, and gold from looted towns—it was in the tradition of the past's glittering knight-at-arms to take what was his by right of conquest. To worry about loss of cohesion, that was beneath him. It was the drumming of hooves, the clash of arms, the fight and the rout, the glory, that mattered to his cousin the king's General of the Horse.

No one could be more opposite than Cromwell, save for the moment when battle was joined. Then the Roundhead leader screamed, sang bits of song, burst into wild laughter; "such a vivacity, hilarity and alacrity," said a contemporary observer, "as another man is when he hath drunken a cup of wine too much." Yet he retained the control of the Roundheads that he had morally molded that Rupert did not have over the Cavaliers, so that they were never to be like a wave rolling up on a shore and there petering out. It was this never letting the reins slip through his fingers in a manner unknown to any cavalryman before, and not practiced with such perfection by any following, that marked him, some have said, as the greatest horse soldier of all time: "Here is a cavalry leader who stands among other cavalry leaders," wrote Hilaire Belloc, "as Milton does among the poets." There is no explanation for his sudden emergence into greatness after forty-three years of routine existence, for the amazing way "he entered fully into his own nature for the first time."

Shouting orders from the saddle, he had, Belloc wrote, "rapidity, lucidity, restraint, judgment of the exact moment" to charge his riders in very close formation, knee to knee, to fire pistols when upon the enemy, then to fling them forward as missiles before drawing swords. At his word they whirled as one to swing left or right to pierce a flank, decimating all in their path, then come about to continue an irresistible assault. Time and again the Parliamentarian cavalry destroyed Royalist armies. The battles Cromwell won—and he never lost—were short in duration, Marston Moor two hours at the most (Cromwell saying of the enemy, "God made them as stubble to our swords"), Naseby at most an hour and a half. He annihilated the king's men; and King Charles knelt at the executioner's block. "Cruel necessity," Cromwell said, looking at the body later.

He went against Scotland, and at Dunbar, blood running down his chin and past the wart from bitten lips, shouted at the top of his lungs as the sun rose just as his troops went in, from Psalm 68, "Let God arise and let His enemies be scattered, let also those that hate

Him flee before Him!" and, a few minutes later, "They fly! I profess they fly!" as his cavalry came sweeping like a scythe into the flank of his opponents to roll them up and go chasing after. The affair took three-quarters of an hour, the Scottish army ceasing to be a military machine but becoming rather a fleeing mob. More than three thousand Scots died as against not more than a score of English. They had outnumbered Cromwell by almost two to one, and it was said that the impossible had been accomplished. England's Jews wondered if he was the Messiah, so supernatural were his doings.

He went to Ireland to slaughter Catholics, holding the Irish to be subhuman as well as religiously misguided. Back at home, Lord Protector of the Commonwealth, his men clothed in the scarlet that would forever represent British soldiery, he subjected his country to Puritanism's harsh proscriptions against unworldly activities that outraged God and went against His will: dancing, the theater, card playing, bear baiting. The ban on horse racing, however, he soon lifted, loving equine sports too much. He even bred runners on his estate. His carriage horses, one team reddish-white and the other snow white, were said to be better than any king of England ever had.

Cromwell had come to bring not peace but a sword, to, as was said, form and inform his horsemen—to mold with order and discipline from without and to produce the right spirit within. There are soldiers who can be a flame in battle and show the highest level of personal leadership while lacking tactical or strategic flights of imagination and insight—they are, in short, sluggers of limited range and grasp. Said Napoléon of his greatest cavalryman: "With me he was my right arm—without me he was nothing. Order Murat to attack and destroy four or five thousand men in such a direction, it was done in a moment; leave him to himself, he was an imbecile without judgment. In battle he was perhaps the bravest man in the world: his boiling courage carried him into the midst of the enemy, covered with plumes and glittering with gold, and he returned with his sabre dripping with the blood of those he had slain." (Yes, agreed a cavalry historian of 150 years gone, "Murat was nothing but a bold soldier, with no talent for command.") Cromwell by contrast had all that makes for the flawless horse soldier.

But so great he was as cavalryman, so wrongly was he placed as political leader. Twelve years after King Charles's death what remained of the Lord Protector, himself gone three years, was taken from its grave and hung on a gallows, head severed and stuck on a pole. Once when having his portrait done, Cromwell told the artist he wished to be represented as he was, "warts and all," and the warts are in a larger sense what have come down to us, the term "Puritanism" a pejorative one. He should never have become a political leader, the uncrowned king of England. He was meant only to be a horsed fighter, nothing more. A biographer noted: "He was not a religious enthusiast, a leader of men and all that, who happened to take on the profession of arms—he was rather a cavalry commander who happened also to be a Puritan. Had fate made him a Papist cavalier or an atheist gambler accustomed to the saddle it would have been just the same—his prime quality would have remained that of the cavalry leader." Another wrote: "I say again, had all Cromwell's qualities, not connected with soldiering, been other than they were, had he been profoundly Catholic or cynically indifferent to any creed, had he been as sensual as he was controlled, ambitious, greedy for gain—or any other thing which he was not—yet still he would have been a soldier, a mounted soldier and supreme in that capacity."

A little more than a century on, there appeared one who was, perhaps, if not his equal, then close.

6

"My children, follow me!"

There was never a more coarse, crude, brutish head of state than King Frederick William I of Prussia. He regarded education beyond the ability to read and do simple sums as pointless, as were any of the arts, which he described as "tomfoolery, frivolous, useless." He stood for order, and was never without a rattan cane used for beating anyone who distressed him, including officials two minutes late in reporting for work. If when walking around Berlin he heard two neighbors arguing, or a couple engaged in a domestic dispute, he would apply his cane to the disturbers of the peace.

Civilians he held to be nonentities, his main and indeed sole concern, beyond coarse practical jokes, being the Prussian army. He had what can only be called a mania for tall soldiers. He scoured Europe and parts of Asia for big men, kidnapping monks, doctors, farmers, men of other armies from roads, churches, and schools to be beaten and tortured into joining his forces. The surest way to gain his favor was to present him with a towering young fellow. Prussian diplomats routinely hired such specimens as servants for their embassies, brought them home, and turned them over to the military. Enrolled, they were subjected to discipline unknown since the heyday of Rome's legions, with severe whippings decreed for such offenses as an improperly polished button. For more serious military crimes, ears or noses were cut off, and for capital crimes, men were broken on the wheel, shot, or decapitated.

Possessed by what was called "gigantomania," Frederick William created one of the great curiosities to be seen when visiting Berlin: "Brobdinaganian" soldiers, "Goliaths," "walking colossi" on parade. For them the king's stud farms through selective breeding produced horses of a size never seen before. They made the great destriers of the High Middle Ages look almost like ponies. Horses for Prussia's cavalry were nineteen hands high. Their riders wore helmets resembling bishops' miters, making them appear to be ten feet tall. The king never risked them in combat but once, in a slight skirmish against Swedish troops.

No apple ever fell farther from the tree than the king's eldest son. The heir to the throne, slim offspring of a porcine father, was dreamy, artistic, an omnivorous reader. From earliest childhood he was deeply involved with playing the flute. He seemed specifically constructed to infuriate his father, and he did. Often the king would burst into Prince Frederick's room, seize books and flute, and throw them in the fire. At table he was known to fling plates at his heir, and the rattan cane was no stranger to the prince's head and back, rear end and legs. Commissioned a Prussian army lieutenant at the age of five, as a young man the prince was anything but the perfect representative of a force that was Europe's fourth largest despite its country's being thirteenth in population: he was utterly devoid of *Zucht*—Prussian spit and polish. Sloppy, ill-kempt in artistically Bohemian fashion, he went about with bearing entirely absent of the stiff and erect posture mandatory for his father's soldiers. He did not care for hunting, and to the end of his days was less than a mediocre rider.

His tutors were told by his father, "Impress upon him the conviction that nothing on earth can earn him more glory than the sword and that he will be a contemptible creature if he does not love the sword and does not seek glory solely in it and through it." The king's instructions were ludicrous, noted Austria's ambassador to Berlin; while Prince Frederick might be a musician, a philosopher, a scientist, "what he will never be is a general or a warrior."

In 1740 King Frederick William fell ill. He had himself brought in a wheelchair to a palace window, below which his riding horses were lined up. He told a group of cronies that they each could have one as a last bequest, and died. His successor, Frederick II, was not yet thirty. To the artistic and literary friends forming the set gathered around him, who took it for granted that his court would be a center for sensitivity and intellectuality, he said, "These pastimes are ended." One of their number essayed to tell the new ruler an off-color joke of the type he had always enjoyed (although his relations with women were virtually nonexistent, his arranged marriage seeing him dine once a year with a spouse at all other times sequestered away in a remote castle, to whom on one such occasion he said virtually nothing beyond: "Madame has gained weight"). He fixed the joke-teller with a stony look, and said, "Monsieur, I am now king."

Such changes from the past were trifling when compared with what soon transpired. Within six months he did what his father never had: he made war. He launched a full-out attack against Empress Maria Theresa's Austria. There was no ideological component. It was purely an aggressive land grab. The armies met at Mollwitz, the king aboard a gray horse. Things did not go well for the Prussians, the Austrian horsemen swiftly dispersing the monstrous Prussian ones and then plowing into the infantry, who were so discomfited that they lost all order and wildly fired into their own lines. "Brothers, children, lads!" screamed Frederick. "Your country's honor! Your king's life!"

It didn't work. A Prussian disaster seemed impending, and the king turned his gray and ran for it. He fled fourteen miles, a solitary figure completely lost by the royal escort and fired upon for near misses by a contingent of Hungarian hussars serving in the imperial forces. For ten hours he was alone before being chased down by Prussians, who told him that while his cavalry had been routed, the infantry had re-formed, collected itself, and gone forward as if on parade, masses of men moving as one in machinelike precision as they loosed off volleys in perfect unison. When a man fell to enemy fire, another instantly took his place. The dead Frederick William's discipline had paid off. It was the first victory won by his son, the artistic intellectual wondrously destined to be Frederick the Great. He rode his gray back to Mollwitz, his flight from which he never spoke or wrote of. He established camp there, Silesia now his.

In taking stock of what had occurred, he said, "Our infantry are heroes to a man. As for our cavalry—the devil won't accept it as a gift." He began to work on that cavalry of enormous men and enormous horses, rising at four in the morning to drive and drill and completely retrain his mounted men. Many he summarily dismissed from the service, writing, "They were giants on elephants and could neither move freely nor fight well. There was not a review during which riders because of their clumsiness did not fall off their horses. They were not masters of themselves or of their horses." Soldiers confounded by the new situation who sought to resign their positions but whom he thought salvageable were informed that they would stay on and that there was no appeal from his decision.

He studied his horsemen, taking note of such high-ranking ones as Colonel Hans Joachim von Ziethen as well as a cornet, the lowest commission an officer could hold, whom the king heard saying that while it was unhappily true that a man might be forced to surrender in battle, the act was unthinkable for a mounted soldier so long as his horse was fresh and sound. That was not a concept the junior officer had invented: cavalrymen have ever held so. The king said nothing in response to the observation, but when his party came to a narrow bridge over a river, he ordered the drawbridge raised and then called the young man to him. "See," Frederick said with a laugh, putting his hand on the cornet, "he has his horse, but he is my prisoner for all that!"

The young officer dug in his spurs, put his horse leaping over the bridge rails into the waters deep below, swam him to the shore, and rode up a bank. He had gone into the river a cornet, it was soon said, but emerged a captain; for the king, skipping the rank of lieutenant, gave him a troop in the White Hussars.

The cornet-become-captain, twenty-two at the time, was Frederick William von Seydlitz, son of an army officer and from an old Silesian noble family. Like Ziethen, who as a child each week called upon an ex-soldier to have his hair braided into the queue required by the army—its extreme tightness combining with the rigid neck stock to make it impossible to turn the head so that in approved marionette fashion the whole body must swivel right or left—Seydlitz was from birth destined to be a soldier. His father and his family tradition had so decided. But while Ziethen seems a more conventional being, Seydlitz took a detour before becoming, with Ziethen, the greatest of Frederick the Great's cavalrymen—and with Oliver Cromwell and one other whom we shall meet in good time a member of that trio who perhaps rank above all other soldiers who made war atop horses.

From a young age he had been a notable daredevil, riding a horse through the twirling arms of a windmill, with death or devastating injury in the offing if his timing was wrong. (He continued the practice all his life.) At the age of thirteen he became a page to the Margrave of Schwedt, of whom it was said, "He was as wild as the winds and played the maddest pranks in sheer wantonness of spirit." This "mad desperado" who "outraged all the routines of society," particularly when it came to "risk and danger in his love adventures," set out to make the page a younger version of himself. Seydlitz was put to riding the most unmanageable and vicious horses in the Duchy of Schwedt, threatened with punishment if he fell off. He seems never to have done that, so the margrave corralled stags from the herd in his park and put the boy on them. Seydlitz proved proficient even in "this novel school of riding."

It was the margrave's pleasure to have himself driven in a four-horse coach to a rough stretch of country. There the coachmen and attending postillons were dismissed and the reins tossed over the horses' heads. Then the margrave and his guests stood on the footboard, and with long whips and shouts demanded utmost speed. The carriage shot up and down hills and over streams and rocks and fallen trees and stumps until it began to break apart. The object of the sport—which seems in spirit similar to modernity's teenage game of "chicken," in which drivers aim their cars at each other—was to remain aboard until the last possible instant before the carriage's final moment. The margrave and his page equally displayed great aptitude for their pastime, neither ever being injured—unlike decades later the Duke of Orleans, son and heir to France's King Louis Philippe, who missed his footing to meet his death after jumping off. Seydlitz spent four years at the court of his mentor, attaining as a result of his activities there, it was said, a degree of presence of mind when in danger not often found, along with unlimited vices, the least of which was a passion for tobacco that found him rarely without a pipe in his mouth.

When Seydlitz turned seventeen the margrave gave him a commission in a cuirassier regiment taking part in King Frederick's land grab against Austria. He came to the monarch's attention when, viewing an enemy artillery barrage, Frederick wondered aloud about the caliber of the Austrian guns. Young Seydlitz rode forward into the line of fire, waited until a salvo came down, and dismounted to pick up a ball, which he wrapped in a handkerchief for presentation to the king. There followed the leap on the horse into the river, and the promotion.

The First Silesian War was followed by the equally victorious Second as the erstwhile aesthete, esteemed before taking the throne as anything but a warrior, led Prussia in battle against France, Russia, Poland, Sweden, and Austria—sometimes several simultaneously. Combating an Austrian-Saxon force, the tall and powerfully built Seydlitz—he looked like a tree, it was said—personally captured an enemy general, garnering him a promotion to major. He was twenty-four, and somewhat gentle by the military standards of the time. It was not unknown to force a local inhabitant of an unknown area into service as a guide, and then mercilessly kill him when he had performed his duties. (He might if freed speak to members of an opposing force.) Frederick William von Seydlitz did not do that, and indeed restrained his officers from riding over crops, and was diplomatic and seemingly thoughtful, presenting the appearance of an earnest and dignified, if obviously ambitious, soldier.

His master, the king, never returned to the form and manner of the days when he was the prince of Prussia, but became an autocrat no less demanding of absolute obedience than his father. Once, in camp, Frederick saw a candle burning in a tent. The time for lights-out was past. He found a young officer writing to his recent bride. "Add that, for the good of discipline, tomorrow, at the same hour, you will have ceased to live."

As brutal as he could be with his officers, who were almost uniformly of high birth—at his death those from major up consisted of 689 nobles as opposed to 22 bourgeois—he having got rid of those whose "conduct or birth," he said, "did not accord with the gentlemanly standards of their profession," the king was equally intolerant of any dereliction from duty on the part of his enlisted men. They must be, he decreed, as well behaved as a community of monks. That meant ferocious discipline: "In general the soldier must fear his officer more than the enemy." His drills for the men were fearsome; of bones broken in them he said, "What signifies that if it should mean the gaining of a victory?" Seydlitz was capable of exceeding the king's view of such matters. Once, Frederick expressed reservations regarding the toll on horses and men of an exercise his subordinate was conducting; the field was littered with dead or wounded bodies of animals and men. "If you make so much fuss about a few broken necks," Seydlitz observed, "Your Majesty will never have the horsemen you require."

He was alone in all the army in addressing the king in such fashion, having in victory after victory attained a status with the monarch that no other officer enjoyed, his views perfectly consistent with those of his master regarding the manner in which cavalry should be employed. In direct opposition to his late father's way of seeing things, Frederick rejected the concept that the Prussian horsed soldiery should be ludicrously heavy, ponderous, unimaginative, and clumsy—it must instead be swift and vigorous and always on the attack, with severe punishment ordered for any officer who allowed the enemy to strike him: Prussia's riders must go forward first. His father's mounted troops "excelled in varnishing their bridles, saddles and boots, and plaiting ribbons in their horses' manes, but nothing had been done to teach them riding and to make them formidable in close combat. They dared not move on uneven ground, and charged at a walk or creeping trot"—and, as noted earlier, solely or almost solely in drill, Frederick William never risking them in war save for the trifling skirmish against Sweden. Like King Frederick, Seydlitz was a serious soldier out for business. Appearing sleepy-eyed upon occasion, as dissolute as his mentor, the Margrave of Schwedt (once, he was absent from duty for having contacted "the pox" from "the society of a lady of high birth but lowly conduct"), his handling of mounted men of war was remarkable. "Out of all the commanders I have seen, he is the only one who can exploit the full potential of his cavalry," Frederick said.

His enlisted soldiers, unlike the officers, who had been accustomed to riding from childhood, were illiterate peasants from towns none of whose other inhabitants had ever been more than a mile from home, but from them Seydlitz made cavalrymen. There was a large stone watering trough in front of his house, surrounded by a three-foot-high iron railing. Each day he was in residence he sent for a squadron, snow, ice, or mud notwithstanding. The troopers were ordered to get their horses over railing and trough, water them, and depart as they came. "Whoever fell with or from his horse was severely punished." Arriving officer-couriers, day or night, were required to gain entrance to the estate by getting their mounts over high closed gates. (Their assignments in the first place to the cavalry Seydlitz commanded when a major general at thirty-six were contingent upon display of capacity to ride entirely unbroken horses.) The concept of large-scale maneuvers was unknown before the king and his cavalry chief invented them, along with the horse artillery, which found light six-pound guns racing along in close attendance to moving squadrons. To lighten the load draught horses pulled, gunners did not sit on the limbers, but rode alongside. Seydlitz was always concerned about weight; his hussars could not exceed five feet five inches in height. Hussar horses were light and not to be more than 14.3 hands high. All horses when not on campaign were ridden daily and given a thorough grooming, doctrine holding it to be as important as exercise for condition.

Along with the maneuvers involving great masses of men and horses, Seydlitz put enormous effort into making each of his men into a finished rider. This applied equally to the hussars flitting about like clouds and akin to, the king said, the reach of a spider registering any disturbance in the web, and the heavy cuirassiers charging like a great wave hitting the beach. There must be not the slightest disorder in the ranks when the cuirassiers went in, after a run first at a trot and then at the gallop for up to two thousand yards of perfect alignment, so that the enemy beheld coming through the smoke of the horse artillery's pieces a compact, maneuverable, knee-to-knee moving wall brandishing sabres—the Prussians had put away pistols, drills having shown that cold steel, "the white arm," was more efficient in dispensing slaughter. For even a good marksman could miss his target, firing as he was from the back of a galloping horse, and even if his shot struck home, he was thereafter restricted in use of the weapon, repeaters being in the distant future. But a swordsman with hundreds of hours' training in cutting the heads off straw dummies was less likely to miss, and if he did there was no need to reload. And the use of swords bred, it was held then and a hundred years and more into the future, what was called the "cavalry spirit," meaning the moral and physical superiority of the horseman.

"Every horse and every trooper has been finished with the same care that a watchmaker bestows upon each wheel of the mechanism," the king wrote; and the punishment for failure was immediate and ruthless. Once, Seydlitz saw a captain lose control of his mount as a unit stood in line. It was a cardinal sin. Horses are herd animals. A single one who bounds or rears or curvets about, its rider hanging on the bridle to discomfit it more, his fear and anxiety increasing, can bring an entire squadron into disorder. The general roared up to scream at the offending captain that he should get out, get off, "go to the devil!"

For long stretches of time—witness the Seven Years' War—the Great King fought his army across thousands of miles. His victories numbered, besides untold skirmishes, twenty-two major battles, of which fifteen were won largely by his cavalry. Very little was left of the onetime effete-seeming prince of Prussia save for that he usually spoke French—German, he said, was for soldiers and horses—plus his love of the flute, which he played daily, in the morning, when possible for half an hour after lunch, and in the evening with professional musicians. (In time from this his head permanently tilted to the side.) His flute offered a means of meditation, he said; he got his best thoughts while playing. From the first moments of his reign, those had been directed toward what Frederick saw as the prime aim of rulership: aggrandizement. Such required of all of Prussia, and most especially its army, iron discipline and instant obedience. The master of victory after victory against his host of foes became the image of one-man rule, autocracy, absolutism, militarism—that Prussianism of which the world would learn much as Prussia went on and then expanded into Germany. He might while on campaign sleep upon straw in barns, as did his soldiers, and eat the same sour army bread as they, and permit them to respond to his "Good morning, boys!" with "Good morning, Old Fritz!" or "Good morning, Father!" but his distance from all was the distance of the Great King from all.

Save for one. Seydlitz was the one who made all possible. Without him there would have been no magnificent wins secured by cavalrymen who, one historian records, "astonished the world by their feats of arms, sweeping whole armies away before them as in the battles of Strigan, Kesseldorf, Rossbach, Leuthen, and Zorndorf." The general knew his value. At one point during the Zorndorf fighting, a courier arrived with the king's instructions that the cavalry charge at once. Seydlitz ignored the order. A great soldier knows when to do so. After a time a second courier came to reiterate Frederick's directions. Seydlitz did not put his horsemen into action. A final rider came to say that the king would have the general's head if he did not charge at once. Seydlitz replied, "Tell the king that after the battle my head is at his disposal, but meantime I hope he will permit me to exercise it in his service." At what he knew to be the precise moment, he ordered his men forward, doing so in the curious manner that was his alone: by taking his pipe from his mouth, throwing it in the air, and shouting, "My children, follow me!" The next day it was almost impossible to pick one's way across the battlefield for the bodies of the enemy's horses and men piled in heaps, and the muskets, pistols, and swords.

Seydlitz's great victory at Zorndorf has been compared to Cromwell's Marston Manor and Hasdrubal's Cannae, Hasdrubal being Hannibal's cavalry leader, in that in each case the leader went in first with the left wing of his force, then passed to the right, and so decimated the enemy infantry. "Curious that at such distant periods, under such different circumstances, the same results should have been achieved, and in almost exactly the same manner!" Prussian losses were described as "trifling," as they were at Rossbach, where while taking 548 casualties they inflicted some 10,000 upon the French and their allies from various German states and provinces. "An amusing battle," it was called by the victors. There was never a military triumph so solely won by horsemen alone. The Prussian horse were supported by

Von Seydlitz's fashion of ordering
a charge, as seen here at Rossbach,
was to fling his pipe into the air.

but seven infantry battalions, only two of which fired more than
five rounds. Seydlitz began by driving off the enemy cavalry, held
his men in check and in formation, and then turned on the opposing infantry to convert it into a fleeing mob. There was no wild
chasing after routed men in the fashion of the English Civil War's
Prince Rupert, and others: here was a supreme display of self-
discipline and of discipline over his troops. The historian Walter
Henry Nelson wrote: "This defeat—indeed the utter rout—of
sixty-four thousand enemies by a small force of Prussian horsemen made Frederick the greatest celebrity in Europe and almost a
demigod in England"—which consistently financed Prussia's fights
against foes deemed opposed to London's interests.

"I can now die in peace," the king wrote his sister Wilhelmine;
but of course he did no such thing, sitting his horse for the presentation of captured colors and standards as kettledrums thundered
away and pipes shrilled and trumpets blared. (Captured enemy soldiers were beaten and starved into joining Prussia's army.) Frederick
remained, as he always had been, a most indifferent horseman, not

infrequently falling off. Seeing himself as now he did to be in the mold of Alexander and Caesar, he affected scarcely to notice that he was unhorsed and, never injured, stood in his snuff-stained and worn and mended and sometimes torn uniform and disreputable old tricorn hat—"I'm a bit of a slob," he said—and waited for someone to get his horse, or bring another one, and assist him up. His cavalry chief upon such occasions would look away and tell others not to take notice. He was less able to contain himself when noting the king's riding technique, which found him never wearing spurs but getting speed from his mount by tone of voice and by hitting the animal between the ears with a cane—"to the outrage of Seydlitz." The king owned thirty-six horses of English blood, fifteen hands or more and somewhat heavy-boned, schooled to be calm and responsive. He did not like horses of delicate, slight conformation. He slouched badly and liked short stirrups as opposed to Seydlitz's ruling that the cavalry use stirrups of such length that even when a man stood in them a single hand's breadth was all that appeared between seat and saddle. (When Frederick said the riders' stirrups were too long, Seydlitz in his cheeky fashion observed that that was the way the men rode at Rossbach.)

Joined to the general's rigorous discipline of his men was his understanding of the strategic use of the Prussian horse. To attempt to combat all enemies simultaneously was to lose all, Frederick held, and so the role of his cavalry was that of a highly mobile force able to project power far distant from the slow-moving infantry and heavy artillery. Often they were on their own, to return to the main force ready to join it in another effort against new foes. Once arrived at the site of an impending battle, Seydlitz was masterful in using the layout of the ground, so deploying that the enemy would find swamps or impassable woods or rocky inclines blocking the way of an advance or indeed a fighting retreat. He was adept at barring an enemy movement by having his horses eat out whole areas of grassland, which in an era before railroads and of roads hardly more than paths and therefore impractical for transport of fodder was the only source of food for the animals. Rivers could be utilized to move bulky hay bales, so he made sure waterways were not accessible to the enemy. The topographical features of a stretch of countryside were to him as the black and red squares of the chess board are to the grand master.

There came a time when Prussia's wars ended. He would, the king had said, "thrash around" until his "damned enemies" lost heart. That moment arrived. He was in direst straits when his great enemy Empress Elizabeth of Russia unexpectedly died, and the dead ruler's forces left off fighting and went home: the Miracle of the House of Brandenburg in Prussian history. Two centuries on, the matter came instantly to the mind of Germany's Third Reich minister of propaganda, Joseph Goebbels, when he learned that Franklin D. Roosevelt was gone. He rushed to Adolf Hitler to declare that a second Miracle had occurred and that now the Americans would end their participation in the Second World War. The Great King often came to the mind of Germany's greatest tank commander of that conflict, Heinz Guderian, the genius of armored attack and Seylidtz's direct heir, who, in his youth a horsed cavalry officer, adapted the light cavalry tactics and manner of operation of a thousand years past for the 1940 tank drive into France that brought that country to its knees. Arguing with Hitler when the fighting went against Germany, and the Führer made mad mistake after mad mistake, each costing the lives of thousands of German soldiers as well as civilians, Guderian remembered looking at Frederick's picture on the wall; and it seemed to him it was asking, "What are you doing with my country?"

After a quarter century of almost uninterrupted war, Prussia was at peace. The king concerned himself with the improvement of roads and canals, agricultural and industrial advancements, financial and taxation matters. His great cavalry commander, residing on an estate bestowed upon him by his sovereign, devoted himself to polishing the Prussian horsed forces. A review of his horsemen was always on tap at an appropriate time. "It may very well happen that their parade before foreign sovereigns or their representatives may exercise a greater influence on the course of politics than many a fight in war."

As he always had, Seydlitz continued his pursuit of women. At one point in the past he had seemed close to marrying, his intended a young woman who among other accomplishments played the piano "with wonderful precision" but whose proficiency doomed the romance. "Whilst sitting by the side of Seydlitz, the lady attempted to rise from her chair that she might strike with more force on the pedal, but so slipped as to break her foot. Physicians declared that lameness would be the ultimate result," recorded the general's biographer Captain Robert Neville Lawley of Great Britain's 2nd Life Guards.

"Seydlitz believed the maiden no longer suited for so rash and brilliant a man as himself, and therefore declined the union. The attachment was soon forgotten." Another candidate appeared, the half-his-age seventeen-year-old Countess of Hacke, daughter of a distinguished soldier. A marriage proposal was made and accepted. The king was put out: there was a war going on, as usual, and the general's service with troops was required. He would beg, Seydlitz wrote Frederick, one day from duty to marry and then be with the army. Permission was granted. The couple was together for four years; had two daughters, in whom neither parent expressed much interest; and separated. The general had never relinquished what his biographer termed his "sensual habits" involving other women, and his wife found the "easy friendship of younger officers agreeable . . . Everyone wished to be a Seydlitz in love adventures." That was quite the norm for cavalry officers of the day, and for a century and more into the future in European cavalry regiments. Gallantry, dandyism, vain dress, and wild disorder in their personal lives were virtually required of the headstrong, dashing, and rich young men. (For decades it was held that no graduate of the French cavalry school at Saumur was really a graduate unless he passed an unofficial test: he must in three hours ride three horses thirty miles, drink three bottles of champagne, and successfully avail himself of the services of three prostitutes.)

The general's health declined. It was venereal disease, although the king did not know, believing the fiction that the problem was apoplexy. When Frederick called upon the invalid in the last stages of his life, Seydlitz turned his head to one side in an attempt to hide a nose hideously ravaged by his disease. It was August of 1773; Seydlitz would be gone in November's first week. The two men had had their differences over the years, the general making it clear that he would not tolerate the clever, mocking persiflage with which the monarch addressed other officers, and the king resenting implications that he never would have achieved what he had if Seydlitz never lived. But Frederick knew what was owed. Detesting the use of tobacco while knowing the general's love of his pipe, he not only permitted but actually urged Seydlitz to smoke in his presence. That was the least of it; "I cannot do without you!" he cried when last they met. He departed wondering how he would replace Seydlitz, who died as he lived, involved with horses and women to the very end, indeed the last minutes. An officer sent to Turkey to fetch animals for the Prussian remount service received from the general "an express order to bring him two handsome Circassian girls," the biographer Captain Lawley recorded. Delivered, "they became doubly injurious to him." He was buried on his estate grounds beneath a sculpture of a sleeping lion, in his fifty-third year. The Prussian infantry thereafter took precedence, for the cavalry was never the same.

7
Light-Horse Harry

Long after having fled the Americas for Asia, horses returned, carried in slings on a conquistador's ship. There were some dozen and a half of them. The natives took them to be a monstrous new species of being.

Arriving in Mexico in 1519, Hernando Cortés with his few riders routinely defeated native forces outnumbering him by three hundred to one. Even greater odds had been faced four years before by Diego Valázquez de Cuéllar in what we today call Cuba. Once Valázquez sent a party of thirty bowmen and one hidalgo—knight-at-arms—on a reconnaissance mission. They were attacked by natives whose number they estimated at seven thousand. The hidalgo leaped on his mount and charged. The people ran, so terrified that when Velázquez came up with the main body of his force, he found the whole province "entirely depopulated with the exception of some very old and sick people."

Sometimes Cortés found it unnecessary actually to employ his horses in combat to arrange desired ends. When a group of hostile-looking people gathered at his camp, the conquistador told one of his men to conceal an in-heat mare behind a building, and then led a stallion to the people. Scenting the mare, the horse reared, snorted, whinnied, and pawed the ground. Let the people note such frenzy, Cortés declaimed. This display, he explained, derived from the animal's belief that the gathered assemblage contemplated harm to the Spanish. Let them consider what might occur if the beast broke loose to wreak such havoc as could scarcely be imagined.

The reaction was what Cortés desired, and he signaled one of his men to get the hidden mare away even as he whispered into the stallion's ear. That he was brave cannot be a matter of discussion—he had burned his ships at the beach to show his men there was no turning back—but never can he have showed greater courage than when dealing so with a male horse ready to mate with a ready mare, such being, as horse people know, no less dangerous than a flared cobra. With the mare gone, the stallion calmed down. Cortés announced that he had informed the monster that the people meant no harm. The area was peaceful thereafter. Second only to God, Cortés wrote Emperor Charles V, "we owe our successes to our horses." A contemporary chronicler agreed: "Horses are the most necessary things in the New Country, because they frighten the enemy most, and after God, to them belongs the victory." Writing the emperor about a skirmish, Cortés bemoaned the loss of one of his mounts: "God alone knows how great its value was to us, and what pain we suffered at its death; because, after God, our only security was the horses."

It was entirely different in the English colonies when the American Revolution came. To deploy cavalry either heavy or light in the classic European manner, the leaders of both sides of the conflict decided, was an impossibility in heavily forested and almost trackless terrain. The use of cavalry played no role in George Washington's mind. His frontier-land military experience in the French and Indian War was entirely innocent of anything involving horsed combat; and when in the early days of the rising of the colonists against England his sole cavalry unit, a group of four hundred Connecticut volunteers, declared that as men of "reputation and property" and as would-be cavalrymen of centuries-old traditional social superiority they must be "exempt from guard duty and unpleasant fatigue details," he sent them home. For more than a year and a half he made no move to create a horsed unit. It was only after he was driven out of Long Island and into Manhattan and then down into New Jersey did it come to him that if he'd had some outlying horsemen ranging about to discover what was occurring away from headquarters he might have held Long Island. He delegated a twenty-nine-year-old Polish soldier-of-fortune nobleman, Count Kasimierz Pulaski, to form a cavalry detachment at the head of which, leading a charge, he was shortly killed. He is remembered as the founding father of American cavalry—remembered, that is, in but slightest fashion. (One wonders what percentage of people driving over today's Pulaski Skyway, which spans the Hudson River, would be able to identify him.) There arrived to replace him a man who would be far more greatly recalled, he the Revolution's most glamorous, exciting, striking leader of horse, and also, ultimately, its most tragic.

Henry Lee, of the Lees of Virginia, was at Princeton preparatory to going to the Inns of Court in London for law studies when the tensions between the mother country and her American colonies became ever more fevered. His college chums Alexander Hamilton and James Madison would soon enough put their energies and talents into the cause of American independence, but young Lee hesitated to do so, saying he thought the idea illegal. He dithered, three times booking passage for England and three times canceling. It was very strange that he quailed at the idea of a war, as for years he had followed a self-imposed training schedule aimed at making him into a finished cavalryman. (Wielding a heavily weighted sabre, he rode about slashing and thrusting, wrote his biographer Noel Gerson.) When Washington came to the realization that he required horsed soldiers and authorized the raising of dragoon outfits, Henry Lee enlisted as a private in one commanded by a cousin. He was swiftly promoted to a captaincy, with orders to raise a troop. Twenty years old, he tested applicants for his projected force by leading each candidate in the wildest type of ride, which concluded with Captain Lee suddenly turning around with a drawn sword. Anyone unable to keep up or who flinched from the blade was politely told there were no vacancies. There was always that about Henry Lee that implied danger. His cousin George Lee felt he would run through with a rapier or shoot anyone who disagreed with him on a serious matter, and related having been told by a woman who knew Henry that she pitied any girl he married, "for he is certain to beat her if she disputes his word in any manner." The men wishing to serve under him would have sensed that although he was intellectual and well read and a brilliant speaker, albeit one who all his life dominated every conversation, there was violence beneath. When Washington midway through the war offered him a high staff position, Lee respectfully declined, saying, "I am wedded to my sword," and "I have a zeal for the honor of the Cavalry." It would have been danger, dash, the desire to be with and follow a swashbuckler, that drew men to him—to be of the glory of the cavalry. It was ever so, before and after, in places and situations we have seen and shall see.

He outfitted his one hundred selectees, at his family's expense, in a bright-green jacket; a high, frilled stock; tight lambskin breeches; polished boots to the knee; and a leather cap topped by a flaring horsehair plume. He and his officers wore short blue capes lined with buff-colored silk.

His work was quintessentially that of light cavalry. There were no swords-lowered, crashing-into-the-enemy, shock-action charges. Instead he went raiding. Once he took note of a British column

Henry Lee, father of Robert E. No apple fell farther from the tree, for Light-Horse Harry was liar, thief, conniver, jailbird, and womanizer—but withal the American Revolution's premier horse soldier.

pushing Washington south from New Jersey into Pennsylvania, its more than twenty supply wagons following the infantry half a mile behind. He rushed in, commandeered them and the mules that drew them, and delivered all to American headquarters. Washington was awakened to be told the good news. Three days later Lee relieved the British of seventeen wagons, mostly loaded with beef. With no formal military training and never having commanded men before, he instinctively understood reconnaissance, speed, stealth, the feint, the flank attack, the sudden change of direction, when to be bold and when cautious, and that from caution comes daring. History knows few soldiers more adept at displaying the matador's cloak in such a manner that the bull charges into air and so exposes itself for the sword's fatal thrust. In one two-month period he conducted fifteen fruitful raids at a cost of two men slightly wounded and one horse killed. Alexander Hamilton, serving close to Washington, said, "Captain Lee warms the blood of the footsore more than would casks of brandywine or rum." The British commander Sir William Howe: "An American named Lee is a damned nuisance. I expect the rebels to nip at our heels, but this fellow always draws blood." Sir Henry Clinton: "The wretched fellow gives me no peace of mind." That was Lee's aim. He wanted, he said, to rattle their teeth. On two separate occasions he netted four hundred British supply carts. He scouted out New Jersey's Hessian mercenaries' positions in December 1776, reporting all to Washington so that the general was able to launch a devastating Christmas Eve attack across the Delaware, one of the great moments in American history.

Lee was raised to the rank of major, commanding what was now termed the Partisan Force of Cavalry and reporting only to Washington, who desperately needed his foraging skills. "The Americans at Valley Forge could not have survived without his unfailing help," an historian notes. He lifted forty wagonloads of bolts of scarlet uniform cloth from a British supply column to be turned into blankets for the Americans. His intelligence reports, offered by Washington to others as models, were crisp, authoritative, and complete, garnered from reconnaissance missions personally conducted, and from spy rings he organized. It was a flitting-about light cavalry display of flawless, classic nature. He was not yet twenty-one, a commander alternating severe tongue-lashings, eloquent as he was, with displays of hopeful cheerfulness. He seemed unhesitatingly always to know what he was doing: his instinct, said the eminent American general Nathanael Greene, was "as sure and swift as that of the eagle that drops out of the sky to snatch its prey."

His force became known as Lee's Legion, and he as Light-Horse Harry. Most of his men began the war as teenagers; the oldest among them the sergeant major at twenty-four. In that fashion of the knightly aristocracy that had always officered cavalry, Lee being of the type of what used to be called the FFV—First Families of Virginia—he dined off family plate with silver bearing his monogram and drank from cups of sterling. Although his was the premier cavalry force the American Revolution produced, its numbers were tiny—reduced from sickness at one point to fewer than fifty men. (He picked up for recruits eleven Iroquois, who joined for the sport of the thing even as he for love of knowledge for its own sake learned to speak their language.) Desertion was always a problem for American units during the long years of fighting, but it was almost unknown in the distinctive, filled-with-pride-and-esprit-de-corps Lee's Legion of dashing raid, clever ambush, scouting, feint, and speed. It was great fun abundantly spiced with the thrill of danger. Once Lee and Alexander Hamilton were chased by a British patrol. The two scattered, Light-Horse Harry racing away on his mount, Hamilton plunging into the Schuylkill River for a swim to safety. After three years of constant action, the always slightly built lieutenant colonel was dangerously thin and worn down, but it required a direct order from Washington to force him to let off of his duties and go home to Virginia's Northern Neck for a rest.

The British cavalry equivalent to Light-Horse Harry Lee was Banastre Tarleton of Manchester, born in 1754 to a very rich merchant, the running of whose business did not appeal to the young man. He opted for the army, and became a member of the enormous expeditionary force, the largest in its history to that time, that Great Britain dispatched for putting down the rebellion in the American colonies. It contained but two horsed units, for the British, like Washington in the early stages of the war, did not regard the eastern seaboard terrain that would see the fighting as a suitable location for cavalry deployment. Additionally, the six- to eight-week voyage across the Atlantic was very costly in terms of horse wastage, a great percentage of them dying en route. Thomas Lobster of the Artillery and the Foot—later Tommy Atkins—would take care of the matter of suppressing the rebels, London felt.

Young Tarleton garnered command of one of the dragoon regiments and very shortly appeared in American eyes to justify the term for those trained to fight on foot and horseback alike, which derived from the flash and smoke of the pistol's discharge so like the fiery blast and vapor exuded by the dragon of ancient legend. For, so history as recorded by the Americans tells us, Tarleton was "vile, despicable, evil incarnate." Perhaps. But only perhaps—a recent biography is subtitled with reference to the "myth and reality" of his doings. Certainly he was brutal. But who in the British army of the eighteenth century was not? Its enlisted men were regarded as but marginally superior in nature to the mules and draught horses drawing the wagons. Soldiers committing the slightest of military offenses were routinely given a minimum of twenty-five lashes with a cat-o'-nine-tails, sometimes of six, often with knots tied in. To brush a fly from one's face when on parade could bring one hundred; something more serious one thousand, the time needed for completion of which could reach four hours. A drummer tapped five or ten times, slowly, between strokes. If an observing doctor felt a man was in danger of dying, he was taken away to be given time for recovery and then the punishment was completed. "Booting" was a common action: flogging on the soles of the feet with a belt. When done with a stick it was "bastinadoing." The soldier, British army doctrine held, was a crude, brutalized, unthinking lout and a ruffian and pariah of the lowest social order.

Given such a culture, tenderness toward the rebels, traitors ungrateful for all the mother country had done for them, could hardly be expected from the leader of the Green Dragoons, the Green Horse, so named for the color of their tunics, worn with elbow-length gauntlets, stiff leather breeches, over-the-knee boots, and caps with swan feathers. Tarleton knew—all the king's men knew—that one third of the colonists were Loyalists, and one third indifferent to or unknowing of the dispute at issue. The remaining third were seen as lawless insurrectionists—what modernity would call terrorists. It was not always easy to distinguish such from the mass of the populace, and so the Green Dragoons leader took horses as he needed them, and if a farmer or a plantation owner had some too young for use, his men slit the animals' throats. It was monstrous that this was done, said Thomas Jefferson, to which Tarleton observed that Mr. Jefferson was a very genteel person. The cry "Tarleton is coming!" panicked all who heard it, for it often meant forced enrollment in his forces. A likely young fellow was offered a choice: join up or see his family's home and fields put to the torch. This method of recruitment was quite familiar to officers of the Royal Navy, who routinely sent out armed shore parties to scour waterfront taverns for people who, drugged or beaten into insensibility, were dragged away to man warships. (Indeed, one of the causes of the War of 1812 was forced impressment into Britain's navy of American merchant seamen taken off their high-seas ships at gunpoint.)

Short, swarthy, alert, vigorous, ambitious, sometimes deploying with infantrymen running alongside his horses while clinging to their manes for aid in getting over the ground, Tarleton was not unaware of his reputation among his foes. Americans "entertained dreadful apprehensions" of him, remembered Light-Horse Harry Lee, and that suited the Green Horse commander's aims. He was serving the cause of "brutal virtue," he said, and in doing so must display a "disagreeable exertion of authority." He was very good at that, very good at his work. (When their commander fell ill with either malaria or yellow fever and so was out of action for a time, the British commander Lord Cornwallis observed that the men of the Green Dragoons were "very different.") He ranged about, hitting and running, an enterprising daredevil who only just failed making a prisoner of Thomas Jefferson: the intended detainee was warned that Tarleton was coming and took to his heels. That he was cold and ruthless is not arguable; a grim little poem was said to define the attitude of the Green Dragoons commander: "Tarleton's quarter means slaughter." But the same could be said of Lee, who dealt with one of the very few cases of desertion from his unit by cutting off the man's head and sticking it up on a pole, and who screamed, "No quarter!" in response to attempts to surrender by an enemy unit that wantonly slew an innocent young boy. Lee the polished gentleman of light persiflage and high gentility vanished when occasion demanded it, to be replaced by a hectoring martinet unsparing of troops or horses. When speed was required, his men, remembered one of his officers, moved "as though the Hounds of Hell were nipping at our heels. There was no sedate pace for us, no pleasantries, no lazy dawdling under the trees. The colonel was an impatient man who goaded us again and again, until, unable to tolerate the verbal lashing any longer, we responded by marching until ready to drop in our tracks."

Lee and Tarleton were two of a kind—professionally indistinguishable, really. They were officers of light cavalry. The charge of heavy cavalry all through history was a psychological as well as a physical assault, the sight of sun rays flickering off the sabres or the lances reminiscent of light on moving waters terrible to behold as the line advanced closer and closer to those who had to await it, only iron discipline and nerves of steel offering even a hope of survival. There was never any of that in the American Revolution, only Lieutenant Colonel Lee and Lieutenant Colonel Tarleton hovering wraithlike about their respective enemies psychologically to unbalance them, to dislocate them, to disrupt their communications, to make them look over their shoulders and hear menace in every sound in the night. Ideology had nothing to do with it in the moment of action. Their work was akin to that of the fighter pilots of later day who swooped and skimmed to harry the enemy bomber or to scout out the dispositions of his infantry far below, and who in World War I were termed Knights of the Sky.

That they were mirror images the one of the other, yes; but history, as has been said, is written by winners, and so the leader of the Green Dragoons, known during the war as Bloody Tarleton, has in the many years succeeding been dubbed Butcher Tarleton. It is an after-the-fact appellation: there is not a single contemporary allusion to him by that term. Yet he knew the Americans' detestation for him well enough to request after Lord Cornwallis's Yorktown capitulation that the victors furnish him with a guard for protection against those who might wish to do him harm. When long after the Revolution the author Stephen Vincent Benét came to write his renowned short story "The Devil and Daniel Webster," in which Satan impanels a selection of the most loathsome individuals ever to tread American soil, Lieutenant Colonel Tarleton was given a place in the jury box.

To those at home who had known him as the Princeton college boy leaving to join the Patriot army, so it was called, the Henry Lee who took time off at General Washington's direct order was almost unrecognizable. Thin, drawn, intense, he talked of nothing but the war. His parents were notably unintelligent despite their high social position—when people asked their quick-minded and verbal son how it was he was so different, he replied in his clever way that here was proof that two negatives produced a positive—but even they saw the need for him to get some relaxation. Mrs. Washington (Aunt Martha, as he had always addressed her) wished him to call, his mother told him, and he did so. Then he paid another call, to a sixteen-year-old distant cousin so genuinely beautiful that she was known as the Divine Matilda. She was heiress to a ten-thousand-acre estate, a mill, a quarry, slaves. He returned to duty to reveal himself no less a grand strategist of war than a leader of cavalry in the field. It was largely due to his plans that Lord Cornwallis was led into a situation where with the French fleet at his rear and the Americans before him he had no choice but surrender. (The Englishman showed poor form in the manner in which he did so, Lee sniffed, for instead of offering Washington his sword himself he delegated the task to a subordinate officer.)

Light-Horse Harry on that day when the Revolution effectively ended could be counted as one of the two or three most outstanding American officers looking on as the British laid down their arms. Nathanael Greene, commander of the Continental army in the South, said he was more in debt to Lee than to any other man who served under him. But something strange was happening to Lee's view of the world, himself, and the army in which he had found so brilliant an existence. He did not understand why he was as he was. "He referred to his stupid conduct" by saying, "I am candid to acknowledge my imbecility of mind" as he turned sulky and petulant and melancholy. They had not done enough for him, he said, resentment mixing with self-pity. His work had gone unappreciated. His health was not good, he claimed; but Greene told people that whatever the problem was, it was not of a physical nature.

Although the peace treaty would not be signed for ten months, Lee resigned his commission and went home. Greene tried to mollify him and urge continuance of a military career so outstandingly begun, but to no avail. Green wrote him: "You are going home; and you will get married; but you cannot cease to be a Soldier."

His marriage would be to the Divine Matilda. There were four hundred guests for the first great social event northern Virginia had known since the war began, and then the newlyweds took up residence in what formed a part of the nineteen-year-old bride's great inheritance. Westmoreland County's tidewater Stratford Hall had a forty-foot-square entrance hall, a Green Room, a White Room, a Blue Room, a cherry-tree room, and a schoolroom and a nursery housed in an enormous brick mansion sitting on terraced broad lawns dotted with outbuildings sloping down to the Potomac. With the aura of his great name and his wartime glory draped about him, and the money come to him through marriage to his stunning wife, Lee's prospects could not have been more brilliant. Then he destroyed himself.

There are situations, conditions, professions for which the absolute requirement is that one be young. The movie starlet is forbidden wrinkles, the starring athlete must not lose even the slightest portion of his lightning reflexes. This is equally true for the leader of horsed soldiers, as the history of cavalry tells, Oliver Cromwell coming to his destiny when in his forties the sole exception. Henry Lee knew that. "The season of youth is the season for battle," he once said. His days on a horse with a sword in his hand were gone, although periodically he dreamed that they might return, that back in uniform he might lead an expedition to put down a threatened tax revolt in Pennsylvania, that he might head a force to suppress Indian outbreaks off to the frontier, or take a major generalcy in the army of the French Revolution. He was not yet twenty-six years of age when he resigned from the Continental army. What next to do? He became governor, a congressman, his main achievement when in office to write the House's statement on Washington's passing—"First in war, first in peace, and first in the hearts of his countrymen."

But both his elective positions bored him. What were vapid debates on taxes or spending to one who for years knew the thrill of the raid, the chase, the great game of war on horseback? Light-Horse Harry found new arenas of combat. The young United States was bursting with the impulse to do great things, to expand its territory off to the west, to build roads and canals and new cities. That meant floating bond issues, land speculation, the issuance of stocks, lending and borrowing, a frenzy of dueling with financial competitors in an atmosphere of chance-taking. Lee was perfectly suited for all that, he thought, a man unafraid of risk, a conqueror. He burst forth with an orgy of deals proposed, accepted, declined. He dreamed to control water sources, construct hotels, erect warehouses and mills, own thousands of acres of undeveloped lands the sale of which in time would earn him millions. He had been denied a full measure of glory in the war, he felt, made to do with a mere lieutenant colonelcy when he should have been accorded a generalcy, but now he would come triumphant to the fore upon another field of battle. Daring and dash and necessary recklessness, the marks of the victorious cavalry leader, had served him well when in uniform. Now they would be put to new use.

But it was precisely what had made him great when he was young that ruined him as he grew older. There are men, the military historian Sir John Keegan has observed, who are meant to be soldiers and nothing more. Henry Lee the ex-cavalryman off his horse and away from his troops was one. Isolated from what he had been, he took from his past what would be fatal to his future, and plunged into investments in coal mines, ore fields, and canals; currency transactions; the offering of interest-bearing loans; and, in breathtakingly unrestricted fashion, the ownership of vast tracts of land. So enormous became his holdings that when he took a fancy to one of Washington's mares, Magnolia, he was able to give five thousand acres as purchase price. In that matter all went well, but in another he baldly defrauded his former commander, making good on a loan with bonds equal to the borrowed amount according to their face value but actually far below when it came to trading or redeeming them. Such a performance soon typified all he did, for he became shifty, offering a ghastly parody of wartime evasion and flight in the form of bad checks, stalling on debts, deceptions, misrepresentations, claims that he could not at the moment find requested documentation. Hazy surveying practices, imprecise descriptions and inflated assurances, the sale of lands encumbered with mortgages—sometimes the sale of the same property to two individual purchasers—alleged ownership of properties by virtue of unauthenticated or dubious deeds, increasingly jumbled accounts of loans he said he made: it was recorded that all titles of land he held could be "supposed as precarious." He seemed never to have learned from the multitude of misadventures, but remained always certain that his next venture would work out. It never did.

He had four children with the Divine Matilda. When they were able to sit and control a horse "his sons learned to ride like cavalrymen, wield sabres like cavalrymen and shoot like cavalrymen," wrote his biographer Noel Gerson. Yet his mad financial dealings were endangering their futures, and so their maternal grandfather moved to secure for them funds beyond their father's reach. Nothing was beneath Henry Lee; he appealed to his Princeton and Continental army chum Alexander Hamilton, secretary of the treasury now, for advance information on forthcoming governmental monetary policies, the knowledge of which might enable him to make successful speculations. Hamilton replied that he could not do such a thing, even for Harry.

Matilda died, the fortune she had brought to her marriage almost entirely dissipated. Soon enough Lee was writing Hamilton to say he was "in love with every sweet nymph" he saw. Eventually he picked one for his second wife. Ann Carter's father was perhaps the richest man in Virginia. The wedding was on June 30, 1793, at her family's Shirley Plantation on the James River, the magnificent center of the miles-long Carter estate serviced by thousand slaves. The twenty-year-old bride knew nothing of life beyond that of the mansion in which she had been raised amid polished mahogany and old silver and the portraits of her ancestors. She saw the glamorous hero-governor but not the self-indulgent dreamer who had gone through one wife's fortune and would immediately set to work on that of a second. He had deceived her in respect to finances and now he deceived her in other ways. "Her affections were trampled upon by a heartless and depraved profligate," wrote a relative. "I am right as to time. One fortnight was her dream of happiness from which she awoke to a lifetime of misery."

They lived in Stratford Hall when not in the governor's mansion in Richmond, but it could be regarded as only a temporary residence, for the Divine Matilda had left it to her son Henry, who could take possession when he reached his maturity. Governor Lee was frequently off on long trips, his speculations and mishaps ever more wild and ever more destructive to his wife's inheritances. He failed in everything, sold her lands, horses, all she had. Weeds grew in the walks and the formal park after the unpaid overseer packed up and left, and where ocean-going ships had once tied up, wharves sank into the Potomac. Often Ann went with the four children he gave her back to Shirley Plantation to live the life she had known and lost, while Lee—so it was said—asked the loan of a pair of horses from a friend. He had to take another of those endless trips in connection with another speculation. The friend sent along a slave to care for the animals. Weeks passed. The horses' owner by chance ran into his slave. He demanded to know where the horses were. "Well, you see," the man said, "Marse Henry sold those horses." "He did, did he? Why didn't you come back and tell me about it?" "Well, you see, Marse Henry sold me, too."

Lee made a giant plunge into land speculation, and by pulling all possible strings raised $40,000. The enterprise, like all his enterprises, failed. He was utterly ruined. One of Stratford Hall's many dependencies collapsed, but there was no one to put back the bricks that tumbled to the ground, no one to till the fields. Vines engulfed the carriage house whose horses were long departed. By the winter of 1806 there was no money to pay a doctor to attend to the pregnant Ann Carter Lee, who huddled for warmth over a portable brazier in the Great Room empty of the sold-off paintings and furniture; and her husband dodged down alleys for fear of creditors when he went to Alexandria or Richmond in attempts to raise money for new harebrained schemes. He was away when on January 19 she gave birth to a baby boy, whom she named for her brothers, Robert and Edward.

Light-Horse Harry owed for his hat, some rope, gun flints, powder, and Peter would no longer lend him sufficient to pay Paul; and what had menaced him for years materialized: debtors' prison. For almost a year he was behind bars, and when let out he had nothing, nothing at all, and his wife had nothing beyond the income of not overly large trust funds willed her by her father and a sister. Even the decaying roof over their heads was no longer available to shelter them, for the ex-convict's son Henry by the Divine Matilda had come into his maturity and wished to take possession of his property. Lee and Ann went to Alexandria to settle in modest lodgings rented to them for a pittance by a pitying relative. Lee was more the guest in his wife's establishment than the head of the house, and Alexandria looked upon him as the model of a hero long outliving his exploits to become a professional ex-soldier turned something of a nuisance. A King Street merchant used to play chess with him occasionally, but the merchant had duties to perform also, and often his clerk was instructed to say he was out. The day came when Light-Horse Harry resented it. "You lie, young man, and know he is in, and you are trying to deny me to him!" But the day was past when people were in awe of Henry Lee, and the clerk sprang forward and pointed to the door and said, "Leave this store immediately or I'll find a way to make you." Lee turned, folded his old military cloak about himself, and walked slowly but majestically out.

In 1812 there came a final cruel blow. A friend's newspaper was threatened by political enemies, and Light-Horse Harry went to the rescue. The affair turned ugly—more than ugly—and a crowd broke down the door to get to the newspaper editor and his defenders. They were beaten unconscious and thrown out into the street, where thugs battered them. A drunk flung hot candle grease in Lee's eyes and then slashed his face with a knife. Taken home, he was insensible for days. Within twenty-four hours his old friend President James Madison called, and Secretary of State James Monroe and Chief Justice John Marshall. Not everybody had forgotten what he had been, and the president said to five-and-a-half-year-old Robert Edward what the boy always remembered, that he was never to forget his father's "honor and matchless gallantry."

White-haired and staring-eyed in his shabby hat and worn clothing, Lee appealed to Madison and Monroe for aid to go to the warm islands of the Caribbean, where perhaps he might recover his health. They gave help, and always short of money and lonely for the past and for his children, he wandered for six years in the sun, through Barbados, San Juan, Santo Domingo, Nassau, Turks Island, an old bronchial condition bothering him along with pains in the back. In Alexandria his wife referred to herself as Widow Lee. He decided to go home, but on the ship he fell deathly ill, and at his request it docked at Cumberland Island off the Georgia coast, where Nathanael Greene was buried on what had been his estate in life. At the dock there was a fifteen-year-old boy, the nephew of Greene's daughter. "Tell your aunt," Light-Horse Harry said, "I am come purposely to die in the house and in the arms of my old friend and compatriot."

She tended to him and he recovered sufficiently to walk at times in the garden, leaning on the nephew's arm and speaking of the old days, of Washington and Lafayette, what Hamilton had said to him and he to Patrick Henry. Then his final illness came upon him and he lay in bed unable to utter anything but terrible sounds of agony. He was two weeks dying—to the nephew it seemed like two months. It was March 1818. He was sixty-two years of age. The United States Army garrison at Savannah sent men to the funeral, and a detachment off a Navy squadron fired minute guns for the military funeral in the Greene family plot. The grave was left unmarked for fifteen years until his son Henry sent money for foot- and head-stones. Forty-four years passed before any of his children visited the grave. Then Robert came. Robert was a general then. All his life, despite being raised in genteel poverty because of his father's copious financial incapacity, he had revered his memory, telling stories he had heard about his father, memorizing letters written during the long Caribbean wanderings. Of course, Light-Horse Harry was long dead when F. Scott Fitzgerald said, "Show me a hero and I'll write you a tragedy."

8

The Highest Calling a Soldier Could Know

"What is the use of cavalry in modern war but to lend tone to what would otherwise be a vulgar brawl?" asked an officer of the Napoleonic Era. Even in times before the remark was made, there was no shortage of those who in one form or another offered a similar inquiry. Really, was cavalry actually needed? In the fifteenth century and before, certainly, for no one could stand against the charging behemoth who was the knight-at-arms in coat of chain mail and helmet, and, later, shining impenetrable armor. But, and here was the point of the question, the modern war alluded to had massed armies of unskilled men who, although in the eyes of the gentry on their chargers were louts, brutes, serfs, and peasants, had proved entirely capable of treading the flower of chivalry into the dust. The hooked halberd yanked from his saddle even the most highly trained son of a duke; the crossbow put paid to the life of the heir to fifty thousand acres. And the age of gunpowder had arrived. Don Quixote was of course ridiculous and insane, but an entire class agreed with what he said of the firearm: "This cursed invention, which is the cause that very often a cowardly base hand takes away the life of the bravest gentleman; and in the midst of that vigor and resolution which animates and inflames the bold, a chance bullet (shot perhaps by one who fled, and was frightened by the very flash the mischievous piece gave when it went off) coming nobody knows how, or from where, in a moment puts a period to the brave designs and the life of one that deserved to have survived many years." Cervantes's creation was far from alone in looking back to the "happy ages that were strangers to the dreadful fury of these devilish instruments."

There was the crux of the matter, stated in perhaps not very economical manner. War in the West for hundreds of years had been seen as a finishing school for knightly character, the showplace for the chivalrous ideals of a code of honor, courtliness, splendor, loyalty, richness, color, courage, generosity, self-denial, professed piety, for display of spirit, flair, dash, panache, the whole encased in and indeed born of the concept of pomp and majesty derivative of the flavor of history and tradition. And all this was irretrievably connected with the horse. Logic decrees that the very term that defines the Knights of the Round Table means that if required we visualize them seated; but it is on horseback that we know them best, a Lancelot and a Galahad riding forth in accordance with the high demands of the Arthurian ideal to fulfill knight-errantry's noble, storied duties. It is from atop his white charger that Saint George slays the dragon. "On one aspect of knightly fighting chivalric literature is quite unambiguous," says one authority; "the standard display of all-important prowess takes the form of combat on horseback." That was the ethos of the knightly caste transmitted through centuries, lastingly potent and resonant. Those whose names were preceded by a "von" or a "de" or an inherited title gained such distinction almost in every case through descent from an ancestor making war atop a horse. The time might have passed for the knight in shining armor, a being alluded to not uncommonly even in the twenty-first century, but the social identity of those bearing his name was entirely bound up with that name, which even into the Age of Steam and the Industrial Revolution, and beyond, meant all. So even as the utility of cavalry was increasingly questioned, those who saw it as what it had been for so long, and profited from that—the ruling classes— clutched it ever closer. There was always a completely established and known hierarchy of rating among the military units of Europe's monarchies, and at the top of each, with only a few Guards regiments figuring in, stood the cavalry. Entrance to Vienna's Hofburg for high imperial events was barred to all not of exalted birth—but the most recently commissioned young cavalry cornet was automatically admitted. Any horsed officer socially outranked a Berlin civic counselor. The tsar's cavalry officers, forbidden to appear in public in civilian attire, were required to slay anyone defacing their uniforms—and what uniforms they were, and likewise all the others of every European power.

For the golden age of military tailoring came at about the same time as Napoléon Bonaparte began his spectacular rise. Perhaps it had something to do with the feeling all over the Continent that as the masses making the French Revolution had shown they could throw off their chains, those who yet stood above them needed visual proof of superiority, even if in the French forces it was now gained instead of inherited. (Several of the emperor's marshals had begun their military careers as enlisted men in the Bourbon armies.) No other arm approached the gorgeous attire of the cavalry, although the fact was not greeted with universal approbation. "To me it appears we have too much frippery—too much toggery—too much weight in things worse than useless," wrote the British officer Lewis Edward Nolan. "To a cavalry soldier every ounce is of consequence. I can never believe that our hussar uniform (take which of them you please) is the proper dress in which to do hussar's duty in war—to scramble through thickets, to clear woods, to open the way through forests, to ford or swim rivers, to bivouac, to be nearly always on outpost work, to rough it in every possible manner. Of what use are plumes, bandoliers, sabretashes, sheepskins, shabraques, &c?"

Said the eminent general Sir Charles Napier: "The hardships of war are by our dressers of cavalry thought too little for the animal's strength; they add a bag with the Frenchified name of valise, containing an epitome of a Jew's old-clothes shop. Our hussars' old-clothes bag contains jackets, breeches of all dimensions, drawers, snuff boxes, stockings, pink boots, yellow boots, eau-de-Cologne, Windsor soap, brandy, satin waistcoats, cigars, kid gloves, tooth brushes, hair brushes, dancing spurs." The British physician William Fergusson, inspector-general of military hospitals, felt light cavalrymen were putting their health at risk by foregoing the use of a simple waterproof cloak in favor of exoticism for exoticism's sake: "It seems decreed that the hussar is ever to be a popinjay, a show of foreign fooleries, so looped and braided that the uninitiated bystander wonders how he can either get into his uniform or come out of it. A woman's muff upon his head, with something like a red jelly bag at the top, has been substituted for the warrior's helm, and the plume, so unlike the waving horsehair of the Roman casque, would seem better suited for the trappings of the undertaker than the horseman's brow."

It was not the extravagance in dress that required for the men of the mid-1840s hussar regiment commanded by the third Earl of Cardigan his personal annual expenditure of ten thousand pounds to adorn them with cherry-red trousers, jackets of royal blue edged with gold, capes glittering with bullion braid and gold lace, stunning epaulettes, and great flaring white- and scarlet-plumed headgear that brought into question the use and value of cavalry. Such dispersal of monies from private fortunes excited no more comment than the regulated purchase of rank long familiar to the British army—indeed, Lord Cardigan paid sixty thousand pounds for the colonelship of the Light Brigade of the Cavalry Division, which he

Military tailoring. Great Britain's 7th Hussars circa 1825.

so disastrously led against the emplaced Russian guns and lined-up infantry on both sides of his well-nigh insane line of advance at Balaklava during the Crimean War. (Not every mounted officer possessed the earl's resources, but all required family financial investment in their careers: what with purchase of horses and uniforms for the field, ballroom and mess charges, contributions to elegant soirees, disbursements for additions to the regimental silver, accoutrements for polo and, when on Indian service, pig-sticking, and near-mandatory hunting during one's leave, a subaltern's expenses exceeded his government salary by a ratio of at least five to one.) Similar conditions applied to every young man of what was called the Officer Class of every army in Europe. And for every marriageable young woman thought to be eligible for membership in the Ladies of the Regiment her antecedence, manners, appearance, capabilities, charms—and what amount her father could bestow upon her—were given careful study before a determination was made as to her suitability.

Such matters were not worthy of public note or remark; they were for the individual to deal with. But there was the fact that cavalry was always enormously expensive for the state, both in its creation—it took ten years to produce a competent trooper, said France's Marshal de Saxe—and its maintenance, which required the breeding of proper horses, their training, provision for their feed, their veterinary and farriers' care, and the equipment required for them to fulfill their role in war: saddles, bridles, cuirassier armor, stabling, watering, lower animals (mules, oxen, draught horses) to pull wagons full of what they needed.

For hundreds of years the cavalry had been exclusively used as a heavy detachment, a great battering ram flung at an enemy with no subtlety at all, simply a frontal-attack rush. It was of limited defensive use. The whole point of heavy cavalry was to go forward. In the siege situations common to warfare for centuries, it did nothing but eat of provisions inevitably to be increasingly depleted. In time, taught at great cost by exposure to the fighting techniques of the warriors of the East, those of the West learned better methods, and what came to be called light cavalry came to the armies of England, France, and the Germanies. Properly trained and employed, it was of great value, as Prussia's Frederick the Great showed. But Frederick had

Seydlitz, and such men were very rare. (He was after his death, one historian records, remembered as a "godlike" figure.) No comparable cavalry officer was ever to appear in Europe. Napoléon's Prince Joachim Murat was perhaps the closest approximation, but, as mentioned earlier, he was a very limited soldier.

The emperor's eventual opponent at Waterloo also had his issues with horsed soldiers. His cavalry was always getting him into trouble, the Duke of Wellington complained. His cavalry losses in the Peninsula War, which found him opposing the French under marshals subordinate to Napoléon, who was elsewhere, were stupendous—his 14th Light Dragoons landed in Lisbon in 1808 with 720 mounts, and during the campaign received 1,120 remounts. Their horse strength when returned home was 278. Wellington himself lost one dozen chargers, slain as he rode them. "The graveyard of horses," he called Spain and Portugal. Yet he knew when confronted with an out-of-the-past cavalry display in the form of Polish lancers in French service that England must have such units also. For two centuries and more, the lance had been seen as the outdated weapon of the Late Middle Ages, something that went along with great heavy lumbering mounts going forward cumbersomely bearing men in burdensome armor. But the Poles, lightly accoutered and on swift horses, were fearsome to oppose. They had refuted the traditional objection to the weapon they wielded, that it was easily parried, awkward under any circumstances, and requiring so much room for employment as to make it impractical for riders in column or line and prone to entanglement in trees. In their flat plains with scarcely a hill to be seen from Warsaw for hundreds of miles westward, ideal country for horsed operations, the Poles had kept to and perfected the use of a slim spear tipped with steel. In five minutes they slew two thirds of a British infantry brigade, fatally stabbing anyone who fell or tried to run. England quickly formed its own lancer regiments, and soon they ranked with the hussars and cuirassiers in social eminence, glorious uniforms, and pomp and panoply.

And so it seemed that cavalry *was* more than an elegant anachronism existing purely "to lend tone to what otherwise be a vulgar brawl." Wellington imported foxes to the Peninsula, they being scarce in that area, so that his officers could work on their riding skills by tallyhoing their way across the countryside behind similarly brought-in hounds; and in France his eventual Waterloo opponent was deeply involved in elaborating upon the curriculum of his army's school for cavalry leaders at Saumur. There the horsemen worked on changes of pace, alteration of stride and variation in leading foreleg, the pirouette, the passage, and the *piaffe*. "The horse, for Napoleon, was the finest expression of his attitude to war; swift, decisive, omnipotent." (Paintings he authorized almost inevitably portrayed him in the saddle atop one of the white Arab stallions that were his preference over thoroughbreds, although David's familiar rendition of young General Bonaparte crossing the Alps on that type of rearing charger is notably inaccurate; for in actuality he went over riding a mule.) The accomplished cavalry officer of precision in drill and horsemanship, doctrine held, should be able to turn his mount on a sixpence or a franc, make him supple and responsive and with man and animal matching each other in rhythm and balance as the former deployed a sabre sharpened to cut in half the flimsiest scarf floated down on it. Seydlitz had always emphasized such work in what came to be known as dressage, from the French verb for short-rein control—*dresser*. (Attendees at today's three-day-event horse shows see along with dressage competition what was originally created for military training: the cross-country of barriers to be risen to or, if of water, to be gotten through with banks to be scrambled up, ditches, woods, and then the stadium jumping over hedges and rail fences.)

The issue of cavalry's value was debated as early as the fifteenth century. The question was not definitively answered during the Napoleonic Era. The emperor took to Russia some hundred thousand horses of all types except light cavalry, and its lack severely hampered his operations. In earlier days he had been fully aware of the role played by mounted scouts, but then there came a time when he placed his reliance solely on riders trained and equipped for the boot-to-boot charge launched to the accompaniment of screams and yells described as akin to the sounds of wild beasts in cages. There was little opportunity for such display during the Russian campaign, for the enemy refused to mass in front of the emperor's forces, fading away and vanishing. There was nothing to charge against. When the Grande Armée concluded its disastrous retreat from Moscow it brought away but twelve thousand horses. All along the way west it was plagued in murderous fashion by the tsar's Cossacks on their swift and sturdy little ponies. "They swarmed about like savage bees engaged in tormenting and exhausting a roaring lion with their innumerable stings," wrote General Charles Antoine Morand. Napoléon's heavy cavalry, unwieldy and cumbersome, a sledgehammer fruitlessly striking out, was unable to counter. "His deficiency in light cavalry, more than any other cause, therefore, contributed to his downfall," wrote the American officer of cavalry Captain Malin Craig, who eventually rose to be United States Army chief of staff.

At Waterloo, later, Marshal Michel Ney, France's "bravest of the brave," his view of the field obscured by smoke from artillery fire, mistook a movement to the rear of wounded British soldiers and French prisoners under escort for a general retreat of Wellington's men. It had been an axiom for centuries back to the Romans that infantry intact and of highest morale and well supplied with ammunition could not be broken by a cavalry charge. Such conditions were very rarely found, and could be negated by missile fire, clouds of arrows or slung rocks, or great boulders flung by mechanical devices in early days and by artillery shells later. Then gaps appeared in formations so that horsemen deploying seven times the weight and infinitely greater thrusting or slashing impact from the high and stable platform their saddles offered got in among the men on foot (if indeed these did not run even before being reached), ruptured their formation, and downed all within reach to send them flying to be slaughtered as they ran. To Ney it appeared that the first requirement for success had been met, and that the British were already out of formation and on a backward move. He did not call for an artillery barrage, but launched five thousand sabre-wielding cuirassiers in glittering breast- and back-plate, only to behold, when the wounded and prisoners scattered out of the way, twenty squares of British infantry—rectangles, actually—with the front rows of men kneeling with musket butts firmly grounded so that a thicket of bayonets pointed up.

The whole meaning of a charge of heavy cavalry was that its impetus could not be stopped, that this was the very genesis of its being; and so the French roared on. Doctrine held that since a horse's vital organs were sheltered behind heavy layers of muscle, it would even if stabbed or shot plummet forward to fall among defenders with hoofs lashing out in death throes, likely disabling sufficient men so that a gap would open into which other horses with their riders could pour. Then all would be well for the attackers, and the charge would have been driven home. But the stolid British held as men behind the kneeling bayonet-holders discharged their muskets and then stepped back to reload as others stepped forward to fire. Ney's thousands kept coming like, it was said, waves smashing on rocks, with dead men and dead horses piling up like breastworks in front of the British. In the end it came down to individual French riders circling the squares forlornly looking for a way in. It is odd that from far away, Light-Horse Harry Lee correctly estimated the situation, writing James Monroe from San Juan that the British would conquer Napoléon when they learned to contain his cavalry.

The Battle of Waterloo, and the career of Napoléon, came to its climax. The French gathered all their horses and launched a final, losing drive. Wellington countered with a charge by the Scots Greys, the riders ordered to take the bits out of their horses' mouths so that even if a man thought to slow the pace he could not, being somewhat in the position, to use a modern simile, of a driver whose brakes are inoperative and whose gas pedal is flattened down. With reins useless, the Greys roared forward, each with one hand holding a fistful of mane and the other a sabre. An epic painting by Lady Elizabeth Butler, greatly esteemed in the world-dominating England that followed, was posed for by veterans she hired to show what they had done. It is seen from the vantage point of the waiting French. They were of the Imperial Guard, France's premier soldiers. At the order "Prepare to receive cavalry!" the front row stepped back to set their musket butts to earth, bayonets pointing up. But the retrograde move, slight as it was, transfixed other, lesser, French units—and a tremor went through others of the emperor's men at the thought that the Guard was in retreat; and in a little while Napoléon was flying for Paris amid an army turned into a routed mob. All was accomplished at some cost for both sides—in horses no less than men. Captain A. C. Mercer of the Royal Horse Artillery (all European armies by then had the quick-moving pieces introduced by the Prussian cavalry of King Frederick and General von Seydlitz) remembered as he headed off the field the sight of a horse with both hind legs gone. Captain Mercer lost 140 of his 200 horses so that the British could conquer at Waterloo, and of blood he had had enough, he wrote, and more. He listened to the "protracted melancholy neighing" of the fatally wounded animal, and it came to him that he should unleash a shot to end such misery. He could not. No more blood. So he went on his way, hearing then and later in memory the horse "neighing after us, as if reproaching our desertion in his hour of need."

"A damned near run thing, the nearest run thing you ever saw in your life," Wellington said of the day's events. He had been sixteen straight hours in the saddle when he dismounted from his chestnut thoroughbred, Copenhagen, to offer a pat on the hindquarters answered with a kick only by the very slightest margin failing to make one more casualty for marking down against England's great victory. The triumphant commander did not hold the act against his steed, but took him back home to be a great pet of Lady Wellington's: "He trots after me eating bread out of my hand, and wagging his tail like a little dog." When, two decades later, Copenhagen died, at twenty-eight, the *Times* of London offered a full obituary. "By the orders of His Grace a salute was fired over his grave, and thus he was buried as he lived, with military honors." The duchess wore a bracelet made from Copenhagen's hair. By then, in 1836, uniforms of British horse soldiers exceeded in operatic splendor almost anything she or any other woman might wear. "Cavalrymen suffered more than other soldiers," noted a recent work. "The head-dresses they were obliged to wear make wonderful collectors' pieces today because of their fantastic shapes. The horse soldiers were loaded with all kinds of dashing trappings—dolmans, pelisses and jackets cut so exquisitely and slung so elaborately that even women's tailors would be envious of their line." That Dickens and Thackeray ridiculed them was of no consequence. The cavalry, elegant and aristocratic, the province of the well-born and socially superior, retained its high place, with the most minute attention paid to details of dress—and mustaches. William IV allowed only members of certain regiments to wear them, with Victoria in 1839 ruling that all must.

Britain's storied charge of the 1854–56 Crimean War, immortalized by Alfred, Lord Tennyson—"Theirs not to reason why / Theirs but to do and die / Into the valley of Death / Rode the six hundred"—is perhaps the most famous horsed movement in history. It came about from matters so diverse as the question of whether a gentleman decants his wine and whether he should be denounced if he does not; and the ferocious enmity between the brothers-in-law the 3rd Lord Lucan and 7th Lord Cardigan, one the commander of the entire cavalry division sent to Balaklava, the other heading its light brigade; and enigmatic, ill-written, and contradictory orders. The route of the disastrous advance can be likened to a bowling alley, with Russian infantry lining the gutters and Russian heavy artillery emplaced where the pins sit waiting for the ball. "Here goes the last of the family," Cardigan remarked as he put his horse into motion, his gorgeously attired followers, pipe-clayed, polished, the horses glossy, at a controlled trot in flawless alignment behind. It was a day of brilliant sunshine and no clouds, light glittering from the brass ornaments on epaulettes, buttons, pouches and shakos, sabres and lances.

They had a mile and a quarter to go to the guns, and had covered some fifty yards when Captain Lewis Edward Nolan, in the most astonishing fashion imaginable, broke ranks to gallop on a diagonal in front of his commanding officer, waving his sword and shouting. Nolan was a recognized authority on mounted operations, author of two highly respected books on the subject, *Nolan's System for Training Cavalry Horses*, which stressed kindness rather than punishment, and *Cavalry: Its History and Tactics*. It was unthinkable that he commit such a breach of military etiquette—"That won't do, Nolan!" shouted a fellow officer—and why he did it was never to be known, for a Russian shot took him in the chest, exposing his heart. He kept his seat even as his sword fell to the ground and he voiced a terrible scream. His horse wheeled and raced back through the oncoming 4th Light Dragoons as the erect rider's protracted cry chilled the blood of all who heard it. Then he fell dead to the ground. A century and a half has gone by, and those who study the Charge of the Light Brigade wonder yet if Captain Nolan, from the depths of his cavalry expertise, realized that only disaster could attend so catastrophic a move, and died attempting to halt it. But he was not alone in seeing what impended. "It is magnificent, but it is not war," said a French general as he viewed the serried ranks going on to certain annihilation in slow, disciplined fashion.

They broke into a faster pace, men constantly dropping from their saddles as the Russian fire took effect. Lord George Paget found himself galloping in the midst of seven riderless horses, obedient to their training that they not break ranks in a charge. It was as if their fallen masters were still aboard, Paget thought. In the end some two thirds of the brigade's 673 soldiers were dead or wounded, and 470 horses gone. As those soldiers who survived the fruitless arrival at the Russian guns and then returned stood for roll calls unresponded to by so many of their fellows, the sound of farriers' pistols putting an end to the misery of dozens of fatally wounded animals rolled over the field. Men gathered to speak of what had occurred. "They especially mourned their horses. Sergeant-Major Loy Smith of the Hussars was 'moved to tears when I thought of my beautiful horse; she was a light bay, nearly thoroughbred, I became her master nearly three years before.'" Crimean horrors had not yet ended, for the British medical and provisioning services were not close to being able to prevent widespread hunger among the troops, with death from disease and exposure the fate of no small number. As for the horses, they were in their picket line and corrals so ravaged by hunger as to chew on one another's manes and tails.

The disaster and its fearsome aftermath followed an even more costly British cavalry misadventure five years earlier, at Chillianwallah in the Punjab. Leading elements charging a contingent of Sikhs mistakenly got the idea that a retreat had been ordered, and turning around collided with the men behind them, confusion turning into panic as the enemy came on. A stampede ensued, with Sikhs wielding kirpans, razor-sharp blades, to inflict gory damage. The battle cost England 750 cavalrymen and 2,000 horses. Yet it and the events at Balaklava did not serve to bring to an end the conviction that cavalry service was the highest calling a soldier could know; and the uniforms grew ever more wondrous as Europe entered a long period of peace. Across the Atlantic Ocean, forms of cavalry warfare never seen before came into being.

9

"The crimes of this guilty land will never be purged away but with Blood"

In the decades following the Revolution, the United States Army, such as it was, less than five thousand men, possessed no cavalry. Local militia had what they called that, with horses bearing riders for Fourth of July parades given a day off from their duties of pulling a plow or logs meant for a new cabin or shed. The performances of such units can hardly be noted with admiration: militia dragoons sent to oppose War of 1812 British forces successfully aiming to take Washington, wrote the historian Fletcher Pratt, "acquired the well-deserved reputation of being the fastest-running cavalry in the world."

In time, the United States Military Academy at West Point offered cavalry training, under primitive conditions. "The present cooped up place is very dangerous," Cadet James Stuart of Virginia wrote his parents in February 1854. Outdoor instruction, he added, was made difficult by inability to hear commands from three paces away for the wind blowing off the Hudson, and, while perhaps appropriate "for a Russian Napoleonic campaign," snows two feet deep did not help. Mr. Stuart, as a student was addressed, possibly offered his opinions to the academy superintendent over dinner, for he was a great favorite of the superintendent's wife. She often had him over, along with her cadet son and cadet nephew. Likely the superintendent, Lieutenant Colonel Robert E. Lee, who had risen to his father's rank through stellar showing during the 1846–48 war with Mexico, did not have to be told. An enclosed riding hall was constructed in 1855 under his supervision, at a cost of $22,000.

In it, cadets on galloping horses swung or thrust swords, including the big dragoon one they termed "Old Wrist Breaker," at leather bags stuffed with straw set on poles about the level of a man's head, leaned over to get at ones on the ground, pointed their weapons through rings and bars, took jumps, performed stunts involving leaping off or facing backward or standing erect on the horse's back or with one foot on one horse and the other on a second. To drill without saddles or stirrups was so commonplace as not to excite comment. Yet of course things did not always go well; it was not uncommon for someone to swat his horse with a sword by mistake, which could lead to equine retaliation. Another man's mount took revenge for his rider's error on the nearby Cadet John Pelham of Alabama, getting him with both rear hooves and sending him to the hospital. Like Stuart, Pelham had written home about the difficulties of riding outside on snow and ice, and like Stuart he was a born horseman. The same could not be said of the future artist James McNeill Whistler, one of West Point's two most noted dropouts, the other being Edgar Allan Poe. Tossed from his mount three times in one session, Mr. Whistler got up from the floor to say, "I don't see how people can ever ride for pleasure." His equitation problems may not have been exclusively his fault, for only first classmen, seniors, got their pick of what they chose to ride; other cadets, like Whistler, were ordered onto animals possibly balky or given to rearing and plunging. The matter soon became of no interest to him, for his cadet days were coming to an end. Asked in chemistry class to discuss silicon, he began by defining it as a gas. "That will do," said the instructor. Shortly Superintendent Lee suggested that Whistler's future would best be of a nonmilitary nature. "If silicon had been a gas, I would have been a major general," Whistler loved to say in later years. (To the bemusement of some who see it, a metal plaque in the West Point library commemorates the nongraduates Poe and Whistler.)

Another cadet wrote of the results of a riding lesson: "I could not lie down with any comfort, neither could I walk, nor sit down. The inside of my thighs, clear down to my knees, was completely black and blue. Every muscle and nerve in my body seemed twisted out of place. I can only hope no mortal will ever suffer as I did during the next week."

Cadet Stuart would have been as amused to read those words as he was at "seeing what ridiculous figures these Yankees cut on horseback." (The distinction between riders from north of the Mason-Dixon line and those from its south would one day be of such importance in the history of the United States as none could have guessed.) Stuart himself was so anxious to be taken into the mounted forces upon graduation that family legend says he deliberately slackened his academic endeavors for fear of ranking so high as to find himself in the engineers, where the best students were assigned. His plan worked. By 1854, the year of Stuart's graduation, the army had maintained horsed units for more than two decades, the first a dragoon regiment formed in 1833. Its officers, serving infantrymen, studied European manuals and practiced drilling one another prior to working with enlisted men. The army then formed the Regiment of Mounted Riflemen, plus regiments designated as Cavalry. Although all were considered distinct arms of the service, with orange trim for the dragoons, green for the riflemen, and yellow for the cavalry, everything effectively blurred together, the men really dragoon-like in that they were trained to fight afoot or mounted. There was nothing in any way reminiscent of Europe's accepted social superiority of cavalry officers uniformly descended from the noble knight-at-arms of the hatchment, the raised oriflamme floating at the tip of a lance, the coat of arms, the glory of the past, heritage, historical memory, the suit of armor standing in the entryway of manse or castle of the family holding. All the Americans were, regardless of background, products of the West Point educational system of individual recital every day in every class, with the grades, along with soldiery smartness, determining class rank and resulting assignment after graduation. Still less was there concern with nor emphasis upon gorgeous uniforms, for all the men had done their riding at the Point in their most disreputable clothing, no uniforms being issued for that, and the tradition of wearing what one wanted when in the field persisted throughout the long years of America's use of mounted forces.

None of the horsed units upon formation, or indeed ever afterward, were based on the thousand-year-old European shock model of speed and weight hitting home so heavily and with such impact that the shattered enemy was sent flying to be lanced or sabred down as he ran. For whom were they designated to deal with, the first of the country's reasonably large-scale mounted forces? It is a question that hardly needs asking. The first major armed hostilities between Europeans and Indians living in what would be called the United States dates from 1622, when a man identified as Trader Morgan vanished from a Virginia settlement on the James River. Soon afterward an Indian was observed wearing the trader's hat. He was killed by the missing man's associates. Masses of Indians avenged his death with an attack that in one day saw the deaths of 347 settlers, men, women, and children alike—the commencement, it has been said, of a war destined to last two and a half centuries. It went on, with rises and falls in intensity, but always constantly, as the whites pushed west from the tideland areas of the original thirteen colonies, their progress unstoppable despite occasional government promises to Indians that it would be restricted.

In time the wave of emigrants left the eastern forestlands and came to great flatlands, where, unlike at the scenes of previous encounters, Indians made war on horseback, having over centuries bred little resilient ponies from animals taken from or left behind by Spanish conquistadors. The horses made tribesmen mobile and able to follow buffalo herds; and this produced a new culture for the Plains Indians. "An entirely new pattern of life developed, complete with a new religious orientation, new dances, and new games," wrote the historian William Osborn. One thing did not change. The Indian was of Stone Age development in all things save one. That was mastery of war. He harked back millennia to the fabled Assyrians of old, to whom there had never been superior warriors. Like them, Indians needed no saddles, using blankets instead, and like them they moved a horse in the desired direction solely by use of the calves and knees. An Indian could keep eight arrows in the air at one time at a range up to one hundred yards. He and his swarmed about, the frequently voiced observation was, like a swarm of bees, never bunching up but individually darting in, going back, vanishing behind a rise or through a defile and then coming on again. Against such—again a familiar phrase, "the finest light cavalry the world ever saw"—artillery was useless and infantry even more so. Only cavalry would do, and its need was intensified when in the wake of the war with Mexico the United States came into possession of vast western territories.

To the settlers going west, the Indians were fiends who burned, plundered, pillaged, ravished, and murdered as a matter of course. The Indian view was that invaders were coming upon the land that had always been theirs, aiming to destroy a way of life dating back to prehistoric times, to rebuke the wisdom of their fathers, to trample on their habits and customs, their values, the old order of things. The United States Cavalry was caught in the middle. Europe's extensive literature of military theory offered no hints about how to deal with the situation.

Stuart at West Point was remarked for his high spirits and conviviality, combined with a love of physical confrontations—"an immediate and almost thankful acceptance of a challenge to fight from any cadet," remembered Cadet Fitz Lee, the superintendent's nephew; Stuart was "vivacious, exuberant, romantic and overflowing with good spirits, but quick to provocation," remembered Cadet William Woods Averell, who won the award for premier horseman of his class in his final year at West Point. There was an academy tradition that no man could be so named if ever in his four years he was thrown from the saddle, which fate overtook Cadet Lewis Merrill. There was a horse, Turk, remembered Averell, who had his own ideas of when a class should end, and demonstrated them by depositing many a rider on the ground. "I will now show you how this horse should be handled," Merrill declaimed, and stayed aboard until it came to Turk that as he could not throw this cadet, the best course was to take him elsewhere. Turk roared out of the riding hall and careered along a crest to make a spectacularly sudden right turn that left Merrill tumbling down the slope. It was a matter of sorrow for

Stuart when a horse he particularly fancied, Tony, was retired from service; he wrote he would wear a mourning ribbon around his pinky for a week.

Assignment to the cavalry was not based strictly upon riding capability, as one cadet brilliant atop a horse found out to his great sorrow. The West Point of his day was dedicated, along with graded recitation every day in every class, to constant, rigidly meticulous adherence to rules regarding dress, manner of speaking, marching, smartness, promptness, and absolute precision in performance of every duty. All of these were entirely beyond the capabilities of the Ohioan Hiram Ulysses Grant, whose congressman when appointing him had misstated his name as Ulysses S. Grant, a name the notably passive and inarticulate seventeen-year-old then and there accepted as his own. An upperclassman reading the posted list of entering cadets saw "U. S. Grant" and said the new man, obviously, was United States Grant. No, said Cadet William T. Sherman, he was Uncle Sam Grant. The Uncle Sam got shortened to Sam, and those who had known him there always called him that. (Many cadets had nicknames. William Woods Averell was "Swell"; James Stuart was "Beauty," in direct contrast to his actual appearance, said his friend Cadet Fitz Lee—in apparent jest, for the young Stuart's face and frame were perfectly presentable.) Grant was always a tremendous rider—as a child he won five dollars offered by the ringmaster of a traveling circus to anyone who could stay on a particular bucking pony and keep his seat even when the ringmaster tossed a monkey on his back to climb up on his head and claw his face. West Point had a horse, York, so unmanageable that only one other cadet was even allowed to approach him. "Sam," said Cadet Charles Hamilton, "that horse will kill you someday."

"Well, I can't die but once," Grant replied, and tamed the animal. On graduation day he gave a jumping exhibition aboard York, sitting so securely in the saddle that it seemed to the first-year cadet James B. Fry as if horse and rider were welded together. "Very well done, sir!" cried the sergeant-instructor in admiration of a spectacular leap. It was the sole moment of distinction in Sam Grant's academy career, insufficient in light of other manifold and manifest failings to earn him the cavalry assignment he coveted, and he took up infantry duties, which he performed in a generally indifferent fashion for several years until, given a choice of involuntary discharge for drunkenness or resignation of his commission, he elected the latter.

William Averell was luckier in getting what he desired upon graduation, for he was assigned to the Regiment of Mounted Riflemen, dispersed in Texas and New Mexico. Before joining his command he put in some teaching and learning time at the Cavalry School, which formed part of the army's recruiting depot at Jefferson Barracks, some eleven miles outside of Saint Louis. There men intended for the mounted service were daily instructed in the basics of their future duties in troop, squadron, and regiment; how to care for horses, arms, and equipment; how to pitch camp or establish bivouac and guard the same; and how to handle their rations and prepare food. Entering enlisted men were hardly a prepossessing lot. Almost uniformly illiterate, they traditionally joined up for one of three reasons: they'd gotten a girl in trouble and had to get out of town fast; harvesting season had given out and they needed what was termed three hots and a flop; or a judge had given them a choice between jail and the army. It was extremely difficult to acquire men sufficiently competent in writing and arithmetic to perform the work of clerk to a cavalry company or a troop, the two words being alternately used, and when found they were inevitably drunkards who had been unable to keep a civilian job. Subjected to harsh military discipline, they might be kept sober enough to perform their duties. Sometimes men who had gotten themselves west on their own enlisted directly into outfits patrolling the vast spaces, but often they proved to be what the army called "snowbirds," men who signed up when cold weather came, and could be depended upon to desert once spring arrived.

After his Jefferson Barracks stint, Averell went to Carlisle Barracks in Pennsylvania, where he put in time sitting on courts-martial. It was not pleasant duty, and he remembered what officers felt when leaving punishment sites featuring whippings. They cursed the regulations compelling them to officiate, and went away silent and depressed. Once the former West Point superintendent of Averell's cadet days, Robert E. Lee, came to be president of a court-martial.

He was no longer the Engineers officer he had been for all his career before taking on the academy post, but had transferred to the cavalry. Lieutenant Averell made a call upon him, which the lieutenant colonel returned, in a blue dress coat with metal buttons, the tails of which he parted as he stood with his back to Averell's fire. "He was bright, genial and easy, while I remember I was a little embarrassed," Averell wrote, thinking it "seemed somehow incongruous to find him in the cavalry service." Lee asked if his host liked being with horses, and after receiving an affirmative reply said, "Well, I was always fond of horses and liked the outdoor life the same as you." He went on to chat about his riding experiences during the war with Mexico, in which he was the right arm of the commanding general, Winfield Scott, saying somewhat improbably, "We young fellows of the Engineers"—he was forty when the war ended—"had to ride a great deal and were glad to get a mule sometimes." (That general and future president Zachary Taylor, "Old Rough and Ready," in a manner inconceivable for any European of high military rank habitually wore a battered flannel shirt and traveled about sitting sideways on a mule during the Mexican campaign is a matter of record—but Lee?)

Averell's classmate James Stuart was sent west to the 2nd Dragoons, based at Fort Riley, Kansas, Colonel Philip St. George Cooke, West Point 1827, commanding. Along with his close friend Jefferson Davis, both lieutenants then, Cooke had been one of the original officers of the first mounted regiments back in 1833. Davis left the army to be secretary of war, successfully pushing for extension of the horsed outfits, and also to arrange the importation of camels for use in the western deserts. His championship of horsed soldiers earned him their affection, the 2nd Cavalry being informally known as Jeff Davis's Own. The camel project had a less fortunate result. Secretary Davis, told the animals could go two days in the hottest conditions without water, and regularly cover 250 miles between watering, pictured them as welcome replacements for the supply mules that accompanied cavalry patrols, those with a "P" branded on the left front hoof used for pack purposes, those with a "W" schooled to pull wagons. Mules were never easy to deal with, given at inopportune moments to balking, kicking, and rolling on the ground. Working them into their duties was a lengthy and chancy business, with in-training neophytes having their tails denuded so as to warn all approaching to take care. (Second lieutenants, by definition new to service, are to this day denoted as "shavetails.")

But the army had no choice but to go on with them, for Davis's camels did not work out, and ended, so it was said, as meals for Apache raiders. Their sponsor went on from the War Department to be senator from Mississippi, then president of the Confederate States of America. Philip St. George Cooke remained in the army to earn the title the Grand Old Man of the Cavalry, the author of the definitive book on horsed tactics, written after a two-year assignment abroad to study European mounted units. A Virginian, stern, demanding, notably inarticulate, he was taken for a soldier's soldier, his motto for his horsemen, "Sharp sabres and sharp spurs." Colonel Cooke had three daughters, the oldest of whom, Flora, attracted the eye of the 2nd Dragoons' new Lieutenant Stuart the moment he first saw her. It was at a regimental review she attended aboard a fractious horse. Perhaps the brute would run away with her, Stuart thought. That would offer him an opportunity to gallop after, grab the reins, effect a gallant rescue, and, to say the least, make a striking first impression. His hopeful fantasy evaporated when he saw that Miss Cooke was an outstanding horsewoman able to control her mount without his aid. Shortly he found other ways to be with her, and she with him; and in two months' time they agreed to be Lieutenant and Mrs. James Ewell Brown Stuart. She had gone from being a cook to a steward, the bride punned in reasonably amusing fashion.

They were six years at various posts west of the Mississippi— Fort Riley, Fort Leavenworth, Fort Clark in Texas—he transferring in and out of various horsed units, as was commonly done. They had a girl who died and then a son who lived, Philip St. George Cooke Stuart. The lieutenant grew a great beard, in later years described as "Jovian," which he said impelled people to declare that he was the only man in the world made more attractive by a crop of whiskers. Always religiously inclined, a Methodist, he found when reporting for duty with the Mounted Rifles that the chaplain was an Episcopalian aiming to build a church. He aided in the eventually successful endeavor, additionally having himself confirmed in the new place of worship's denomination. How many of the civilians whose relations with Indians it was the cavalry's duty to regulate attended services there would be depressing to calculate. For while a percentage of the people coming west were decent family folk seeking to farm or raise cattle, or open stores or ply a trade, no less a number were of the churned-out type that always washes up on a frontier: criminals on the run from the law, people who didn't fit in with established eastern seaboard society, the perpetually dissatisfied, debtors, swindlers, men leaving their wives, girls kicked out by families with too many mouths to feed who heard cow-town bordellos meant good money. To such, in a harsh land and unforgiving world, the Indian was a creature whose practices marked him as less than human. Scalping had never been heard of in all the thousands of years of European history; in the New World the natives routinely did it, sometimes taking ears and all. Indians swooped down to kill the man of an isolated homestead or, even worse, take him away for ghastly torture and a dreadful death; his wife they ravished and his children they enslaved or, sometimes, raised as their own so that in a little while all traces and remembrance of a former life vanished. To kill an Indian for his horse or for whatever else he had, or perhaps just for the sport of it, was not really a crime, most people felt.

That was not a viewpoint shared by many of the cavalry officers doing their duty as their government gave them to see that duty in the countless skirmishes and officially itemized twenty-two little Indian wars of the decade between 1850 and 1860. Back east, they knew, there was no little sense of guilt about what was being done to those portrayed by James Fenimore Cooper and Henry Wadsworth Longfellow as the noble red man. Should it come to pass that one of these exotics killed him, ruefully mused Lieutenant William Averell, any paper that "deigns to notice the affair" would "express the world's regret" by saying it served him right. A rider galloped to the tiny windblown one-troop post to say Indians had slaughtered a settler family or attacked a wagon train, and one's bugler sounded "Boots and Saddles," and with the command presence and parade ground manner learned on the Plain over the Hudson one shouted, "Stand to horse! Prepare to mount! Mount! March!" The column of twos or fours moved out behind the held-aloft guidons, mule train following, most efforts to no effect whatsoever for finding those sought, who had slipped through defile up into unassailable rocky mountain fastness, or down into deep canyon labyrinth. "Notwithstanding we have threaded every trail, clambered over every precipice and penetrated every ravine for hundreds of miles around, we have not been able to find Mr. Comanche," Lieutenant Stuart wrote a cousin at home back in Virginia. Yet not seeing, he knew, as did all other soldiers, that he was very likely seen: if signs of Indians were detected, frontier wisdom dictated, be careful; if not, be *very* careful.

There came a moment when a cavalry detachment beheld something almost never seen in the West: a bunched group of hostiles. They were Cheyennes. It was along the Solomon River in northwest Kansas. Stuart expected the officer commanding to order withdrawal of pistols from holsters and carbines from saddle buckets and was surprised to hear, "Draw sabres! Charge!" They roared forward in the classic manner of a thousand European battlefields. A fellow officer was off his horse. There was an Indian on foot, firearm in his hand, approaching the downed man. Stuart swung his blade as simultaneously the Indian fired at him. Both fell, the Indian dead and Stuart with a chest wound that proved minor. He was taken away on a travois, a slanted stretcher of two poles with one set of ends lashed to a mule and the others dragging on the ground. Four sabres stuck in the ground to hold a blanket protecting him from the sun formed his shelter for a while, he wrote his wife, his only diversions reading his Book of Common Prayer, "which I must say has not been neglected," and a copy of the army regulations.

Soldiers had duties not involving Indians in what in the 1850s was called Bloody Kansas, for there was murderous enmity between those who stood for what was called Free Soil and those who were proslavery. Adherents of one policy or the other were dragged from their homes to be hacked or beaten to death or shot in front of their families as the army thrashed about attempting to keep the peace. It was the most unpleasant of obligations, and Stuart must have been happy to be away from it when in 1859 he took a leave from Fort Riley to attend an Episcopal conference in Richmond as a lay delegate. He additionally went east in an attempt to sell the

War Department his patented invention of a device expediting the removal of sabre from sword belt for swift attachment to saddle when a cavalryman got off his horse to take up ground duties, military doctrine holding that use of a blade was exclusively reserved for a rider, and not someone who had dismounted. (In time the War Department bought his patent for $5,000.)

The lieutenant was sitting in an anteroom waiting to demonstrate his invention to Secretary of War John Floyd when he was told the matter must be put off. An extreme emergency had arisen, information regarding which must immediately be conveyed to Lieutenant Colonel Robert E. Lee, on leave from his post as officer commanding the 1st Regiment of Cavalry at San Antonio, Texas, in order that he clear up the tangled state of affairs left by the death of his father-in-law, George Washington Custis, Martha Washington's heir through her first husband, and the first president's adopted grandson. Stuart volunteered to gallop to Arlington House, seat of one of the three estates forming part of the inheritance of Mary Custis Lee, Mrs. Robert E. Lee, to hand her husband a sealed note from the chief clerk of the War Department. Arrived, he was informed that the colonel had gone to nearby Alexandria. He tracked him to an apothecary shop, where he was making some purchases. Lee opened the letter to read that he was to report at once to Secretary Floyd. There was trouble at Harper's Ferry, Virginia, at the federal armory and arsenal there. A man calling himself Captain Smith had with followers of unknown number seized the property, taken hostages from leading families of the region, and sent out word that he was going to lead a slave rebellion that would end bondage in America. Local blacks must rally to him. He would lead them south, liberating others as he went, storming through Virginia and into Tennessee, an army growing by the hour, burning and shooting, into Alabama and then the coastal states, Georgia, South Carolina, North Carolina. When he was finished slavery would be dead in America.

It appeared to President James Buchanan that a full-scale insurrection, an apocalyptic race war, was at hand. There was not a single enlisted man of the army in Washington, and the only troops at all in the capital consisted of ninety United States Marines of the

Navy Yard whose commander was a lieutenant. They were ordered to entrain at once for Harper's Ferry. But a lieutenant could not be entrusted with putting down what might amount to a revolution. A more seasoned officer by far was needed, and hence the summons to Colonel Lee. He and Stuart passed through District of Columbia policemen told to watch the roads for invading armies of slaves and went to Secretary of War Floyd and then President Buchanan, who ordered Lee to Harper's Ferry. Stuart volunteered to accompany the colonel as an aide, and the two got on a waiting steam-up Baltimore & Ohio locomotive and sped to where the marines awaited them, along with Virginia and Maryland militia outfits and every local white man who owned a gun. Firing could be heard directed at and coming from the complex of buildings where the insurgent leader and his men were barricaded. No slaves had rallied to them.

It was eleven at night, October 17, 1859. Thirteen hostages were with the invaders in a brick building that housed the post fire engines. It had thick walls and heavy oak doors. There was no way of knowing the number of men in the insurgent party (it proved to be eighteen), and storming the engine house in the dark would be dangerous and perhaps futile. Lee decided to await morning before doing anything. When the sun began to rise he sent Stuart with a white flag to the engine-house door, which opened a crack. The lieutenant found himself looking down the barrel of a cocked Sharps rifle. In the half-light of a misty morning he saw a face he recognized from his service with the peacekeeping forces from which he had so recently taken leave.

"Why, aren't you old Osawatomie Brown of Kansas, whom I once had there as my prisoner?"

"Yes, but you didn't keep me," said John Brown. His nickname came from a town where he perpetuated a particularly notable massacre. Other than Stuart, no man of Lee's force and almost certainly no one else in Harper's Ferry would have known Brown. Stuart read out a note Lee had written calling for a peaceable surrender and warning that failure to comply would compel measures making Lee unable to answer for the safety of the barricaded men. Brown said he could not accept the demand, and requested safe passage out of Harper's Ferry. Stuart replied that that was out of the question. They argued the point to no avail, and then Stuart stepped back and took off his hat and waved it at Lee, a prearranged signal that sent the marines running at the building to the sound of more than two thousand spectators screaming for blood. The men bashed down the door and rushed in. Lee had ordered that there should be no gunfire; one insurgent had a bayonet driven through him and died pinioned up against a wall, and Brown was slightly wounded. A marine was shot to death. The insurgents were brought out as spectators shouted they should be lynched. Lee had the marines escort them to the post paymaster's office and there, as newspaper and magazine reporters looked on, later to file stories appearing under headlines screaming of insurrection, riot, and rebellion, officials told Brown he was a madman and fanatic and deranged criminal. He replied that God, not man, was his judge, and that the slaves should be free.

What wages did he pay his followers? inquired U.S. Senator James Mason. "None."

"The wages of sin is death," said Stuart.

"I would not have made such a remark to you, if you had been a prisoner and wounded in my hands," Brown said. A trial followed with the expected verdict leading some in the North to say that the scaffold was now made glorious, as once the cross was similarly. As he walked down prison steps on his way to execution, the condemned man handed a note to a jailor: *I John Brown am now quite certain that the crimes of this guilty land will never be purged away but with Blood. I had as I now think vainly flattered myself that without very much bloodshed it might be done.* A moment later he swung at the end of a rope. Six months later the war came.

10

"The best damned cavalryman ever foaled in America"

Of the five officers commanding the horsed regiments of the United States Army in 1861, four tendered their resignations to Secretary of War Simon Cameron when the Confederate States of America came into being. In their number was Colonel Robert E. Lee of the 1st Cavalry. Offered field command of the force that would be raised to suppress the rebellion by an emissary speaking in the names of President Lincoln and the army chief, General Winfield Scott, Lee asked for time to consider, prayed, anguished, and made his decision that Virginia and not the United States came first. Her husband had wept tears of blood over this, Mrs. Lee wrote. No such reservations attended Lieutenant Stuart's resignation, and he went to Richmond to seek a Confederate army commission. He was astounded, he wrote his wife, that her father, Colonel Cooke, was not also there in the capital of their mutual home state and soon-to-be capital of the Confederate States of America. High position awaited "Pa," the "ne plus ultra," Stuart wrote, of a cavalry officer. "Why doesn't he come?"

But Cooke would never come. Like the Virginian Winfield Scott, he saw his first loyalty as being to the flag of the United

States and not to that of the Confederacy. He was horrified when he learned that his son-in-law and his Harvard University–graduate son, John, had elected to go South: "Those mad boys!" Stuart could not come close to accepting his father-in-law's attitude, and he and his wife changed their little son's name from Philip St. George Cooke Stuart to James Ewell Brown Stuart Jr. For a time Flora Cooke Stuart retained the habit of referring to the child by what he had originally been called, and her husband wrote, "My Darling, don't call our boy by his old name if you please—we settled that when together, it is not right to revive it in your letters." Harvard's John Cooke rose in time to be a rebel brigadier general. It was not until twenty years after the war that he reconciled with his father.

Colonel Cooke's 2nd Dragoons were in Utah Territory when the country went to war, and the fashion in which he got them back to Washington lived in the memory of Lieutenant Wesley Merritt, West Point 1860, as the most flawless example he ever knew of how a cavalry leader comported himself. So precise and so exacting was the discipline regarding mounting too early or dismounting too late, march times, rests, unsaddling, feeding, watering, grooming, and attention to hooves and all other aspects of the animals' condition that upon arrival after so long a journey, the horses and men were ready to go into battle immediately. All that could be learned of horse management, Merritt thought, had been displayed. Cooke was given the two stars of a major general and command of all the horsed units in and around Washington, his intensive drilling of which, it was said, made the open grounds north and east of the Capitol shake. But in fact the Union authorities expected cavalry to play the most minor of roles in the conflict that was getting under way. Winfield Scott had performed brilliantly in the war with Mexico a decade and a half earlier—"He is the greatest soldier of the age," the old Duke of Wellington had said, Waterloo more than thirty years in the past—but Scott's work had involved the investment of walled cities and assaults upon fortresses, not horsed operations. His War Department planned to form the Regular Army men remaining loyal to the Union, and the seventy-five thousand volunteers President Lincoln had called for, into thirty-nine regiments of infantry. There would be only one of cavalry, for the fighting would see but little of its use.

That was not the view held in the South. In the days before the war, Mark Twain wrote, people there lived in a romantic dream world based on novels of Sir Walter Scott telling of gallant knights-at-arms upon their chargers. How much this applied to the farmers making up the preponderance of the Confederate army is a matter of speculation, but it did occupy the imagery of the leaders. They saw themselves as modernity's representations of the Age of Chivalry, and at home in peacetime were known to hold mock tournaments with blunted pole jousting and flowery professions of devotion to Honor, Gallantry, Truth, a Lady Fair. "Chivalrons," they called themselves. To them it was evident that it was cavalry that would disperse the Yankee clerks and mechanics and shopkeepers. Southerners knew how to ride, the roads of their vast region hardly more than paths, and unsuitable for wheeled vehicles. In the North, with its macadamized highways and extensive railroad lines, one could grow to manhood never having sat a horse.

Within a short time the leaders of the Union army decided that they too must have cavalry, for the war, they realized, was going to be a lengthy affair fought over very widespread areas, and would require soldiers of all stripes. The North was rich and energetic. In the first two years of the Civil War it issued to its troops nearly three hundred thousand horses. The majority were never of any use, for as all of history had shown, it was no easy matter to teach men to care for and utilize their mounts. And those doing the teaching were very frequently learners themselves, the greater proportion of pre-war professionals of the Southerner-dominated mounted regiments having resigned their commissions to join the Confederate army. A civilian recruited to be captain of the 10th New York Cavalry remembered the early days of his regiment: "We drew everything on the list—watering-bridles, lariat ropes and pins—in fact there was nothing on the printed list that we did not get. Many men had extra blankets, nice large quilts presented by some fond mother or maiden aunt (dear souls), sabres and belts, together with the straps that pass over the shoulders, carbines and slings, pockets full of cartridges, nose bags and extra little bags for carrying oats, haversacks, canteens, and spurs—curry-combs, brushes, ponchos, button tents, overcoats, frying pans, cups, coffee pots."

Regarding the moment men were ordered to mount, he wrote:

> Such a rattling, jingling, jerking, scrabbling, cursing, I nev-er heard before. Green horses—some of them had never been ridden—turned round and round, backed up against each other, jumped up or stood like trained circus horses. Some of the boys had a pile in front on their saddles, and one in the rear, so high and heavy it took two men to saddle one horse and two men to help the fellow into his place. The horses sheered out, going sidewise, pushing the well-disposed animals out of position. Some of the boys had never ridden anything since they galloped on a hobby horse, and they clasped their legs close together, thus un-consciously sticking their spurs into their horses' sides.
>
> Blankets slipped from under saddles and hung from one corner; saddles slipped back until they were on the rumps of horses; others turned and were on the underside of the animals; horses running and kicking; tin pans, mess ket-tles flying through the air; and all I could do was to give a hasty glance to the rear and sing out at the top of my voice, "C-L-O-S-E U-P!"

A recent Harvard valedictorian of no military experience given a cavalry commission wrote his wife about what occurred when the division commander ordered the troops to gallop around a field: "I smiled, for I thought of Casey's probable fate—one major gen-eral less, dead of a review, ridden over by wild horses." The riders got going and the order was given to draw sabres. The men waved them over the horses' heads, which produced shying, bolting, men being thrown. The out-of-formation column raced around, rider-less mounts keeping up. Such was the Union cavalry. Its men knew nothing of horse management, and countless animals were incapaci-tated for being ridden with improperly positioned saddlecloths, wrin-kled ones coming off with horsehair adhering from the galled back. That one drink of water too many could founder an overheated horse came as news. What was called "greased heel," "foot rot," "sore-mouth," and "foot-evil," and glanders, distemper, mange, and distended barrels from improper food ravaged the animals. (Charles Francis Adams, great-grandson of President John Adams and grandson of President John Quincy Adams, came to feel himself no less a veterinarian than a captain of horse.)

A board was set up in Washington to select men for cavalry commissions. The president of the board, a newly minted colonel, remembered William Averell, wore a fresh and very becoming uniform, and gave charming dinners. "That he had seen no military service and knew nothing of cavalry, even theoretically, did not prevent him making a very imposing president." Averell and Hugh Judson Kilpatrick of New Jersey interviewed applicants, hoping to prevent "the idle and shiftless dependents of influential, social or political connections" from putting on the uniform of a cavalry officer. Kilpatrick had not completed his West Point education: when the fighting began in April of 1861, he and other Northern cadets successfully petitioned the War Department to let them join the colors while forgoing the June graduation. By then almost all of the Southerners who had been their fellow students were gone. The last two to leave were the first classmen roommates John Pelham of Alabama and Thomas Rosser of Texas, who together took the ferry across the Hudson for the cars south to New York and then Richmond. Pelham was deeply regretful to leave without a diploma and a commission after all the years spent at the academy. But he could not resist the pressure put on him by his friends, he said. He had not known he had so many friends, all averring that his first duty was to his home state. He was not alone in his sadness— Jefferson Davis, academy graduate, Mexican War stalwart, cavalry officer and then champion of the branch when secretary of war, cried when he gave up his seat as senator from Mississippi and went to be president of the Confederate States of America. Averell himself missed the Virginian Fitz Lee, his dear friend at the Point and in army service afterward. Along with another officer, they used to sing together. Fitz had tears in his eyes when they parted. They would meet again, or at least be in contact, when a detachment of Fitz's cavalry captured several of Averell's riders at Kelly's Ford along the Rappahannock. Fitz left behind a note: "If you won't go home, return my visit and bring me a sack of coffee." Three weeks later Averell crossed the stream to engage his old friend's force in an inconclusive melee of swinging sabres, and departed leaving behind the requested item and a reply: "Dear Fitz. Here's your coffee. Here's your visit. How do you like it?"

The same tone came into an exchange between two other old West Point and army friends now of opposing sides skirmishing in northern Virginia. "Dear Beauty," wrote the Union army's Orlando Poe. "Come and see me some time. I invite you to dine with me at dinner at Willard's Hotel in Washington next Saturday night." The RSVP was a horsed attack scattering the Yankees back. Perhaps Captain Poe had sped away to make arrangement for the meal, James Ewell Brown Stuart dryly observed, "Beauty" still perhaps to those who had known him in the past, but soon known to the world and to history as Jeb.

He was called "the best damned cavalryman ever foaled in America," and it was said of him that "some men are born to write

Jeb Stuart, Richmond. *Beau sabreur*, the Last Cavalier, his South has always said.

great works, others to paint great pictures, others to rule over
nations. Stuart was born to fight cavalry" and that he was "wonderfully endowed by nature with the qualities necessary for an officer of
cavalry." Stuart loved the war. He had never been happier. There was
always a smile, a laugh, a song, some dancing around, a leg flung over
the arm of a chair as, humming a tune, he attended to paperwork. He
exhibited the seemingly careless gaiety of a man with not a care in
the world. In the beginning his horsemen thought him insane, for he
led them about in full view of the Yankees to show how inaccurate
their fire was. Then, his point made, he said, "A gallop is unbecoming a soldier unless he is going toward the enemy. Remember that.
We gallop toward the enemy, and trot away, always. Steady now!
Don't break ranks." He seemed so reckless but seemed also a magi-
cian at getting safely out of the potentially most dangerous situations,
always desirous of being in close proximity of the enemy, ordering
that saddled horses be fed by hand so as to be instantly ready to slip
bridles on if Yankees suddenly appeared in force. "You don't want to
go back to camp, I know; it's stupid there, and all the fun is out here,"
he told his men. Stuart seemed impervious to danger or to fear, and
gave the appearance of thinking about something else in the most
perilous moments. Once he and his aide George Cary Eggleston
were caught in a hail of Yankee bullets. They had earlier exchanged
mounts. "Did you ever time this horse for a half mile?" Jeb inquired
as they went away with rounds whistling around their ears. He said
to Eggleston, "All I ask of fate is that I may be killed leading a cavalry charge," who remembered that the remark was "made quietly,
cheerfully, almost eagerly, and it impressed me at the time with the
feeling that the man's idea of happiness was what the French call
glory."

Yes, but in fact Jeb from the start realized that the role of the
Confederate cavalry in the War Between the States had far less to
do with European-style, Napoleonic, massed shock-impact charges
hitting home than it did with reconnaissance, patrolling to study
enemy troop dispositions, deductions from concealed or fleeting
in-motion observations, the questioning of locals or prisoners, the
noting of Yankee supply depots, and an Indian-like attention to a
trail's indication of how many men had passed over it, and when.

Mixed in were sudden swoops aimed at disrupting supply lines, cutting railroad or telegraph lines, and burning bridges. From the start of hostilities the rebels were short of every kind of supply, and so Stuart made it his business to relieve the well-supplied Union army of anything he could in the way of food, ammunition, clothing, arms, equipment. It was never his mission to fight major battles and even less to take and hold territory—he conducted what were called raids. To those Europeans who cared to be informed about the martial developments across the Atlantic, their number being not overwhelming, with the Prussian military genius Helmuth von Moltke dismissing the whole business as consisting of "two armed mobs chasing each other around the countryside," Stuart became the subject of interest. One's heart "beat quicker" when reading of raids by horsemen independently covering great distances while relying on their own resources to appear, surprise their foes, and vanish; such "caused much astonishment and won much renown" wrote Heros von Borcke of Prussia's 2nd Brandenburg Dragoons. "This new word 'raid.' Who does not feel what a vein of poetry there is in such raids?" Like every officer of European horsed regiments, Borcke was dependent upon family money to meet his military obligations, but his father supplied it in quantities the son felt insufficient. So he took a ship to America and presented himself, a gigantic man several inches over six feet in height and weighing more than 250 pounds, to Stuart. He bore with him a colossal broadsword of the type in fashion hundreds of years earlier.

So exotic a specimen attracted Jeb as a worthy addition to a crew that included his band of banjo player, guitarist, drummer, and his slave "Mulatto Bob" to work the bones, with his jongleur, the joyous minstrel Sam Sweeney, whose brother Joe invented the modern banjo, leading all in song as a column rode along. Stuart combed the rebel army for dancers, actors, vocalists, acrobats, and whistlers to be couriers when needed, and performers the rest of the time. He seemed to his officers like the cheery leader of a happy hunting party, "the gayest of companions, full of fun, frolic, laughter, courage, hope, buoyancy, and a certain youthful joyousness which made his presence like the sunshine," remembered his aide the writer John Esten Cooke, dedicating his life of his leader to "the Flower of Cavaliers." The war was a lark to Stuart. He took it as supremely great sport to discomfit the fumbling Union cavalry, laughably inept as its leaders and men were, and pathetic as the horses were that the Union remount depots supplied. It was different for the Confederates. Men and officers alike furnished their own horses, the government at Richmond compensating them for use at forty cents a day. That arrangement suited Stuart's followers. The stock they rode was so superior to that of the Yankees as not remotely to bear comparison. "Virginia was full of horses of noble blood," wrote stuart's aide Major Henry B. McClellan. "The descendants of such racers as Sir Archy, Boston, Eclipse, Timoleon, Diomede, Exchequer, Red-Eye, and many others more or less famous on the turf were scattered all over the state. Gentlemen fond of following the hounds had raised these horses for their own use. They knew their fine qualities, their speed, endurance and surefootedness, and they greatly preferred to entrust their safety in battle to their favorite steeds rather than to any that the government could furnish."

On June 12, 1862, Stuart told his soldiers in their camp near Richmond, "Gentlemen, every man must be in his saddle in ten minutes." It was two in the morning. The column of twelve hundred riders headed north. A spectator asked how long they'd be gone, and Stuart sang a line from a popular song: " 'It may be tomorrow and it may be forever.' " Winfield Scott was gone by then, replaced by George B. McClellan. On the basis of minor victories in northwestern Virginia, he had been acclaimed as a new Napoléon. Earlier he had in an official capacity observed the Crimean War, writing penetrating reports of the contending forces' arms and tactics and mastering several European languages, including Russian. He designed a new army saddle using a Cossack model, which lasted until horses were eliminated from America's armed forces. "The people call upon me to save the country. I must save it," he wrote his wife upon taking command. He was not yet thirty-five. McClellan when returning home late at night was capable of ignoring the information that the president was waiting in the parlor in favor of going straight up to bed. It did not matter, Lincoln said. He would hold the general's horse if that would bring victories. But no victories came. The general assembled a force of colossal size, magnificently equipped. He drilled it to perfection and held grand reviews, galloping past gleaming bayonets and burnished field pieces, rolled telegraph wires, straight wagon trains, trim men and officers in French-style kepis, "Little Mac" to his men, who loved him. Yet he made no move to engage the rebel forces not a day's march from Washington. People asked just when he was going to put this host into action, but he did not care to answer. Seasons passed, the autumn of 1861 and that year's and 1862's winter; by early spring of 1862, he still had not fired a shot. Finally he gathered 400 boats, steamers, and barges, and transported 120,000 men and 15,000 horses and mules two hundred miles to the foot of the Virginia peninsula. He had gunboats on each side of his force in the James and the York. Thrusting between the rivers, he said, his sword would go straight up to penetrate Richmond's heart. Arrived and unloaded, he spent weeks erecting fortifications. Then he began to creep forward with glacial slowness.

In front of him the rebel general Joseph E. Johnston, late of the United States Cavalry, drifted back, seemingly planless, until the Yankees were within five miles of the Confederate capital, close enough to hear the city's church bells when they rang the hours. Finally the two armies opened upon each other, and Johnston was hit by a musket ball and, a moment later, a shell fragment. Conscious but in great pain, he was carried away moaning that he had lost the pistols and the sword that his father had carried as a major in the Revolution under Light-Horse Harry Lee. Someone went for them, and Light-Horse Harry's son, who had been serving as military advisor to President Jefferson Davis, succeeded as commander of what had been called "the Potomac Army" and "the Army of Richmond" but which now the new leader termed the Army of Northern Virginia. The fighting died down. A Confederate officer wondered aloud if Lee possessed the audacity his position required, and Colonel Joseph Ives, knowing him, said, "His name might be Audacity." It was that quality that prompted Lee to put Jeb Stuart and his twelve hundred riders in motion. Unlike Joseph Johnston—of whom it was said, "retreat is his trade"—Lee thought of attack. McClellan's force lay in a great swath reaching toward the Confederate capital, regarding which the North cried, "On to Richmond!" The Yankee left and center were thick with troops and supply. Their right's situation was hard to know, and the topography there—wet, swampy, filled with copperhead snake–infested streams—might be but indifferently staffed with Union forces. It seemed to Lee that if Stonewall Jackson's forces operating in the Shenandoah Valley could come down to fall upon his opponent's right wing, while, he, Lee, pushed at his front, the Northerners could be evicted from the Peninsula. But he must know what dispositions McClellan had or had not made to forestall such a move. He directed Stuart to go find out. Only Stuart knew the mission's intent. Most of his men put into motion assumed they were moving to join Stonewall Jackson's force in the Valley, and it came as a decided shock when Stuart, leading the column with his two chief subordinates, Colonels W. H. F. Lee, the general's son, and Fitz Lee, his nephew, abruptly turned right and headed directly toward McClellan. It was only then that he told the two colonels what he and they and their little force were to do.

The information sifted down to the troops. They were appalled. Outnumbered one hundred to one, they were entering the heart of the enemy's citadel. Filled with cheer, singing as he rode—he favored "Her Bright Smile Haunts Me Still," "Lorena," and "The Corn Top's Ripe"—and resplendent in his trim gray uniform of short braided jacket with red rose in the button hole, breeches and high boots, white buckskin gauntlets, and flowing red-satin lined cape, and with a slouch hat surmounted by a dancing black ostrich feather fixed on with a gold pin, a light French sabre with elaborate filigreed basket attached to his sword belt, and a tasseled gold sash around his waist, their leader, they thought, had taken leave of his senses. "General Stuart is going to get his command destroyed," Captain John Esten Cooke heard. "This movement is mad."

They moved on, paralyzing by their entirely unexpected and unsuspected appearance scattered Union detachments astounded suddenly to behold the rebels confidently supposed to be supinely awaiting McClellan's annihilating assault. There was almost no attendant fighting, for Stuart had with him soldiers native to the region familiar with little off-the-map trails utilized to fall from the sides and rear upon relaxed Yankees who never had a thought that they were in any danger. A line of prisoners and captured mules and horses formed at the rear of the Confederate column. Telegraph lines were ripped down that news of their coming might not be sent ahead. All around, almost within shouting distance, or at most a few minutes' ride away, were masses of Union horse and foot, and great artillery parks of big guns. Stuart had with him a couple of little horse-drawn field pieces under the command of John Pelham, the cadet who had reluctantly left West Point because all his alleged friends told him he should. In earlier skirmishes the Alabaman had proved himself wondrous at selecting sites for fields of fire, and for moving his guns at the exact moment before the enemy zeroed in on them. He was slim, slight, mild in manner, boyish-looking, hardly more than twenty years of age. But then, they were all young, those who rode with Jeb on what would be called the Ride Around McClellan, the Chickahominy Raid. It is the fulsome beards in the old pictures that throw us off and make us think them aged and appropriately dignified—that and the high ranks we today associate with gray hair. Jeb was thirty, the full colonels W. H. F. Lee, always called Rooney, and Fitz Lee twenty-seven and twenty-four, respectively. The boys in the long line behind them—and "boys" is the proper term—were for the most part not out of their teenage years, and uniformly light in weight. In other words, cavalrymen. Every ounce counted on the horse upon whom your life depended. If your reins seemed long, you cut off the ends, ripped leather from the saddle tree, took off the hoods of the stirrups. One had but a tin can for stew and coffee, a spoon. They sufficed for gastronomical needs.

As they went along, generally at a slow trot, on what was later remembered as the most romantic, intrepid, rakish, adventurous, daring and dashing event of the Civil War, the riders fired upon trains and Union gunboats, Pelham's howitzers bursting shells over one, *Marblehead*, which, unable to bring its big guns to bear on a target so close, ignominiously steamed off to jeers and catcalls. They burned tons of enemy supplies in depots, and ate and drank lavishly; a cache of crates revealed a seemingly endless quantity of citrus fruits for an orgy of lemonade production to allay the sultry lowland heat, with the ground left yellow by skin and pulp. John Esten Cooke recalled eating in succession figs, beef tongue, pickles, tomato catsup, preserves, more lemons, and cakes. Heros von Borcke remembered champagne, smoked oysters, preserved fruits, oranges, lemons, and cigars. A rebel major saw a captured Union captain filling his pipe, and leaning from his saddle, requested it. "I want to smoke," said the Yankee.

"So do I."

"This pipe is my property."

"Oh! What a mistake." The Confederate reached out and gently took it. Thirty acres of loaded wagons were put to the torch, with towers of flame lighting up the sky, and immediately a bridge was crossed, columns of smoke rose in the air. Numerous little Union detachments stationed in small rural settlements were taken in hand before they could spread the alarm or send for aid, with rebel soldiers of the region who knew the byways taking detours to halt anyone who might try to slip away. One contingent, captured at Hanover Court House, where Patrick Henry spoke, proved to be from Fitz Lee's troop of the lst United States Cavalry in what men in both blue and gray had come to call the Old Army. He had a happy reunion and the "most friendly imaginable" talk with them, asking about soldiers he'd served with who stayed with the Union, the prisoners addressing him by his old rank of lieutenant. They and their horses and mules then joined the long line in the rear of the column.

At the town of Old Church, Stuart paused. He had fulfilled his mission, which was to ascertain the strength, or lack of it, of McClellan's right wing. There was, he saw, very little strength at all, no fortifications worth mentioning and no natural defensive positions of hill or impassable river. That meant, he knew, that the way was open for an assault on the Federal right by Stonewall Jackson's men should Lee bring them down from the Shenandoah Valley as he, Lee, pushed forward at their center and left from Richmond, the two bodies of Confederate troops combining to evict the Federals from the Peninsula. But if he turned back now, Stuart reasoned, he would make perfectly clear the meaning of his journey to the enemy. They would understand why he had come, to then reverse course, and would throw up fortifications and dig entrenchments to ward off an anticipated blow. Stuart had local civilians brought to him for questioning about all the alternate ways back, knowing that eventually the Yankees would learn the tenor of his inquiries. That would confirm in their minds the reason for his trip.

But in fact it was a ruse and he was not going back, for going forward would entirely confuse his opponents' minds. There was of his doings what was not unlike the sword-concealing wave of the matador's cloak at the bull, or the three-card-monte deceptionist's concealment of the winning card. If he went forward when expected to go back, he would distract enemy concerns about a possible Confederate drive upon their right—and it would be infinitely more fun. Jeb knew Little Mac very well. For months the two had been tentmates of the 1st Cavalry out on the Kansas plains, prone during the day to scrabbling at each other and quibbling over trifles as young men will, remembered an officer who served with them; but when retiring for the night they always made up, Stuart throwing his arm around McClellan's shoulders to make things right. What could be a happier turn of events than to play a great trick on his old comrade—a grand "prank," said Captain Cooke—and run through and around his forces? The Confederates went on, their beloved theme song frequently rising from their throats: "If you want to smell hell / If you want to have fun / If you want to catch the devil / Jine the cavalry." At the frequent parties and dances and theatricals back at camp its rendition always ended the festivities, invited girls lustily joining in. Saturday night affairs promptly concluded at the stroke of midnight, for Stuart allowed no merrymaking on the Sabbath. He did not smoke or ever take a drink, and it was unknown to hear from him a word of profanity, still less of blasphemy. He loved his two setters, Nip and Tuck, and had an enormous raccoon whom he tethered to an artillery piece standing before his Camp Qui Vive, French for Who goes there. (Others he titled Camp Quién Sabe—meaning Who knows? in Spanish—Camp No Camp, and the Wigwam.) "His owner regarded him as the pearl of sentinels, the paragon of coons," wrote John Esten Cooke. It was very sad "that this animal, so trusted and admired, who had become like a member of the staff, chewed his rope and deserted, never to be seen again."

The command compactly closed up and perfectly in hand, as Stuart's forces always were, its members broke open barrels filled with sugar, and eggs packed in salt, which they found to be delicious; got for themselves new boots and pants and blankets and pistols, and relished a keg of whiskey that had been placed atop one of Pelham's guns to encourage its bodily lifting by thirsty drinkers from where it was mired in a stream. Everything was done to the accompaniment of song and signs of joy, with Stuart's great mustache "curled with laughter at the slightest provocation," John Esten Cooke recorded, as it was so very frequently all his days. (Later in the war there came a moment when his laughter was unaccompanied by movement from one of the mustache's tips, for what caused his mirth was that a bullet had sliced it off as neatly, people said, as a barber might have done.) "One who has never participated in such a scene," remembered Stuart's aide William Willis Blackford, "can form but a faint idea of the careless gayety of the men, and gayest among the gay, and apparently most unconcerned among the careless, was he upon whom all the responsibility rested . . . Who will ever forget the fun, the frolic, the romance—and the peril too—of that fine journey?"

There was no stopping for more than a few minutes at a time, for there was always the danger that the "blue birds," their "Northern friends," would gather themselves and, with the overwhelming disparity of numbers that was theirs, crush the incursion of this slight force. But that did not happen, and in the course of a ride of three days' duration over a distance of more than a hundred miles through and around the Union army, the travelers suffered but a single fatality, that of a physician turned cavalry captain who took a bullet from a Yankee detachment come upon along a woodland trail. His body was entrusted for burial to women of the area, some thrilled to see their sons, husbands, and brothers suddenly appearing in wholly unexpected fashion at their doorsteps. The men slept in their saddles as the column went along thin and twisting country roads, into and out of swamps and forests, their leader with one leg hooked over his pommel and his head down on his chest.

In time the news reached General McClellan that the outer lines and central body of his vast army had been and were being penetrated by riders looting and then burning his depots, ripping down his telegraph lines, pulling up his railroad tracks. He looked to his cavalry commander, General Philip St. John Cooke, Stuart's father-in-law, to stop this. For all the long months when Little Mac, the young Napoléon, sat with his army supine in and around Washington, General Cooke, the Grand Old Man of the prewar cavalry, had waited for an opportunity to put his drilled and polished horsemen into action. He had lived with his wife in a hotel, with their daughter Flora, Stuart's wife, never absent from their thoughts, along with their grandson originally named for his grandfather but renamed for his father when the older man elected to cast his lot with the Union. The child's mother in turn missed her parents. Jeb understood, and told his wife to write a note, which he would have put under her mother's plate when she came down to breakfast in the hotel. He would do it via "Underground Railroad," he said—a secretly Southern sympathizer in the Union capital performing the duty. Stuart was always good at handling agents and spies, the latter a term Robert E. Lee did not care for, preferring "scouts." (The Prussian Heros von Borcke in later years remembered how he and Jeb, alone, rode to remote places to rendezvous with people who for money or devotion to the cause of the Southern Confederacy would do as asked.)

Now, with his son-in-law's riders outrageously running amok, it seemed General Cooke's moment of performance and response and retribution had come. George B. McClellan, for all the year of his command of the North's main army, had parceled out its cavalry as little disunited contingents of headquarters guards, orderlies, escorts, guides, grooms. Nothing could be more obvious than that in this extraordinary situation unparalleled in military history what was called for was that they join together to pursue and engage Stuart's men, these invaders who having completed half of their circling journey—one can almost say jaunt—around the Union army were now heading north back to rebel territory. McClellan of course recognized that. He ordered Cooke to get his men after his onetime Kansas plains tentmate.

But what he saw as the correct manner to do so horrified those receiving his orders. McClellan, Lincoln had observed in the homey fashion he sometimes affected, had "the slows." Never had the general's actions more justified the characterization than now, for he stipulated that Cooke's riders move with infantry detachments closely accompanying. That meant a plodding march and almost certain abandonment of any hope of catching the raiders, who were streaking north to safety. It was a complete refutation of what light cavalry was meant to do and could do. McClellan was completely deleting mobility from the equation. He was going against a thousand years of doctrine; he was throwing away the canon. Cooke consulted with his staff—should he blatantly disregard a direct order and swiftly chase after Stuart? To Lieutenant Wesley Merritt the answer was yes, since as he coldly pointed out in later years after rising to very high rank, General McClellan "was especially deficient in the instincts which characterized the great army commanders of history with reference to the proper uses of cavalry." Never forgetting or forgiving what McClellan had done, Merritt dearly wished that he and others had urged utmost speed upon Cooke. But he and they did not, and so at a sluggish walk accommodating the slow infantry the Union cavalry trudged along.

Up ahead the Confederates came to the Chickahominy to find the ford at which they planned to cross not shallow as expected, but instead deep and filled with rushing water. There had been heavy mountain snows during the winter, which due to unusual weather had not yet finished melting. Rooney Lee volunteered to see if perhaps the situation was not as bad as it looked, and put his horse into the water. He was strongly built and knew very well how to swim—his father had taught all his sons when they were young—but he and his mount came near to losing their lives, Rooney just about making it across and the horse having to be rescued from entangling roots and snags. The ford was clearly impassable for Stuart's command. Worried looks appeared on everyone's face save for that of the leader, who showed no emotion, but, they saw, twisted his beard in a preoccupied fashion. That the Yankees in overwhelming force were coming they knew from their scouts to the rear. "What do you think of the situation, Colonel?" John Esten Cooke asked the soaked Rooney Lee, back on the southern side of the Chickahominy. "Well, Captain, I think we are caught," Lee replied. During the ride, Cooke had remarked to Jeb, his cousin through marriage for his relation to Flora Cooke Stuart, that it was certainly not an impossibility that the enemy of tens and tens of thousands in whose domain they were with hardly more than one thousand men might easily trap them and compel a surrender. Stuart replied there was another course left: "To die game."

But it had not yet come to that. A soldier reported that there was an old bridge in ruins but with stone abutments still in place not far off. Perhaps it could be put in order. There was an abandoned warehouse nearby whose timbers were quickly ripped off, Stuart laboring along with the others and singing. They had very little time. The enemy was practically breathing down their necks. But whatever happened, they knew, they had raced to sow destruction for supplies and communications through masses of opposing soldiery while suffering but the loss of a single man, the doctor-turned-captain, and that their trip meant permanent discomfiture for the Union army ranged before Richmond from the lowliest private up to Little Mac, the young Napoléon. No Yankee could rest easy, for perhaps Stuart might come again. In Washington the authorities trembled. He might suddenly appear there.

The makeshift bridge began to take form. It was Sunday, and save for dozing-off naps on the moving horses, the men had not slept since Friday night. A rear guard was sent to try to delay the Yankees when they came, as they must and would in a very short while. At a height of more than thirty feet above the water, the Confederates got a footbridge up, got men across, then enlarged the construction so as to permit horses over. Men erupted in cheers at the sight, and at the sound of clattering hooves. The prisoners, mounted on hundreds of captured mules, followed. Rooney Lee with the rear guard rushed up and got over, Fitz Lee the last man, and ten minutes later the Union army arrived, guns firing over the bridge put to the torch by the Southerners then running off to fling themselves on safe ground for some sleep. Jeb was not among them. After lying down for a few minutes to roll around with laughter at what he called the prank, the joke, he had played on McClellan, he rode with one accompanying orderly for Richmond, twenty-eight miles away, to report to General Lee and President Davis, stopping once for fifteen minutes to drink a cup of coffee from the silver cup he always carried. He loved coffee. General Philip St. George Cooke said he wished a bullet had taken him, and asked to be relieved.

Stonewall Jackson came down from the Shenandoah Valley to be guided by Stuart in striking at the right wing of McClellan's army, which had been found to be vulnerable, Lee pushed forward from Richmond, and the Yankees departed the Virginia Peninsula. (He was making a change of base, McClellan blandly explained; and afterward any rebel horseman who tumbled off his mount could expect inquiries as to why he was changing his base.) Jeb and his headquarters staff of about a hundred men in all, including grooms, couriers, and servants, encamped with their two hundred horses on the grounds of the Bower, a mansion some eight miles from Martinsburg and ten from Charlestown in what was then Virginia, now West Virginia, on a hill along the Opequon. It was owned by the member of the gentry Stephen Dandridge, and was "full of daughters and nieces," remembered William Willis Blackford, "all grown and all attractive—some very handsome."

No mise-en-scène can better depict Jeb Stuart—the stupendous and unexampled performance of great military value instantly become legendary, the grand and to him hilarious befuddlement of the enemy with loss of but one life—and now what his officers ever after recalled as their golden October at the Bower. Where the evening before only a squirrel might have disturbed the quiet of the park of noble oaks a few hundred yards off from the house, Blackford wrote, there of a moment appeared "to the eyes of the lovely girls who peeped through the curtains of their chambers in the light of the early morn" a "camp of war awakened to life at sunrise by the stirring strains of martial music," a "brilliant scene" of "white tents and gay uniforms" with "heroes of romance fresh from fields of glory."

"It would have been strange indeed if the handsome young men of the staff"—for Stuart always wanted good-looking men on good-looking horses around him, esteeming, Blackford said, masculine attractiveness almost as much as he did feminine—"and the gay and gallant commander of our cavalry failed to win the friendship of our charming neighbors." Strange? Inconceivable. Women flocked about Jeb in such a manner that a passerby might have thought a dance around a maypole was under way, and if he had honored every request for a lock of his hair, he would soon have been bald. "He dearly loved," Blackford wrote, "as any good soldier should, to kiss a pretty girl, and the pretty girls dearly loved to kiss him."

The cavalrymen and the girls rode, took walks, went on fishing expeditions, and after afternoon tea "came music, singing, dancing and games of every description, mingled with moonlight strolls along the banks of the beautiful Opequon or boating upon its crystal surface. Never was there a more beautiful moon or more exquisite weather." (War can be terrible, but it has its compensations.) Upon occasion the cavalrymen departed to skirmish with and harass the Yankees along the line from Harpers Ferry to Williamsport, sent on their way by the Bower's young ladies with what Blackford recalled as "consternation and tears," adding, "We assured them it would soon be over and we would not all be killed." At Williamsport a young woman asked if she could not fire an artillery piece, and Jeb gave her the lanyard, and afterward always referred to the cannon as the Lady of Williamsport, its cheery designation akin to one with which he dubbed himself when some Baltimore women sent him a set of spurs made of gold perfect for wear at a dance: the Knight of the Golden Spurs. (In private letters he put under his signature K.G.S.) He titled a Northern girl visiting Southern relatives who expressed support for the Confederacy with French nomenclature: the New York Rebelle. He produced a piece of doggerel about one of his horses, "My Maryland":

I feel secure upon your back
Maryland, My Maryland
While cannon roar and rifle crack
Maryland, My Maryland
You bore me o'er the Po-to-mac
You circumvented Little Mac
Oh may I never know your lack
Maryland My Maryland.

Stuart was a brilliant rider of always-straight back and glued-in-the-saddle seat, as unregarding of fearsome jumps as he was of bullets singing about his ears, but he was unsentimental about his various mounts, hunters, and sometimes thoroughbreds—Lady Margrave, Skylark, Star of the West—regarding them as utensils, not pets. Few of them lasted long, shot as they were or disabled or killed by artillery fire, or gone lame, ill, or simply worn out from the exertions required of them from their indefatigable master.

For two years the Major General Commanding the Cavalry Corps of the Army of Northern Virginia, as now he was, knew nothing but triumph as he rampaged about confounding one after the other the hapless generals to whom in vain Lincoln looked for suppression of the South. Once, he did have a bad moment. When John Pope succeeded McClellan, Jeb was for an instant very close to coming a cropper: he awoke from sleeping on a porch—he never slept indoors, saying that if all his men could not he would not—to discover that the approaching hooves he heard were not those of his own riders but instead those of the Yankees. He leaped on an unbridled horse and ran for it, like his staff officers jumping the fence enclosing the house, but leaving behind his hat with its distinctive plume attached by a gold clip. Sheltered by a clump of trees, he saw it carried away on the tip of a raised Yankee sabre. It was taken as a valued spoils-of-war trophy to Pope; and with a handkerchief covering his head in its place, Jeb repeatedly heard from his men, he wrote his wife, laughingly shouted inquiries of "Where's your hat?"

He would get back at the Union commander for this, he vowed, and he did. Of a night, Yankee officers encamped at Verdiersville were enjoying an evening of drink and pleasantry. "This is something like comfort," one of them remembered saying as toddy was passed around. "I hope Jeb Stuart won't disturb us tonight." The moment the words left his mouth, pistol shots rang out and rebel shouts resounded as rebel sabres slashed at the cords holding tents, which collapsed on the Yankees inside. "There he is, by God!" a Union officer cried. The raiders almost laughed themselves out of their saddles at seeing Yankees trapped in fallen tents like fish in a net, or struggling to get out over overturned tables. In the chaos the Confederates drove off horses for later retrievement, shot up the encampment, and ran off with a box of General Pope's papers and, to Jeb's delight, the commander's coat. "I have had my revenge on Pope," he wrote his wife of the Union general reduced to so wildly sending his cavalry after phantoms that the horses could barely stand up. He wrote across the opposing lines: "General: You have my hat. I have your coat. I propose a cartel to exchange the prisoners." He liked sending messages to the enemy. A telegraph operator always accompanied him, and after surprising Union communications outposts, Jeb frequently had him send off complaints to Union army quartermaster general Montgomery C. Meigs about the quality of appropriated mules, requesting that Washington issue a higher type. Sometimes he was more generous: "I am much satisfied with the transport of mules lately sent, which I have taken possession of, and ask you to send me soon a new supply."

An officer inadequate for the task assigned him, Pope was removed, and McClellan came back—the hair of the dog that bit you, Lincoln said. As he had on the Peninsula, Jeb wove his way through and around Little Mac's force centered in Pennsylvania, cut apart his lines of supply and communication, relieved him of animals, supplies, guns, and ammunition, made as if to destroy a vital bridge, and then departed unscathed by going eighty miles in twenty-four hours without a halt. His escape was made along a route the Yankees never expected he would utilize, it being long and roundabout—but safe from the forces they dispatched elsewhere, including the defenses around a Washington fearful of his sudden appearance, which were stiffened and then maintained at the price of removing soldiers, material, services, and guns from other duties. He came away with twelve hundred horses taken from Pennsylvania farmers stunned and outraged that their countryside swarming with blue-coated Union soldiers had proven vulnerable to the rebels. The animals, mostly heavy Conestogas bred for the plough and wagon, were handed over to the Confederate infantry and artillery, as they were far too lumbering and cumbersome for use by light cavalry. (Any Pennsylvania horses ridden or driven by ladies were by Jeb's order exempted from confiscation.) The service to Stuart himself of his new acquisitions was confined to pulling wagons bringing guests to a ball at his headquarters the night following his return.

It was Stuart's genius that with what amounted to a force of but slight number he could befuddle and confuse and regularly confound a far stronger enemy. The Confederacy, largely blockaded by the Union navy along almost all of its shoreline and of most modest manufacturing capacity, was increasingly unable adequately to supply him with guns or ordnance, or even such basics as horseshoes or bridles, but he made do. He would personally join in removing from the enemy's dead horses or mules their reins, bridles, and traces to drape around his horse's neck for transport back to camp. (It was a common sight to see his riders bearing the amputated hooves of animals slain in the North's cause to rebel farriers for removal with nippers and then reuse of precious horseshoes.)

For a second and final time McClellan was removed from command after a lackluster performance against Lee at Antietam, with a following months-long cessation of activity, explainable, he told Lincoln, by the fact that his horses were fatigued, to which the president replied, "Will you pardon me for asking what the horses of your army have done since the Battle of Antietam that fatigues anything?" His replacement knew and defined himself to others as not up to his job. Ambrose Burnside in his move upon Fredericksburg was never out of sight by Jeb's riders, the result being that Robert E. Lee was in position to receive him and inflict so disastrous a rebuff as history has rarely recorded. The hapless Burnside was succeeded by Joseph Hooker, "Fighting Joe," assertive, dynamic, inspiring, as confident as his predecessor was feckless, who interrupted Lincoln when he said, "If you get to Richmond, General—" with, "There is no 'if' in this case." He drilled the Army of the Potomac to perfection and instituted all sorts of valuable reforms to its structure. Stuart with his raids was of course very much on his mind. "You have got to stop these disgraceful cavalry surprises," he raged at George Stoneman, the most recent commander of the Army of the Potomac's horsed soldiers. There had been a succession of them, William Averell succeeding Philip St. George Cooke to be found wanting, too cautious, always ready in McClellan-like fashion to pull back, entrench, refit, think things over, others slow, hesitant, dilatory—exactly Jeb's opposites.

In the spring of 1863 Hooker struck with what he termed "the finest army on the planet." His early moves were stunning, the Army of the Potomac never more well-positioned, never up in such strength and style, the infantry and artillery by Hooker's plan seizing

commanding ground and with his cavalry off to block Lee's anticipated retreat. He held the Army of Northern Virginia in his grasp and
would crush it like *that*, he said, closing his hand firmly. It must "inglo-
riously fly" or face "certain destruction."

But the Union cavalry, as so many times before, was slow and hesitant, with its leader, George Stoneman, esteeming road and weather
conditions to be so intimidating as to reduce his forward motion to
a crawl. He had been Stonewall Jackson's roommate at West Point,
but no two men ever turned out more differently, Jackson being so
swift in moving his forces that his infantry was termed "foot cavalry."
In Washington, President Lincoln telegraphed Hooker that word of
Stoneman's slow progress deeply alarmed him. But Hooker was soon
and of a moment to go beyond presidential appeal or even gravest
enemy threat. All vigor, logic, intellect, and fighting spirit suddenly
vanished, and he huddled within himself and became a lethargic,
depressed, paralyzed shadow rising up only to decide to withdraw his
forward elements from their previously selected and strongly held
positions. It was a decision so at odds with rational thinking that
officers receiving the order initially refused to accept it, one general
threatening to shoot the courier bringing the instructions. In later
days Hooker said that he had simply ceased to be Hooker, but now he
crouched down and numbly awaited a blow, his men drawn in upon
themselves like a turtle in its shell in a thickly wooded area known
locally as the Wilderness while around them swirled Jeb Stuart's cavalry, their leader singing out to the tune of "Old Dan Tucker," his
banjo player, Sam Sweeney, accompanying, "Old Joe Hooker, won't
you come out the Wilderness, come out the Wilderness, come out
the Wilderness, come out the Wilderness; Old Joe Hooker, won't you
come out the Wilderness now?"

The blow Hooker supinely awaited came, Stonewall Jackson falling upon the soldiers of the Union right wing to send them flying
from the field of what came to be seen as Lee's most brilliant victory,
Chancellorsville. Stuart was very fond of Jackson, although the con-
trasts between them could not have been more acute. The latter was a
solemn, awkward, odd personality of unusual dietary and physical practices involving lemons and water cures and prone to holding one hand
pointed to the sky for lengthy periods as he rode his nondescript horse

Little Sorrel, who was as unimpressive in appearance as he. Seer and mystic and well-nigh fanatic when it came to religion, he went about in battered Virginia Military Institute attire. He had been a professor there before the war, known to the students as Mad Tom and Tom Fool. When Stuart, with his showy sash, golden spurs on glittering high boots, and floating plume on dashing hat, gave a try to inducting Jackson into the brotherhood of correctly if not flamboyantly attired officers and presented him with an elegant uniform coat, Jackson reacted with a mixture of almost childlike pleasure and concern that wearing the gift would be unbecoming to the austerity he saw called for by his concept of Presbyterianism. Once Stuart called upon Jackson in a house with sporting prints on the walls that was serving as the Jackson's headquarters. It was just after Fredericksburg. Jeb "paused to scan with affected astonishment the horrid pictures of a terrier that could kill so many rats a minute," Jackson's staff officer Captain James P. Smith wrote. "He pretended to believe that they were General Jackson's selections; with great solemnity he looked at the pictures and then at the general.

"He paused and stepped back and in solemn tones said he wished to express his astonishment and grief at the display of General Jackson's low tastes. It would be a sad disappointment to the old ladies of the country, who thought Jackson was a good man." Stonewall "blushed like a girl, and said nothing but to turn aside and direct that a good dinner be prepared for General Stuart." (Any joke, it was said, was a mystery to Jackson). Within half a year he was gone, fatally wounded when with darkness fallen on the fields of Chancellorsville, he was shot by his own men, who mistook him for a Yankee. Lee named Stuart to take over Jackson's infantry command on a temporary basis while retaining his cavalry duties, a decision that caused some to be uneasy for fear that Jeb, the dashing and impetuous officer of horse, was ill-suited to the command of large bodies of footmen and would do something rash. But he performed well enough before returning to his usual responsibilities, which in a brief pause in action after Chancellorsville principally amounted to keeping an eye on the enemy and reporting back to Lee. "I wonder if the girl is yet alive who rode the general's fine horse and raced with him to charge our station," wrote H. W. Manson in an issue of 1932's *Confederate Veteran*. The old gentleman—for he would have been very old indeed when he wrote his article chronicling events seventy years gone by—had served as member of a two-man lookout team on an observation and signal tower atop a high mountain. "The glorious Stuart would dash up, always with a lady, and a pretty one too. When they reached the level platform, and Stuart left her in the care of one of us and took the other off to one side and questioned the very sweat out of him about the enemy's position he was General Stuart, but when he got back and lifted the beauty into the saddle and rode off humming a breezy air, he was Stuart the beau."

His relations with women were never of the slightest illicit nature, so his aides always maintained, but gossip about them got back to Flora Stuart, as would knowledge of a Charleston *Mercury* article condemning the general for "rollicking, frolicking and running after girls." Yet he never seemed happier than when she and Jimmie and Flora came at quiet times to visit his various camps. Of course Jeb's people made much of the children, Heros von Borcke lifting the boy in front of him on his saddle to go galloping about, but the war was a horror to Mrs. Stuart. Despite being a soldier's daughter and a soldier's wife and the sister of soldiers serving on both sides, she could not bear the sound of gunfire coming from even the most distant points and became distraught when she heard it, bursting into tears. She lived in fear that her husband would be wounded, or worse. "Don't be telegraphing General Lee's staff or anyone else," he wrote her. "If I am hurt you will hear of it very soon." He told her of meeting an old woman who had been at his parents' wedding. One of his officers had remarked that the lady was "never so happy as when she is miserable. She reminds me of my darling when she will insist on looking on the dark side in preference to the bright."

As always whether she was present or not, in moments when there was no combat action, he and his men gave themselves up to great fun. Lights played behind Borcke and another officer in shadow to represent when seen on a sheet hung before viewers a patient whose surgeon forcefully removes from the sufferer's bloated stomach deer and beef horns, cabbages with stalks still attached, quantities of oyster shells, and a pair of boots, all to the Prussian's shrieks of "*Mein Gott, Doktor!*" and with the finale being an uproarious dance by the two. Then there were *tableaux vivant,* with a girl holding a lance standing over the conquered and prostrate figure of Borcke portraying Tyrannis, as in the Virginia motto of Sic Semper Tyrannis (Thus always to tyrants), Jeb praising the scene while saying he knew the Prussian really wanted to be Sic Semper. Another performance found the gigantic Prussian dancing in a ball gown, flowers in his hair, with the colonel commanding the 1st Virginia Cavalry. Stuart could not stop laughing, and said that if he ever forgot Borcke's battlefield doings, he would certainly remember his dancing. To someone come to maturity in the traditions of a Prussian cavalry always mindful of the great Seydlitz, the horse practices of the Southern Confederacy took some getting used to. Borcke on his first night of service with the rebels as a guest of Fitz Lee was taken aback that mounts were not picketed in regular lines in the fashion he was accustomed to, but irregularly scattered around, some tethered to trees or limbs of trees or simply left loose to browse as they might. Their riders were indifferently turned out, he noted, although they uniformly had good seats and hands.

In Richmond, the South's chief of cavalry and his staff acted as stagehands for a pageant, but the major general was relieved of his duties in disgrace after letting the backdrop scenery crash to the floor when while standing on a stepladder he became engrossed in conversation with a girl. He was replaced by Fitz Lee, who averred, "No young lady can make me forget my responsibility as a step ladder." Jeb was more successful when serving as a waiter at a banquet given to feminine guests, he and his officers standing behind the guests' chairs before positions were exchanged, the girls waiting on the men, all done with uproarious joking and laughing.

The war was two years old, and the Cavalry Corps of the Army of Northern Virginia for all that time had had it all its own way; but the horsemen of the North were changing.

II
The War

On the fifth of June, 1863, the brilliant Battle of Chancellorsville gloriously won, Stuart, in the manner almost of a theatrical impresario,
organized the greatest review of troops the Confederacy ever knew. It
would be at Brandy Station, Virginia. For days trains pulled into the
nearby Culpeper station filled with people eager to see the show and to
attend the great Town Hall ball the night before. When in the morning more than ten thousand soldiers were assembled on a vast field free
of fences or trees and with firm and level ground, Stuart and his staff
rode up in the fashion of a great leader of the Age of Chivalry appearing with his vassals, trumpets flourishing to herald their approach,
their horses draped with flowers and with girls showering more in their
path, their sidearms gleaming like burnished silver, military bands blar-
ing. Artillery pieces loaded with blanks thundered deafening salvos,
sending great clouds of smoke into the air. Great lines of rebel horsemen drew sabres from scabbards, with the united action producing
a metallic whoosh, and squadrons moved into a trot, then a canter, and
finally, when bugles trilled the signal, a thunderous all-out charge.

Standing in their stirrups and waving their glittering weapons, thier guidons, pennons, and flags whipping above them, they emitted such shouts as common to all charges throughout the history of
horsed combat. The screaming riders turned and came again, and,
William Willis Blackford wryly noted, maidens in close proximity to male spectators swooned to be caught by strong arms. (Those

with no gentleman near, he saw, confined themselves to exclamations of awe.) In the evening there was a great outdoors ball, with bonfires illuminating the dancers and diners and drinkers. General Lee had not been able to be present at the great review, but when he appeared the next day, Jeb decreed there should be a repeat performance—although at Lee's request the unrestrained galloping of the horses was kept to a minimum, he not wanting them overly stressed. "Stuart was in his glory," the general wrote Mrs. Lee, while mildly indicating to his cavalry commander—for he was almost uniformly mild, offering suggestions and observations rather than orders—that perhaps this sort of panoplied display was more in the line of those many high Union officers who took horse soldiers as mere escorting adornments to their personal and very often spurious paraded glory. It is a part of the great soldier to be prescient as regards the future; and perhaps General Lee perceived that within a few days there would be a very great modification of the fashion in which the horsemen of the North and the horsemen of the South viewed each other.

"Whoever saw a dead cavalryman?" once asked Fighting Joe Hooker, he of the later disastrous Union showing at Chancellorsville. If you saw the Yankee horsemen moving toward the rear, it was related, you knew a fight was in the offing. For a long time, nobody took seriously the shopkeepers and clerks riding plow horses who called themselves the Union cavalry while justifiably deriving for actions or lack thereof, so it was said, the contempt of enemies and terror of friends. By far the greatest percentage of prewar horse officers had gone with the South, as previously remarked. Those who remained with the North to be given high rank were, also as previously remarked, uniformly weak, hesitant, and overly cautious, Cooke, Averell, Stoneman, and Pleasanton, the last named known as the Knight of Romance for the dubious nature of his reports on what he had done and observed on scouting expeditions. (The best way to improve matters, Ulysses S. Grant was to hear from the cavalry officer James Harrison Wilson, was to get an Indian chief, furnish him with a knife and a bottle of bad whiskey, and send him out to scalp all the major generals he could find.)

The Union horse leaders of the first two years of the war were perhaps not overly talented, but a case can be made for their showings when we look at what they had to work with—the fresh-from-civilian-life subordinate officers assigned to the Yankee horsed outfits. Such were, recalled William Forse Scott of the 4th Iowa Cavalry, "inept cadets" from military schools plus political figures "often uniting natural unfitness to a total lack of military training" and with only "the dimmest ideas of the use of cavalry."

The Iowan was harsh in his assessment written three decades after the war, but he had a point when denouncing "vanity generals" using riders for pointless endeavors, "show generals" with horsed escorts and bodyguards performing "wasteful and degrading" service garnering the disdain of infantrymen: "Soldiers who marched on foot carrying their arms and accoutrements seemed to feel their burdens lightened by gibes at the cavalry whose horses covered them with dust or splashed them with mud as they hurried their riders on useless errands." Fighting Joe Hooker, who had proved an outstanding leader earlier in the war, but never a director, as Chancellorsville showed, should have known better—although he himself was far from immune to going about on a great white charger amid a flurry of brilliantly uniformed aides, colonels, and brigadiers, crashing bands, and flaring banners—but he used his cavalry as disunited segments. Horse soldiers were employed to protect wagon trains, as outpost guards, to maintain videttes (mounted picket watch points), as messengers, and as grooms. They served as provost troops—military police—to sit motionless horses in a line while using their sabres on men who sought to run from the battlefield. They were sentries at the multitudinous little forts set up to protect Washington should Jeb Stuart appear.

Then there came a time when Hooker realized he must pull his horsemen together into a mass. It was when he received word of the stupendous two reviews at Brandy Station. The display of what Jeb had and how he deployed it, reports of which swiftly reached Union headquarters from spies in the viewing crowds, was emblematic of the lack of regard the rebel horsemen held for their Federal opponents: they had, in utterly disdainful manner, showed their hand, just what cards they held. Still shattered from the Chancellorsville disaster, Hooker had to react, fearing as he did that the dual reviews portended some great rebel raid greater than anything previously seen, one that might take Washington, Baltimore, even Philadelphia. He had Alfred Pleasanton gather every Union cavalryman he could to go against Stuart, and two great masses of riders met on the same Brandy Station grounds that had witnessed the two reviews to fight the greatest cavalry-only engagement of the nineteenth century. Everything was shrouded in dust kicked up by the hooves of thousands of horses, and difficulty in seeing largely precluded the use of pistols or carbines. Sabres rose and fell in a scene reminiscent of a medieval, or even earlier, passage at arms.

On occasion the dust might for a moment blow away to reveal a target. Wesley Merritt saw a high Confederate officer and rushed over to cry, "Sir, you are my prisoner!"

"The hell I am," the rebel said, and swung his sabre. Merritt parried the blow, but the blade sliced his head, inflicting a minor but bloody wound. He sank his spurs into his horse and raced away, to learn later that his assailant had been either Fitz Lee or W. H. F. "Rooney" Lee, the general's son—he never knew which. (Rooney was later wounded in the leg, captured and taken away to a Northern prisoner-of-war camp.) Just before battle was joined, Brigadier General Hugh Judson Kilpatrick of New Jersey produced a flask of whiskey from his saddle bag, took a swig, and handed it round to his officers. One said, "Here's hoping we will do as well at Brandy Station as we are doing at whiskey station." "Good, blamed good," replied Kilpatrick with a grin. He had been in his final year at West Point when the war came in April 1861, scheduled to graduate in a couple of months. He gathered three dozen cadet signatures on an appeal to Washington for immediate assignment to the army. It was granted, and shortly thereafter, in a skirmish at Big Bethel, Virginia, he became the first Regular army officer to suffer a wound, minor though it was. The Prussian military strategist Alfred von Schlieffen once said that character is the first thing in an officer. No man by his actions ever disputed the words as completely as Kilpatrick, who, as we shall later note in detail, was a liar, a convicted and imprisoned thief, a shameless braggart, a relentless womanizer and whoremaster, and so disregardful of the lives and well-being of his men and horses that he early on earned and always kept the nickname Kill Cavalry. In addition to everything else, he was usually found to be an arrant coward. But on occasion he could rise to a high display against the enemy. Possibly that was accounted for by the resultant publicity assiduously courted from newspapermen in furtherance of his master plan, often stated to his fellows at the Point, which was that he be elected governor of New Jersey and then president of the United States.

In any event, he did very well during the twelve-hour fight at Brandy Station. "Men of Maine!" he screamed at a regiment of that state arriving on the field. "You must save the day! Follow me!" They galloped forward behind him to send an enemy group flying. Kilpatrick was not alone in offering a splendid showing. So did all of the Union's horsemen, to the amazement of the populations of both the Confederate and United States of America. The battle was the making of the Union cavalry. It has always been said that it came of age that day. Two years of humiliation at Stuart's hands had finally weeded out the misfits who officered the Yankee horse, with their replacements young fighters capable of being educated for what was needed. The Brandy Station affair was seen as a draw, although Stuart said it was a rebel victory by virtue of the fact that the Yankees went back to their encampments while he and his, to make his point, pitched their tents on the field amid the dead and swiftly bloating horse carcasses and the swarming bluebottle flies. But important as it was, it has an obscure place in the history of the Civil War—or, as the South called it for one hundred years, the War Between the States and, by those who went to their graves as proudly unreconstructed rebels, so they termed themselves, the War of Northern Aggression. For within days occurred what completely put in the shade Brandy Station and every other of the war's battles. Lee moved north. Endless lines of marching infantry, rolling artillery pieces, wagon trains bearing quartermaster and commissary supplies, ordnance, and portable forges to make horseshoes for replacing ones expected to be worn down by Pennsylvania's macadamized roads, of which the South possessed few or none, got under way. The Confederate chieftain had no precise destination firmly in mind, being as he was an improviser and a counterpuncher who got his ideas about a course of action from his opponents, but it was apparent that he and the Union army would meet somewhere in

Pennsylvania. Joe Hooker moved on a parallel course, confidence and bluster gone, and within days asked to be relieved of his position. His replacement was George G. Meade, an Engineers soldier and a friend of Lee's in the days before the war. Far out in front, Jeb Stuart raced away to scout out Yankee troop dispositions and to select the right place for Lee to make his fight—and also, Jeb being Jeb, to find excitement and fun. He found both at Rockville, Maryland, in the form of a caravan of 125 wagons filled with supplies for the new commander of the Army of the Potomac. Hundreds of sleek mules, six to each wagon, plodded along a thin road, strung out for a mile and a half or more. No more inviting a proposition ever had come Jeb's way. There was no McClellan-like pondering of a course of action: at their commander's joyfully shouted order, the rebel horsemen swooped down yelling, "Halt! Halt! Halt!" What little resistance that was offered was swept away, and when wagons overturned, others piled into them as the entire line dissolved in panicked chaos.

Drivers trying to reverse course or get off the road into surrounding fields crashed into one another, mules became unmanageable, and more wagons went over to bang down on their sides with wheels upward, contents spilling out to the sound and sight of drivers' curses, yells, and futile wielding of their long whips on kicking and bucking mules. Stuart erupted into ungovernable laughter. "Did you ever see anything like that in all your life?" he asked John Esten Cooke, who had not. They got the wagon train straightened out, a trophy of war now, and with it went to Brookville, Maryland, a town of very Southern atmosphere where a "bevy of beautiful girls" gave them baskets of cakes, bread, and meats and hugs and pitchers of ice water. Their horses had feasted on oats from the wagons, and men slung a bag filled with more across their saddles, William Willis Blackford noting how his mount, Magic, "occasionally turned an affectionate glance back towards it." It did his heart good to see Magic eat his fill and to know there were more good meals in the offing, for in the South's straightened circumstances, the animal had become in Blackford's eyes as thin as a snake. Men in the infantry had such a hard time of it, Blackford reflected, and saw so little fun; but the cavalry under Jeb got to join in activities as exciting as a fox hunt.

They went on through Maryland in the general direction of Pennsylvania, the staff served by a home's Southern sympathizers flapjacks, biscuits, buttermilk, coffee, and other treats before gathering with their hosts at the family Steinway to sing "Annie Laurie," "My Old Kentucky Home," and other songs, ending with the inevitable "Jine the Cavalry," Jeb putting "as much enthusiasm into that song," remembered one of their hosts, as into matters of an infinitely more serious nature. "His eyes sparkled and he kept time with his foot, the very personification of fun and spirit."

Lee came to the Pennsylvania hamlet of Cashtown and tentatively selected it as a place to meet Meade, who was thinking of nearby Pipe Creek. The issue was taken out of both generals' hands when an advance party of Confederates got word of an alleged stash of new shoes stored in a reasonably sized crossroads place. They headed there, ran into a detachment of Union soldiers, and got involved in a firefight. Reinforcement troops for both sides dribbled in, and the battle of happenstance encounter swelled of its own momentum. Twenty miles away, Lee was in complete ignorance of what he was facing in the town of supposed shoe storage. (In actuality there were no shoes, or at most very few.) He had no idea, he said, if he was dealing with a trifling skirmish or if the entire Federal army was being committed. For, as was later said, he had been rendered no less sightless than was Samson. It was Jeb Stuart who had achieved this by completely neglecting his duties as an intelligence officer assigned to spy out the enemy's movements, dispositions, intentions. For an entire week he had no contact with Lee, picking up caches of farm horses to add to his mule train booty, burning depots, tearing up railroad tracks, and fighting little bouts with minor Yankee detachments, during one of which he escaped substantial personal danger by leaping his mare, Virginia, across a stream, followed successfully by some of his people but with failure by others, whose mounts dumped them into the water. "The ludicrousness of the situation, notwithstanding the peril, was the source of much merriment at the expense of these unfortunate ones." In Cashtown, Lee paced his tent, asking staff officers, "Have you heard anything about my cavalry? I hope no disaster has overtaken my cavalry."

Crossed over into Pennsylvania from Maryland, his men cheering their arrival on enemy soil, Stuart took it into his head to obtain the surrender of the Union bastion at Carlisle. Its commander, General William "Baldy" Smith, told Fitz Lee, who presented the demand, that he would meet Stuart in hell before he lowered the base's American flag. The riders went on. "Any news to give me about General Stuart?" Lee asked his aides. There was none. It came to him that whether he liked it or not he was going to have to give battle, now that substantial numbers of troops were engaged there, at a place whose topography was entirely inimical to his forces—a fact Stuart would have easily and instantly grasped had he been doing what he was supposed to, instead of going about on what was soon denounced as a "useless, showy parade" calling for, in the opinion of Colonel Charles Marshall, Lee's chief aide, not only a court-martial but a firing squad. He had left on June 25, and it was not until July 2 that he had any contact with his commander: A courtier reached him with news that a great battle had begun at Gettysburg and he was to hasten there as swiftly as possible. He was twenty-five miles distant and encumbered by his slow-moving mule-train convoy, but made as much speed as he could and then went on before his men to meet with Lee.

"General Stuart, where have you been?" The commander's face and the back of his neck were red with rage as he lifted his arm and appeared about to deliver a physical blow. "I have not heard a word from you in days, and you the eyes and ears of my army!"

Jeb wilted. "I have brought you a hundred and twenty-five wagons and their teams, General," he got out.

"They are an impediment to me now." The scene was inexpressibly painful to those who watched and listened. Lee brought himself under control. "Let me ask your help now," he said. "We will not discuss this matter longer. Help me fight these people." Had Jeb not forgotten his primary function of scout and information seeker, Lee would never have fought on Gettysburg's unfavorable terrain. But that was water under the bridge now. "He stopped to capture a wagon train," Lee later said sadly, "and what was a wagon train compared with the tremendous issues we had at stake?" Stuart was told to get behind the Union position on Cemetery Ridge and to strike it from the rear as George Pickett came in from the front. There was a time when the plan would likely have worked. But the affair at Brandy Station had unalterably changed things. They had gotten a draw there with the rebel horsemen, and the years of frustration and humiliation were over, Yankee riders told one another. It came to the minds of those in the inner circles of the Army of the Potomac that it was their cavalry that might now carry the day for the North. Its commander, Alfred Pleasanton, handed out supremely generous promotions left and right to young officers who had not come of age in, or become accustomed to, a tiny, constricted, small-action frontier constabulary, and who were additionally free of before-the-war concepts that only Southerners were horsemen. All available Union cavalry made for Gettysburg to mass in an effort aimed at stopping Stuart from coming in behind Meade's position on Cemetery Ridge.

One group of Yankee horse, the Michigan Cavalry Brigade, exhausted from a long march north, dismounted for its men to get a little sleep, their reins tied to their wrists as they lay on the ground with the horses nibbling grass six inches from their faces. (It was a familiar situation: sometimes you awoke to find that your horse had consumed everything around you, leaving your shape outlined in uneaten greenery. Nobody ever got stepped on.) The unit had been assigned a new commander, jumped from brevet captain to brevet brigadier general three days earlier. He arrived after riding forty-five miles to take up his post. He was West Point 1861, his entrance into the army and the war delayed for a time because he was up on academy charges of observing rather than breaking up a fight between two cadets he was supposed to be supervising. Once in active service, he had performed in such manner that now, at twenty-three, he was the youngest general in the Union army. He was a pet of Alfred Pleasanton's, imitating his mannerisms and the dandyism notable at West Point that irritated Pleasanton's classmate Jeb Stuart, and played up to the cavalry chief by presenting him with a picture of the actress Fanny Fifield, a representation of whose likeness the general had admired in the captain's quarters.

The impression the newly minted brigadier general made on the men of his new command was anything but favorable, for after coldly and in distant and imperious fashion greeting his regimental commanders, he conducted an inspection and found fault with everything: mens' salutes were sloppy, the outfit had too much excess baggage, officers were remiss in superintending the grooming of horses. When he retired for the night, remembered Captain Frederick Whittaker, people competed in speaking ill of this "boy" with long blond locks reaching to his shoulders—"girl's hair"—who was an "affected dandy" and a "popinjay" of "West Point conceit" and accompanying "swagger," offensively put over men old enough to be his father who had abandoned for the Union cause farms and businesses where they had prospered without asking the government for a penny, as opposed to this epauletted poseur who had been supported all his career by citizens' money.

The Michigan Cavalry Brigade, four regiments recruited in that state, moved to take up position in the rear of Meade's Cemetery Ridge position, upon which soon enough the Confederate batteries would open in deadly force, one salvo coming down to kill twenty-one horses of the cavalry escort with which General Meade saw fit to surround himself as he moved about. The new brigade commander was not native to the Wolverine State, having been born in Ohio, but had lived there from the age of ten under the supervision of his sister in Monroe before leaving for the academy. After the first encounter of the war, Bull Run (or, as some called it while thinking the name indelicate, Manassas), he had gone on leave to Monroe and gotten drunk, to be seen staggering down the street under the highly disapproving gaze of a judge looking out his window. The intoxicated young man was in his hometown known as Armstrong, or Autie, from his childhood attempt to pronounce the middle name by which he was always addressed, and Judge Bacon told his daughter Elizabeth, who was very interested in Autie, as he was in her, that she could forget about any future involvement with George Armstrong Custer. That individual then, like Jeb Stuart promising his mother he would never touch liquor, swore that not another drop would pass his lips. One never did. With her father's consent he would marry Elizabeth Bacon—Libbie.

He got his unit into position to come under the view of men distant from the brigade's main encampment. "Fantastic at first sight," remembered James H. Kidd, remarking a youth originally taken for a junior staff officer passing on a superior's orders while attired in such fashion as almost to make Jeb Stuart's flamboyant dress, and that of the garb of gloriously done-up European cavalry officers, appear drab by comparison. General Custer had on a suit of black velvet elaborately trimmed with gold lace down the outer seam of the trousers and almost covering his sleeves. He wore a blue shirt with a wide collar and a necktie of brilliant crimson. His soft black hat had gilt cord and one side rakishly turned down, and sat atop golden hair to the shoulders framing a face that although dramatically mustachioed had the fair and soft complexion of a schoolgirl. (It had brought him the nickname "Fanny" at West Point.)

The Confederate general facing the Union forces atop Cemetery Ridge was ready to launch what would go into history as Pickett's Charge. Stuart's men were ready to attack the Yankee rear behind the Michigan Brigade drawn up to protect it and preparing to attack the Confederate horsemen menacing it. Autie Custer told a captain of a 6th Michigan detachment about to order his bugler to signal an assault against the rebels that he, the brigade commander, would replace the captain at the front of the troops. He wheeled his horse to face the soldiers, and drawing his sabre cried, "I'll lead you this time, boys! Come on! Come on, you Wolverines!"

It was the Custer adored by his Civil War troops, seen as brave but not reckless, self-confident but modest, ambitious but with the highest sense of honor and of duty, cautious when caution was called for, eager for laurels but scornful of wearing them unworthily, resourceful, cool, quick to act but careful of life, highly concerned for his soldiers' comfort and that of their mounts, kind and tolerant and even tenderhearted. A soldier playing at being a soldier, so it would be said, his display of harshest demeanor when first taking command was a performance aimed at producing a concept that he would swiftly dispel by being his real self, to his own benefit and that of his troops. It had been a role in a game that he loved: "I must say that I shall regret to see the war end," he would shortly write a friend. "I would be willing, yes glad, to see a battle every day during my life." His "Come on, boys" as opposed to the "Go in, boys" of other officers ended criticism of his exotic manner of dress, which indeed came to remind men of medieval leaders under banners proclaiming their location, of the white plume of Henry of Navarre showing where the thick of the fight was.

The two charges each directed toward the other got under way, the men of each side yelling and up in their stirrups. The opposing riders were some five hundred yards distant from each other when they dug in spurs. "As the two approached each other the pace of each increased," remembered a Union captain, "when suddenly a crash like the falling of timber betokened the crisis. So sudden and violent was the collision that many of the horses were turned end over end and crushed their riders beneath them. The clashing of sabres, the firing of pistols, the demands for surrender and cries of the combatants filled the air." Fitz Lee, who had been Custer's instructor in West Point days, and South Carolina's richest planter, Wade Hampton, were at the head of the Confederates. They had a portion of their forces dismount to pour carbine fire into the Federals, a volley shooting Custer's horse out from under him. He sailed through the air to arise brushing dust from his velvet. A rebel six feet away leveled his weapon, but a 1st Michigan private fired first and then reached down to pull his brigadier up behind him. The mount raced away, bringing both men to safety, and a replacement horse was found for Custer. A flanking Yankee artillery battery threw shells into the Confederate mass, while across the lines rebel pieces preparing the way for Pickett opened a tremendous barrage, the smoke of landing shells throwing up clouds over the Wolverines in amounts reminiscent of a forest fire. The continual crash of ordnance hitting the ground or exploding in the air was like the sound of reverberating thunder in a fearsome storm as the cavalrymen continued their fight, 7th Michigan riders blindly galloping into a stone wall with rail fence on top. Men and horses became "a mass of pulp," remembered one of the unit's captains. "It is yelling, shooting, swearing, cutting, fight, fight—all fight," recalled a 5th Michigan bugler. "Horses and men are being shot down like dogs." Opponents were so close to each other that powder burns from fired pistols scorched their uniforms.

Custer's men kept going, wheeled as they were hit by a flank charge Stuart led. Later Autie put himself at the head of the 1st Michigan as it prepared to assault eight rebel cavalry regiments. "Colonel Town," he told the 1st's commander, "I shall have to ask you to charge, and I want to go in with you." He spurred his horse almost four lengths in front of anyone else's and for the second time that day shouted, "Come on, you Wolverines!" A bugler remembered, "He is bareheaded and glorious. His yellow locks of hair are flying like a battle flag." His charger stumbled and fell, but he leaped on a riderless horse and continued on. His opponent Wade Hampton was sabred twice in the head and almost blinded by his own blood, and the Southerners fell back. The rebel artillery, after two hours of uninterrupted shelling, fell silent so that Pickett could take his infantry forward. As with Lord Cardigan of the Light Brigade at Balaklava saying that here went the last of his family, Pickett had no anticipation of success. Sitting his horse next to General James Longstreet, the dead Stonewall Jackson's replacement, he handed over a letter to be delivered to his fiancée if he fell during the advance of seven-eighths of a mile across completely open and virtually treeless terrain up to Cemetery Ridge, where, he saw, the Union artillery, while reduced by the long Confederate barrage, was still intact and firing. "General, shall I advance?" he asked. Longstreet did not reply. Tears ran from his eyes down into his beard. Like Pickett, he saw here the most fruitless of endeavors, the product, he said in later years, of a strange, inexplicable bloodlust on the part of Robert E. Lee.

"I am going to move forward, sir," Pickett said as Longstreet remained silent, and got his men moving, fifteen thousand soldiers in forward-march and parade-ground formation esteemed by an observer, Lieutenant Colonel A. J. Lyon of Her Majesty's Coldstream Guards, as the most magnificent thing he had ever seen. Pickett's Charge ended with virtually all of the horsed officers lying prostrate on the ground along with their mounts and perhaps a hundred of the footmen getting through the Yankee infantry and guns to pierce the Union center atop Cemetery Ridge and plant there, for a moment, a Stars and Bars. It was the high-water mark of the Confederacy.

To the rear of the Union line, Jeb Stuart had been held to no gain by Custer and the other horsemen of the North. Had he forgone his fun-filled joyride with its hilarious capture of the mule-train wagons, had he scouted out a better place for Lee to make his fight instead of allowing chance to select a spot where the Union soldiers occupied all the high points, or at least brought his horse-men up in better style and not exhausted from their long trek to Gettysburg—who knows? The South might have won the day, with the Yankee troops sent within days to suppress New York City anti-draft riots instead disarmed by the victors or in rebel prison camps. But then, history is full of buts.

On another portion of the field, Hugh Judson Kilpatrick issued an order that all who heard it, Wesley Merritt included, thought insane. He directed Brigadier General Elon Farnswoth, jumped along with Custer and Merritt from captain to one-star cavalry rank not a week previous, to charge a Confederate stronghold. There never was ground more unsuitable for such an endeavor against emplaced riflemen and artillery, hilly and wooded, laced with ditches, fenced, strewn with great rock outcropping, and with to boot a blazing sun shining directly in attackers' eyes. Farnsworth pointed out the extremely disadvantageous conditions with which his horsemen would have to deal, to which Kilpatrick replied that if his subordinate was afraid to lead, he himself would do so. "Take that back!" Farnsworth cried, rising in his stirrups. Kilpatrick did, and Farnsworth formed his riders and galloped forward. When his body was recovered it was found to have suffered no less than five bullet wounds and possibly more. Sixty-six of his followers lay dead. "For utter recklessness, for self-indulgent folly, the doomed and senseless folly outshone the many other stains on Kilpatrick's record." But then, Kill Cavalry did not very much care. "Charge them, God damn them!" was his almost unvarying answer to all military problems, and afterward he seemed so uninvolved in loss or repulse as to have had nothing to do with the matter.

Jeb Stuart had a more forceful response to what others called failure: he refused to admit such a thing could exist for him; all his people knew that. So when the rebel army, repelled in its invasion of the North, trailed away to its own country, he wrote to his wife, "I had a grand time in Penna. and we return without defeat." A 2nd Virginia Cavalry private noted Jeb's demeanor on the way back: "I was much amused to see Stuart pass through Martinsburg with a large cavalcade of staff and two bugles blowing most furiously." Earlier the private saw the commander of the Army of Northern

Virginia quietly ride down the same road. "Lee passed with one or two persons." When the fighting at Gettysburg came to a halt after three days, Lee knew what it meant that Pickett had failed to break the Union line atop Cemetery Ridge even as Stuart failed to break it from the rear. It was one in the morning when he went to his tent, walking his gray, Traveller, slowly through soft silvery July moonlight. Asked to meet him there discuss details regarding the coming retreat, General John Imboden saw how the effort Lee made to get off his horse revealed utter exhaustion. Lee leaned on Traveller, arm across the saddle, to rest himself a moment. It seemed to Imboden that horse and man stood together as motionless as statues. "General," Imboden said after a long silence, "this has been a hard day on you."

"Yes, it has been a sad, sad day to us." Then, tremulously, he added, "Too bad! *Too bad!* Oh, too bad!"

Across the lines, General Meade considered the situation, thought, temporized, held councils of war. Councils of war never fight. When President Lincoln telegraphed pleas that he fling himself upon the retreating Confederates, all history teaching that a routed and strung-out army is likely to suffer utter destruction from a determined enemy's blow, Meade submitted his resignation, which was refused by the White House. His horse commander, Alfred Pleasanton, said to the Army of the Potomac chief, "I will give you half an hour to prove yourself a great general. Order the army to advance while I will take the cavalry, get in Lee's rear, and we will finish the campaign in a week." It was not in Meade to do so, cautiously calculating as he was and seeing as he did Pleasanton as one staff man among many, authorized to pass on orders to subordinate officers while having no personal contact with combat troops. For days Pleasanton pressed his case, and then the opportunity passed. There were some not very significant cavalry attempts to harry the rebels heading south, Kilpatrick characterizing one of his efforts in his self-glorifying way. "Never under such perilous circumstances did a command behave better," he reported, while Lee called the matter "an unimportant demonstration on our rear which was easily checked." The two armies settled down to rest and refit, although the rebels had little new or reconditioned equipment and fewer provisions to offer their troops or, more particularly, their horses. Confederate stays at cavalry encampments swiftly found all trees of the area stripped of bark, gnawed down to green wood by starving animals for whom there was no grain. Officers issued with a little hay to floor tents often gave it to their mounts instead.

For the horsed units of the Union army there were new saddles, bridles, bits, and stirrups, and plenty of feed brought in by the North's railroad networks from the rich farmlands of the West, the Middle Frontier. The lot of the Yankee cavalry was, however, far from pleasant. George Meade utilized his riders, as largely had his predecessors in the leadership of the Army of the Potomac, in an unimaginative and static manner. They were as in the past wagon-train guards, grooms, couriers, escorts, and, most notably, holders of tightly woven and extensive vidette positions—mounted watchmen in unmoving defensive posture. Continually maintaining no less than sixty miles of a line in all kinds of weather imposed on horsemen the most drearily depressing of duties. Only Hugh Judson Kilpatrick, dynamic and dramatic despite his manifold flaws, saw a way to put the Federal horse to better use.

The enemy capital of Richmond had two dreadful prisoner-of-war camps, Belle Island for Union enlisted men, Libby Prison for officers. Both saw captured soldiers existing, and in horrific number dying, under appalling conditions: the most minimal distribution of food—a cup of worm-ridden bean soup a day—putrid water, beastly heat in summer and deadly cold in winter, rats, lice, disease. The situation was in vague nature known in the North, as was the fact that there were no great numbers of rebel troops stationed in Richmond, but rather a mélange of home guards—crippled casualties, clerks, old men and young boys a few hundred in number. A determined cavalry strike, Kilpatrick reasoned, could briefly invest Richmond to free the captives and so inflict a devastating blow to rebel morale all across the Confederacy while advancing to great Northern acclaim the career of the officer leading such an effort, who would be, Kilpatrick of course schemed, himself. He knew he was most unpopular with Generals Pleasanton and Meade for both professional and personal reasons. Meade's aide Colonel Theodore Lyman called him "a frothy braggart, without brains and not over-stocked with desire to fall on the field" who had gained "all his reputation by newspaper and political influence." As to his personal life (one cannot say his private life, for it was anything but that, the whole army knowing the situation), he had taken a prostitute into his tent and given her a horse to ride as she went about in a major's uniform he provided. Annie Jones, so she called herself, eventually chose Custer's tent over Kilpatrick's while claiming, truthfully or otherwise, that she had at one time captured the attention of Jeb Stuart. Either from that allegation or from pique at being displaced in her affections by Autie, Kilpatrick had her arrested as a spy and confined in Washington's notorious Old Capitol prison.

Knowing his military superiors would never give his plan a hearing, Kilpatrick outlined it to a congressman close to Lincoln, hopeful that it would be communicated to the president. That occurred, and Lincoln took the matter under consideration. Shortly after, a group of Libby Prison inmates, by virtue of the most arduous labor imaginable, tunneled their way out. The first escapees arrived in Washington to say the others would soon be there. That meant newspaper interviews revealing in detail the dreadful imprisonment situation in Richmond with widespread Northern uproar certain to follow. That night Lincoln telegraphed to Brigadier General Kilpatrick an order that he come the next day to the White House. Commander in chief and officer were alone together for a time, and then Secretary of War Edwin M. Stanton directed that four thousand prime cavalry mounts and as many carefully selected riders be put under Kilpatrick for a special mission.

Keeping secrets from wartime Washington's rebel spies was an impossibility, so Kilpatrick hastily set out with his force divided in two, five hundred riders under Colonel Ulric Dahlgren delegated to strike Richmond from one direction in a diversionary manner calculated to draw off such defenders as there were, while Kilpatrick went in with the mass of men from another point. Dahlgren was twenty-one, the son of the Union navy's eminent and famed ordnance expert, Admiral John A. Dahlgren. The young man had lost a leg at Gettysburg and gone into a coma from which it was feared he would never awaken, but he did so to declare himself as able to ride a horse with one leg as he had with two, and returned to active duty with a crutch strapped to his saddle for aid when dismounted. He was a born cavalryman, intense, athletic, involved with hunting and riding, craving action, excitement, challenge. Kilpatrick was happy to accept his services, saying Dahlgren would bring "even more publicity and prestige" to his raid. The youthful colonel's men, and Kilpatrick's, carried on their horses the slimmest of troop rations for three days, the time allotted for both groups to get to Richmond, do their work, and get back: hardtack, sugar, coffee, and salt, but no meat. They had light-horse artillery batteries able to stay with a swift pace, but no cumbersome horse-feed wagon trains, which would inevitably slow things down: their mounts would have to do with but one day's saddle-borne serving of grain. In ostentatious fashion, infantry detachments of long columns complete with extensive hospital and headquarters wagons were marched off in various directions to attract Confederate attention away from their mission, and George Custer angled cavalry distant from Kilpatrick's Richmond destination specifically as a decoy for Jeb Stuart.

February 1864 offered freezing rain and brutal wind-driven sleet, through which Kilpatrick's thirty-five hundred and Dahlgren's five hundred pressed on at great speed, the slowest gait a trot and the horses generally at a gallop. General Meade had always distrusted Kill Cavalry, reading his always grandiose reports of, as Colonel Charles Wainwright told his diary, " 'the most glorious charges ever made'" and "'sabring right and left' and such stuff" with greatest skepticism. But perhaps this dissolute, ruthless, self-glorifying liar, who, after all, when necessary had proved that he could fight, might yet with his men, Meade reflected, succeed in what might be, he wrote his wife, "the greatest feat of the war," which would "immortalize them all."

The smaller of the two columns approaching Richmond from different directions, Dahlgren's, ran into trouble. A ford it hoped to cross was flooded; another could not be found. There was a skirmish with rebels, and the young colonel was killed. A boy rifling through his pockets found what appeared to be an order calling for the freeing of the Union prisoners with the assassination of President Jefferson Davis and all of the Confederate cabinet members to follow. Whether it was a legitimate document or a forgery or even some sort of perverse joke has never been determined, although the South believed it to be a true representation of Kilpatrick's desires. Robert E. Lee sent a note across the lines to his Old Army associate Meade asking if the murder of unarmed civilians was a new function of the U.S. Cavalry.

Said to have been mutilated in fearsome fashion—again the facts are unclear—Colonel Dahlgren is alleged to have been thrown into a hole dug under a crossroads in the fashion reserved in medieval days for those soulless: the murderer, suicide, vampire, witch. His unusual first name was used to hark back to an earlier horsed marauder of the most ruthless type, and Southern papers would come to call him Ulric the Hun. Not knowing his subordinate's fate, Kilpatrick sped on. All horsed operations throughout history show that a long column pushed to make time runs the risk of its rear becoming strung out in rush-and-then-stop manner. When late at night Kilpatrick had his forward elements halt for rest and coffee, two hours passed before his men at the rear made camp. Ice covered beards and overcoats, scabbards and rifles. Horses foundered, their riders going along on foot with one hand gripping a comrade's stirrup to help with forward propulsion. Thirty-six hours after getting under way, with but three hours of rest for the most fortunate, the men were within five miles of Richmond. From their position on the Brook Pike, they saw for one thousand yards open land crisscrossed with earthworks and trenches created much earlier and now but thinly held by defenders of minimum military capacity, the scratched-together home guard of the old, young, and crippled doing duty while the real soldiers of the Confederacy were elsewhere. The riders, it seemed, could charge forward and be in Richmond's streets within the hour headed for prisoner release plus—perhaps—wholesale dispatch of Confederate officialdom. But General Kilpatrick hesitated. He unlimbered his horse artillery to throw a few shells forward and dismounted a slight contingent of soldiers to feel their way into the ground before him. They were met with a scant volume of fire indicative of but a limited number of defenders.

Glory awaited, higher rank, perfectly plausible postwar election to his long-planned governorship of New Jersey, with the American presidency to follow. But something intangible and beyond analysis, as perhaps much of war is, seized Kilpatrick. Like Hooker, whose tastes in women resembled his—although the term descriptive of a certain type of woman is incorrectly connected with Fighting Joe's name, it having come into use two decades before his rise to the command of the Army of the Potomac—Kill Cavalry turned tremulous to quail before the task he had set himself. Hooker at Chancellorsville sat immobile and huddled within himself before Stonewall Jackson's impending blow. Kilpatrick along the Brook Pike simply turned and went away. Autie Custer and his diversionary force aimed at diverting Jeb Stuart had, in an exemplary display of what light cavalry was supposed to do, covered nearly a hundred miles in forty-eight hours through ice, snow, and driving rain, and burned a railroad bridge and a depot while drawing Jeb into a fruitless pursuit. It was all for naught so far as the Richmond venture was concerned, and Kilpatrick and his thirty-five hundred found their way to Union boats for transfer to safe territory, carried along, Meade's aide Colonel Lyman disdainfully recorded, "like a bunch of old women going to market."

The whole incident, begun with hopes of cavalry achievement as has rarely been recorded, slipped away into a Civil War footnote, notable only for bitterness in Southern conceptions of the ruthlessness of a foe perceived as countenancing the brutish slaughter of the Confederacy's civilian leaders. Soon far more significant events blurred its memory. Out in the west, the Union's regularly victorious general Ulysses S. Grant attracted the White House's intense interest. "I like this man; he fights," the president said. Grant was ordered to Washington and given what only George Washington had possessed: three stars. (Winfield Scott had worn that many, but only in brevet, acting as, capacity.) The new Lieutenant General Commanding the Armies of the United States originally planned to oversee the eastern campaigns from afar while resuming his duties in the west, but soon he changed his mind. The officers of the inner circles of the Army of the Potomac were far too occupied, he decided, with describing the supreme capabilities of Bobby Lee, as they called the Army of Northern Virginia leader in imitation of Lincoln's manner of referring to him. General George Meade, shown in the Gettysburg aftermath to be hesitant and cautious, would never be the leader to emancipate them from that view. While leaving him the face-saving title of Army of the Potomac commander, Grant would utilize him as an executive officer following out Grant's orders. And the cavalry commander Alfred Pleasanton was, while being not entirely incapable, of insufficient brilliance, fire, drive, character, to deal with the flashing and inventive dash of Jeb Stuart. So the lieutenant general ruled that he would have William T. Sherman command Union moves away from the Virginia theater of operations while he himself there dealt with Lee. To face Stuart he brought in a strangely and indeed grotesquely formed little man with some hundred days of cavalry experience.

12

Little Phil

It is unknown if Philip Henry Sheridan was born in Boston, in Albany, New York, or on ship coming from Ireland to America. In maturity he gave differing versions of birth circumstances. The third of six children, he grew up in southeastern Ohio's crossroads town of Somerset, where his father worked as a laborer and in construction. He seems to have been outgoing, given to participating in boys' dress-up barn shows in one of which he appeared as an elaborately costumed animal tamer whose charges, a cat and a dog, fell to biting and clawing each other and him, much to the audience's delight. A pal and he balanced a bucket of water atop a schoolroom door to come down and soak the teacher, who identified Phil as one of the culprits, took a stick, and rushed for him. The boy dashed off and into a tin shop, where he begged the tinner to let him hide under a copper kettle. In later days when his water-bucket fellow conspirator, Henry Greiner, heard of General Sheridan's swiftness in reaching battlefield decisions, the immediate selection of the kettle as safe refuge readily came to mind.

He always loved horses, involvement with one, his mother long after related, bringing on the sole physical chastisement of his childhood—a good whipping administered by his father. There was a team member of the stagecoach that regularly came through Somerset who was known for fractious, dangerous behavior. Phil contrived to get on board for a gallop, which although safely concluded, produced the parental ire and punishment. At fourteen he

163

left school to work at a grocery and hardware store, with a salary of $24 a year. He was so pleasant and agreeable a clerk that a rival establishment lured him away with an offer of $60, and he concluded his mercantile career by taking on duties at a third place for $120.

It was to go to the United States Military Academy at West Point that he left Somerset. As boys he and Henry Greiner had taken awed note of a cadet on leave engrossed in conversation with a local young woman, their attention focused on the man's glamorous dress uniform, based on those worn by a unit of the War of 1812 in which Winfield Scott had served, which remains virtually unchanged to the present day. The cadet was William T. Sherman. Memory of his appearance plus attention to the events of the 1846–48 war with Mexico, for which he was too young to volunteer, created in young Sheridan, he wrote, a "sole wish to become a soldier" with his "highest aspiration to go to West Point."

He received an appointment to perform in academically unspectacular fashion, and as a second classman—the equivalent of a junior in a civilian college—got himself a year's suspension. He had, as future occasions would prove, a temper, and it rose up when he was offered a harsh reprimand by a cadet superior. Sheridan lowered a bayonet and rushed forward intending to use it before, he said, "my better judgment recalled me." His offense was too grave to be worked off through punishment tours (during which a cadet, under pack and arms, endlessly marched about the post) or restriction to quarters, and he returned to Somerset for his banishment. Then he was permitted back for a final year and graduation. He was certainly not the physical beau ideal of the brilliantly turned-out and perfect Point cadet-turned-second lieutenant, being as he was under five foot four, 120 pounds or less, and so constructed that Lincoln's estimate when first seeing him a decade and more later was: "Chunky little chap, with a long body, short legs, not enough neck to hang him, and such long arms that if his ankles itch he can scratch them without stooping." The president neglected to mention Sheridan's head. It was so bullet-shaped that he always had trouble keeping on a hat if riding a horse at speed. When he rose to such rank as to be able to wear what he pleased, he sported a squashed two-sizes-too-small little porkpie affair unworn by anyone else in the Union, or any other, army.

Sheridan served eight years as a second lieutenant, stationed in Texas and then the Pacific Northwest. With the coming of the war, he made captain and was assigned to quartermaster duty in Missouri, then to recruiting and training duty at Jefferson Barracks in that state, then to the Army of the Tennessee to work as a topographical engineer. Offered the colonelcy of a cavalry regiment, he accepted, brilliantly to defeat a force of rebel horsemen outnumbering him by four to one. After three months he took on infantry duties. Near Chattanooga, his men were positioned at the base of the Confederate-held Missionary Ridge and Lookout Mountain. The sheerness of the heights made the enemy, under Braxton Bragg, appear unassailable. Looking up, Sheridan poured himself a cup of whiskey. "How are you, Mr. Bragg?" he cried, and a bullet hit and shattered the cup. "That's damned ungenerous!" Sheridan shouted, and rushed forward, his men accompanying. What followed was called the Battle Above the Clouds, which saw the rebels driven away. Looking on in his silent way, Ulysses S. Grant took note, and when he went east to take command of all Union forces and to express to Lincoln dissatisfaction with what he called "the little that has been accomplished by the cavalry so far in the war," Sheridan, despite his limited horse soldier experience, came to Grant's mind as someone able to remedy the situation so far as the Army of the Potomac went.

The new commander arrived with his four personal mounts to find that while the troopers were in good shape, the horses of the units he was to lead were not. General Meade's insistence on their endless cold-weather picket-line duty had gravely worn them down. (Lee, by contrast, had sent his horses off behind his lines for rest and to partake of the grass of 1864's spring.) Sheridan ordered a two-week recuperation period, during which the animals were not ridden while given copious feed. It was the first instance of how his way of looking at things differed from that of the on-paper commander ofthe Army of the Potomac, who was actually subordinate to Grant. Meade saw Sheridan to be, like the relieved-from-command Pleasanton, little more than a staff officer. Meade would dictate cavalry dispositions, which Sheridan would carry out. At best, Sheridan would directly control but a portion of the army's horsemen.

No concept could have accorded less with Sheridan's views. He had been named chieftain of all the cavalry, he said, "and by God I want them all." Ferocious arguments resulted. For his temperament, Meade was—behind his back, to be sure—termed by his officers the Old Snapping Turtle, and Sheridan, as earlier indicated, was subject to all but uncontrollable rages. Late in life he confessed to his old friend Henry Greiner his concern that posterity would remember him as excessively foul-mouthed, but in Civil War days he gave the matter little thought and put no rein on his tongue. "Strange, novel, picturesque oaths, made up on the spot, would burst from him spontaneously," remembered a newspaper artist-correspondent. If he was to be given only severely limited authority, he raged at Meade, he would not issue a single order to anyone. Let Meade himself take care of the cavalry, about which, he added, Meade knew nothing, ridiculously believing as he obviously did that the nimblest arm of the service was useful only in stationary guard and on picket duty. If it was up to him, Sheridan concluded, he would take every last Army of the Potomac horseman and go out and destroy Jeb Stuart. (When someone earlier said that his cavalry mission was purely defensive in nature and solely to keep "Jeb Stuart from getting into trouble," and that the rebel horse leader would "do about as he pleases," Sheridan retorted, "Damn Stuart. I can thrash hell out of him.")

Shouted expletives flew back and forth and Meade went fuming to Grant, complaining about Sheridan's insubordination and his claim that he could destroy Jeb Stuart. "Did he say that?" Grant asked. "Well, he generally knows what he is talking about. Let him start right out and do it." So Little Phil, as he was known to his men (he was also called the Jack of Clubs for his short and squat appearance and his dark hair, which was cut so short it almost looked like a coat of paint roughly slapped onto his skull), set out south with a column of riders some ten thousand and more strong, four abreast and thirteen miles long, with guidon after guidon following his headquarters flag of red with the two stars of a major general.

Little Phil, Washington, aboard Rienzi. "The horse who elected a president."

He was thirty-three, generally untalkative when not given to near-hysterical outbursts. In combat situations he alternated screaming with moments of extreme calm, sitting his horse in a hunched-over posture to issue orders in a low tone. All who served close to him recorded memories of the unique reddish glow that appeared in his eyes when bullets began to fly.

The Union horse had in the past traveled at speed with, as seen in Kilpatrick's venture, the rear often needing to rush to catch up. Doctrine dictated the use of two or three parallel columns along separate routes. Sheridan rejected both techniques; his men proceeded at a measured walk in one long line, and there was something infinitely menacing about this long, slow-crawling snake, which took three hours to pass from front to rear a given point. Dogs barked along the way announcing his passage, Confederate scouts flew off to warn of his coming—he did not care. His two immediate subordinate commanders were the brigadier generals Wesley Merritt and George Custer, Merritt holding superior rank over Autie by virtue of his earlier West Point graduation. Sheridan always played favorites—envious officers called his pets Little Phil's "toadies"—and he was much taken with Autie's high-spirited off-duty cavorting with Mrs. Custer, which found them running around a room to jump over furniture as they chased each other in games they invented. With Merritt, a bachelor like himself, Sheridan made excursions to certain houses in Washington or Baltimore, where, as was said, they "worshipped at the Temple of Venus." On the march, he or one of the two brigadier generals leading, he was relaxed and approachable, as likely to ask a light from an enlisted man's pipe as from an officer's cigar.

Yet he missed nothing, his eyes seeming to rest at one point or another on each man in his command for individual judgment and estimation of capabilities. No soldier understood topography better. Sheridan could look at a map and say there had to be a road from Point A to Point B. But the map indicated none such, his officers retorted. There *must* be, for the lay of the land dictated it, he said, confidently sending off masses of riders who inevitably found that indeed there was such a road for their use and that of the cause their general and they served. A great soldier, like a great pianist, or baseball player, or indeed a great anything or anybody, possesses, as earlier indicated, a talent that it has pleased God, or genetics, or inexplicable chance to bestow. Added to that talent must be a time and a place where it can be utilized. And added to inborn capability and the proper opportunity for its display, what matters for success is work. It is such, we know, that in the end is what counts. We have the letters of the man who can be called the most unusual, unlikely, certainly atypical, and in ways most brilliant of all Yankee cavalry officers to attest to what today would be called the work ethic of Philip Henry Sheridan.

That man was Charles Russell Lowell, son of an illustrious Boston family whose most noted member was his uncle James Russell Lowell, editor of *The Atlantic Monthly*, who even from his nephew's

Charles Russell Lowell, who had
he lived, Sheridan said, would have
ended up commanding the Union
cavalry, to do a better job of it than
Sheridan himself.

childhood days accepted him for his intellectual capacity as an
equal. At fifteen, Charlie, as he always was to friends and family,
entered Harvard, the youngest member of his class and much the
youngest-looking, small and slightly built. He also was academically first among his fellows. The college had no scholarships as we
understand the term, but because of Charlie's performance, no bill
was ever presented for his four years. It was well that it was so, for
his father was a poor earner, with much or likely most of the family's
income deriving from a small girls' finishing school his wife ran from
their home. As valedictorian Charlie spoke of the country's need
for idealism, his words correctly interpreted by listeners as having to
do with the abolition of slavery. Indeed that was the calling of their
generation, he told his friend Henry Lee Higginson.

He was found to be aloof, judgmental, and dauntingly intellectual by most people, and moved in a circle of Boston Brahmin young
men uniformly descended from colonial America's founding fathers.
His own great-grandfather had roomed with James Madison at the
Continental Congress. While a grandfather with whom he was
close was a noted clergyman, Charlie felt and said that organized

religion was the source of most of mankind's ills. With no family money behind him, he set out to earn some, going into railroad work in Iowa. He contracted tuberculosis, the cure for which, the doctors decreed, was a sojourn in warm climates, coupled with outdoor exercise. A grandmother financing it, he set out on an overseas tour whose focus was the riding of horses. Under the North African and then the European sun, in Algeria, Malta, Italy, and Spain, he was for much of every day mounted, saying, "I must secure a certain number of hours of violent exercise."

The disease routed or at least in remission, he returned to the United States to continue a business career, studying German so as to be able to instruct immigrant Maryland ironworkers for whom he also formed choral groups. He continued to ride, two hours every morning of the year regardless of the weather, sitting at his desk late at night to get necessary work done so that he could be free to do so. He married Josephine Shaw, Effie to family and friends, a former student of his mother's from a wealthy and fervidly Abolitionist family. Her brother Robert, called Rob, became when the war came colonel of the 54th United States Colored Volunteer Infantry. To Rob, his brother-in-law was the most brilliant man the Union army came to possess. Charlie had contacted Senator Charles Sumner to ask for a cavalry commission, his qualifications being, he offered, that he was able "to ride a horse as far and bring him in as fresh as any other man." A meeting with Secretary of War Simon Cameron resulted. Cameron saw before him a frail-looking Harvard intellectual extremely youthful in appearance, and asked, "You, young man, what do you know of a horse?"

"Enough to take a hard day's work out of him and to bring him back fresh at night." He was given a captaincy in the Regular army's 6th Cavalry Regiment of men mostly new to service but leavened with a number of hard-bitten old-timers accustomed to seasoned West Pointers as opposed to an almost childlike little fellow who days before had been a civilian and was attired in less than spiffy fashion, being as he always was rather shabbily done up. One baited Charlie and, encouraged by others, appeared to be about to administer a beating. The old soldier had mistaken his man. After giving fair warning, Charlie drew a revolver, put a round through him, and reported himself to a superior ready to face murder charges. The matter was ruled a permissible act.

"I hardly know myself in this new style of life," he wrote a friend, but there was never a man more instinctively an officer of horse, nor more a student of what it was to be one. New recruits to the cavalry, he wrote his father, should never be sent to units without at least four months' training, for tyros corrupted seasoned troopers, being as they were often ignorant of and frightened of horses and so in danger of setting off mass skittishness in a line or column. They had to learn what it was to be a cavalryman. That included: "The horse splashed with clay after three hours' drill is not a cheerful spectacle to the recruit who has to clean him—it opens his eyes to some of the advantages of infantry." As for the animals themselves, he said, "I do not fancy horses who at the outset do not resist; but they must be intelligent enough to know when they are conquered, and to recognize it as an advance in their civilization." McClellan in the Peninsula campaign might display entire incapacity at deploying his horsemen, but Captain Lowell, within the limited scope permitted by the commanding general, showed striking tactical ability. He also possessed unexampled bravery that found him interposed on his horse between advancing rebels and a shaken, about-to-panic Yankee unit, the result being a forward rally that sent the Confederates flying. Seeing a line of leveled enemy rifles poking over a wall, he galloped its length striking each one in turn with his sabre to disarray the lot.

There are intellectuals whose letters, like Charlie Lowell's, are filled with references to Schiller, Spencer, Chaucer, Carlyle, Swedenborg, Dante, Emerson, Kant, and Plato, but not all intellectuals are remarkable judges of men. That was not so in his case. Made an aide to McClellan after the Peninsula campaign, which cost the life of his brother, James, who had succeeded him as a Harvard valedictorian, Captain Lowell's estimations about the high officers he now closely observed proved unerring. About McClellan he observed, "He prepares very well and then doesn't do the best thing—strike hard." About the future loser of the catastrophic battle of Chancellorsville: "Personally I like Hooker very much, but I fear he will do us a mischief if he ever gets a large command. He has got his head in the clouds." And about Sheridan: "The first general I have seen who puts as much heart and time and thought into his work as if he were doing it for his own exclusive profit. He works like a mill owner or ironmaster, not like a soldier—never sleeps, never worries, is never cross, but isn't afraid to come down on a man who deserves it."

Sheridan went south in the direction of Richmond with his great column of horses in the first days of May 1864. It was not the Confederate capital that interested him; it was his opposite number of the rebel cavalry. His coming was of course known to Jeb, who hastened to throw up a line of defense at a crossroads some half dozen miles from Richmond, Yellow Tavern, so named for an abandoned drinking place. En route he paused for a few minutes at Beaver Dam to be with his pregnant wife and their son, Jimmie. Their daughter, Flora, was dead of disease, not yet six at her passing. "I will never get over it," her father told his closest aides, seeing in light blue flowers the color of her eyes and in glancing sunbeams the golden tinge of her hair. La Pet, he had called her in letters to his wife—short for La Petite. He leaned from his horse to kiss his wife and went on.

His men quickly threw up fortifications, behind which they awaited the Yankees, George Custer leading the forward elements across a bridge so narrow as to allow but three horsemen to go over shoulder to shoulder. The rebel horse artillery opened fire. John Pelham, "the Gallant Pelham" as Lee had termed him for a performance at Fredericksburg in which four of his guns combated thirty-six of the enemy's, he constantly shifting and ducking his pieces away, was not present. He had taken a shell splinter to the head when he and Jeb, in Culpeper for court-martial duty, heard there was a fracas with the enemy and went to see the fun. Stuart wept as he bent to kiss the pale and cold forehead of the man whom Southern iconology would term the Great Canoneer. With his death, it was said, something youthful and golden passed from the Confederate army. Heros von Borcke was not at Yellow Tavern. During a skirmish preceding Gettysburg he felt what seemed like a tremendous blow to his neck, saw fiery stars, and felt himself being dragged down by some irresistible force. His horse became fractious. Recalling how the Prussian had once remarked that in his country's cavalry schools one was taught that the best way to control a horse was violently to twist its ear, Borcke's tentmate, William Willis Blackford, did so while the wounded man, insensible, was eased off. Taken to Richmond, he was told that a wound through his windpipe with the bullet lodging in his right lung was mortal, but he lived, though permanently incapacitated and unable ever to ride again. W. H. F. "Rooney" Lee, the general's son, was also not at Yellow Tavern; he was a prisoner of war. The happy jongleur Sweeney, he who had led them all in singing of how if you want to smell hell, if you want to have fun, jine the cavalry, was gone, dead of disease They were gone, most of them, who had joyously ridden with Jeb on the great raid around McClellan, and elsewhere, and indeed it seems to have come to their leader that his own sands and those of his country, the Confederacy, were running out; for as they went along he remarked to his bugler and his aide Theodore S. Garnett that he did not expect to survive the war, and that if the rebels lost he would not wish to. But when someone said that perhaps Sheridan had too many men and was too strong to be beaten, he declaimed "with hot impatience," remembered Garnett, that no! it was not so. "I would rather die then let him go on."

Stuart was off his iron gray, General, and lying under a tree when Custer got sufficient men across the narrow bridge to mount a charge. "Go in, I will give you all the support in my power," Wesley Merritt said, and Autie's buglers rang the order as his band blared "Yankee Doodle" and he shouted his familiar "Come on, you Wolverines!" The Federals had some four hundred yards to go to reach the rebel fortifications, first at a walk, then a trot, and finally an all-out rush, sabres flashing and the men screaming. Sheridan looked on through the dust and the smoke. That bells were tolling in Richmond to sound an alarm bringing the home guard to the city's defense positions did not concern him. He had no designs upon Richmond. It was for this before him that he had come east and for which he had contended with George Meade, what he had told Grant he would do: to deal in cavalry-to-cavalry battle with the rebel horseman as to end their great sweeping and free-ranging untrammeled intimidations of a Union army huddled supine to await their depredations.

The charge swept over the first line of defenders, Yankee horsemen sabring down the Confederate gunners, and broke upon a second one, there to become disorganized and out of formation before Custer in his red tie and flying blond mane (he was known as Old Curly to his troops now) rallied his men to come again in such splendid fashion that Sheridan told Merritt to send a staff officer to give Autie his commander's compliments. Stuart got on General and rode to where dismounted riders were firing from behind a wood-rail fence. He was humming a tune. He put General's nose between the heads of two soldiers firing from a standing position, then drew a revolver and added his shots to theirs, yelling, "Steady men, steady! Give it to them!" Major Reid Venable pointed out that people were being hit and it would be wise to be careful; Jeb laughed and said, "I don't reckon there is any danger."

Unhorsed Yankee soldiers came running by, heading back to their own line. One was Private John A. Huff, Company "E," 5th Michigan Cavalry. At past forty he was old for a trooper. He had earlier served in a sharpshooting unit. He held a .44 Colt pistol. He was some ten or fifteen yards from a target when he discharged the weapon. Jeb Stuart's hat fell off and he lost his grip on General's reins as his legs sagged to lose contact with the mount's flanks. His rider suddenly lumplike, the horse reacted by becoming unmanageable. Captain Gus W. Dorsey attempted to lead him to the rear, but that proved impossible. In another moment a Custer push could result in the capture of the leader of the Confederate cavalry. The entirely incapacitated rider was gotten down and then up on another horse and taken to the rear. The battle raged on. Fitz Lee arrived. "Go ahead, Fitz, old fellow," Stuart got out, relinquishing command with the words. "I know you will do what is right."

He was lifted into a wagon. Private Huff's bullet through the lower abdomen had pierced the liver. It was about ten in the morning. Richmond was seven miles away over bumpy country lanes, and he was in shock and in pain but able to shout at men he saw running from Custer, "Go back! Go back and do your duty as I have done mine, and our country will be safe! Go back! Go back!

"I had rather die than be whipped!"

Lieutenant Walter Hulihen and a trooper got into the wagon, the latter cradling the wounded man's head on his knees. "Honeybun," he asked, using the lieutenant's nickname, "how do I look in the face?"

"General, you are looking right well. You will be all right." They proferred brandy to dull the pain but he refused it, harking back to an always-kept promise to his mother at age twelve that he would never let alcohol pass his lips. Finally, at their urging, he took some. "Well," he said, "I don't know how this will turn out, but if it is God's will that I shall die, I am ready." By nightfall they were in Richmond and at Dr. Charles Brewer's East Grace Street home behind a low wall of red brick, mid-May's yellow roses blooming there. In the long ago days of the Old Army, the doctor had ministered to the young Lieutenant Stuart shot by a footman Indian along Kansas's Solomon River. Now General Stuart, hit by the footman Huff's bullet, came to lie upstairs upon a bed. In the interim between the two weapon discharges he and the doctor had become brothers-in-law, Brewer marrying a sister of the former Flora Cooke, both daughters of the Union general Jeb had so bedeviled in his great ride around McClellan. For a brief time the physician permitted himself to believe that the general's wound was not a fatal one, and that concept wishfully ran about Richmond so that when Heros von Borcke went to the telegraph office to send word to Flora Stuart that her husband had been wounded, the operator took it upon himself to add the word "slightly."

There could not have been a less accurate description for what was bringing death by internal hemorrhaging and peritonitis. The pain was excruciating, with the constant application of ice hardly quelling it. Stuart lapsed into merciful unconsciousness, later awaking to ask about the faint sound of artillery fire. He was told it was Fitz Lee battling the Yankees, and said, "God grant that he be successful. But I must be prepared for another world," wandered in his mind to call out orders, became sufficiently lucid to say he wanted to see his wife, who was on her way by train, railroad handcar, and horse wagon on a roundabout route avoiding Sheridan's horsemen. President Jefferson Davis came to the sufferer, and taking his hand asked, "General, how do you feel?"

"Easy, but willing to die if God and my country think I have fulfilled my destiny and done my duty." At times he spoke as if to his lost daughter, and then, fully rational, told Borcke, "I shall soon be with little Flora again." During the afternoon, some thirty-six hours after taking his wound, he asked Brewer if he could survive the night—surely his wife would be at his bedside by morning. The doctor replied that death was near, and Stuart said, "I am resigned if it be God's will; but I would like to see my wife. But God's will be done." He asked the Reverend Joshua Peterkin of St. James Episcopal Church if he would not lead in singing a hymn, and when it began, feebly and in a broken voice, he tried to join in. Then he said, "I am going fast now; I am resigned; God's will be done." Four hours later Mrs. Stuart arrived to be told nothing more than that he was upstairs. She came into the room to behold his body. When a few months later their child was born, the widow named the fatherless infant Virginia. Never marrying again, Mrs. Stuart outlived her husband by nearly sixty years, running a school in Staunton, Virginia, before dying at eighty-eight in 1923. To a white South soaked in nostalgia for the Lost Cause and for the days that were no more, Jeb Stuart remained forever young, the perfect image of gallantry and romance. He was in fact a figure out of time, an anachronism who in the sixties, as people spoke of that decade of the nineteenth century, represented what had been appropriate for long before: the Last Cavalier. In the history of men on horseback making war, surely Stuart ranks with Cromwell and with Seydlitz.

There was no military escort for the funeral and interment by little Flora's side at Richmond's Hollywood Cemetery, for all available rebel troops were needed to repel Sheridan. Soon they would form in thirty-five-mile-long lines protecting Petersburg and Richmond from Grant, the trenches and dugouts and gun emplacements presaging the dreary siege warfare of 1914–18's Western Front, where cavalry was of no use. Sharply pointed wooden stakes grounded in rows— the precursors of the Great War's barbed wire—and impassable mud churned up by artillery shells, also a forerunner of what would be seen half a century later in France and Belgium, meant mounted units loitering behind the lines. That was not so bad for the Federals.

Their base at City Point, with great piers stretching out into the James River, their abutments still to be seen today, became the busiest port in the world, with ample feed and hay arriving in lavish amounts. It was quite different for the other side. "General Lee, I'm hungry," barefoot Confederate soldiers called to their commander as he rode by on Traveller, and so were their horses. Sheridan had vowed to so arrange things that the rebel cavalry would no longer trouble the Union forces, and his doings and the South's desperately straitened circumstances made the promise come true.

Perhaps it was well that Jeb died when he did, with at least some sort of chance existing that the Confederacy would yet pull through, and with him believing that. He lived in memory of those who knew him as the focus of the best years of their lives. John Esten Cooke likened him to Cromwell's great opponent, Prince Rupert: both "gallant to the echo, cavalrymen in every drop of their blood, fond of brilliant colors, splendid pageants, the notes of the bugle, the glitter of arms, proud, gay, unswerving, indomitable, disdainful of low things, passionately devoted to glory." There would have been little more of that, nor opportunities for following the jaunty plume to joyous exploit in what was coming; yet Lee said, "If Stuart were only here! I can scarcely think of him without weeping."

A protracted siege meant Southern defeat, Lee knew, and so to relieve and perhaps end the pressure on his long Petersburg-Richmond line, he gave General Jubal Early twenty thousand infantrymen and sent him north to menace Washington, hoping that Grant would counter by thinning the Federal forces to dispatch troops for protection of the Yankee capital. Early was the only Confederate officer who used profane language in the presence of the Army of Northern Virginia commander—"my bad old man," Lee called him. He slipped north sheltered by the mountains lining the Shenandoah Valley and emerged at Silver Spring, on the outskirts of Washington, to create panic in that city. A hastily mustered force of government clerks from their offices and wounded soldiers from the hospitals gathered to hold off Early until Grant could send reinforcements. Had Old Jubilee pushed forward with a little more resolve, sabred down everyone found in Washington's streets, burned the Capitol, freed all the city's Confederate prisoners, looted the Treasury—had he been, in short, Jeb

Stuart–like—who can say what might have resulted? But he was slow and hesitant. The late Mr. Early.

President Lincoln came and stood straight up, high hat and all, in what had become a battle zone to hear bullets sing by and to hear, also, young Oliver Wendell Holmes Jr., son of the celebrated writer, shout, "Get down, you God-damned fool!" Another officer was more politic than the future Supreme Court justice: "Mr. President, you are standing within range of five hundred rebel rifles. Please come down to a safer place. If you do not, it will be my duty to call a file of men and make you."

"And you would be quite right, my boy."

The tenuous Union defense held in no small measure by virtue of the doings of young Holmes's cousin. Raised in rank from captain to colonel, Charlie Lowell commanded the 2nd Massachusetts Cavalry. Like his fellow Harvard valedictorian brother, James, who died in the Peninsula campaign, his brother-in-law Robert Gould Shaw was gone, killed leading his 54th United States Colored Volunteer Infantry. (When Union emissaries under a flag of truce asked leave to retrieve the body, the brutal Confederate response was, "We have thrown him into the ditch under his niggers." The family responded that there could be no more noble interment for a leader than that he lie with his fellow warriors. Charlie wrote his wife, Effie, that who stood for what was right, for Emancipation, owed a sacrifice for its achievement; and that with her brother Rob's passing, a part of the debt had been paid with the very best that could be offered. It was said that Rob's sacrifice sanctified the Union cause. His and Effie's younger sister, seeing him for the last time at a march-past of his troops, felt she beheld an angel doomed to die. There is of that belief something in the Augustus Saint-Gaudens sculpture on Boston's Beacon Hill, which rarely fails to move those who see it—and also in the great film *Glory*.)

There came a moment when Early's forces found only Colonel Lowell's horsemen, far inferior in number to the Confederate infantry, facing them at a particular point. It was ages-old doctrine that when riders dismounted to fight on foot from cover or from behind fortifications, one man out of four was told off to hold the horses' reins. Charlie threw away the concept. Needing every soldier to fire,

he simply had the horses turned loose as he held the line. He possessed enormous command presence, perceivable by foe no less than
friend: when a rebel lowered a rifle at him he said, "Drop that!" and
the man did. Early went away.

There followed in the Shenandoah Valley the most brutal kind
of warfare, with guerilla rebel units, that of the Gray Ghost, John
S. Mosby, among them, joining regulars of the Confederate army
to battle the Federals, with hangings and the shooting of prisoners
seen on both sides. Civilians suffered bitterly, their homes and barns
put to the torch if they were believed to have offered aid or even
encouragement to one or the other of the opponents. No horse was
safe from immediate impressment into the force of whoever found
him, regardless of the owner's allegiances. When word came of an
approaching unit, whether Yank or reb, people rushed their mounts
into the woods, or hid them in mountain fastness or cave or, if there
was no time to get them away, in the parlors of their homes.

Taken off, be they pampered ladies' palfrey, gentlemen's hunter,
child's beloved pony, or utilitarian plow horse, the tears and pleas of
their owners unavailing, the animals were put into instant service
carrying a rider or pulling a wagon. They rarely lasted long, unused
as they were to their new lives of irregular and frequently scant feed,
no stabling (with consequent exposure to all kinds of weather), and
relentless hard work. When they faltered, they were slain for fear that
they might be recovered by the enemy and nursed back into health
for use in his service. Philip Sheridan, who departed the stalled
Petersburg-Richmond siege lines to take command in the Valley, was
adamant on the point. Where he went was marked by horses given
a bullet between the eyes: "Sheridan's Milestones." Generally some
two weeks elapsed between a horse's departure from his former life
and his death by the side of the road.

This, the American civil war, the War Between the States, the
War of Southern Secession, the War—to Southern thinking—of
Northern Aggression, was called the last gentlemen's war; but
there was precious little chivalry in the brutalized Valley fighting.
Of medieval warriorlike courtesy, the likes of the gallant English
at Agincourt telling the French please to have the honor of firing
first, there was but a sole example. "There is that General Custer of

whom the Yanks are so proud," said Thomas "Tex" Rosser, who with the Gallant Pelham had been the last of West Point's class of 1861 to leave for Confederate service. "I will give him the worst beating he ever had." Across the lines, Autie made out the figure of Tex, his dearest friend back in the days when they were cadets on the heights above the Hudson. They had had recent written contact, Custer after learning that Rosser had just fled a Southern sympathizer residence in which he, Custer, took breakfast, leaving a note saying he had called to pay his respects and was sorry Tex was not at home, Rosser returning only to flee again after leaving a note saying that as soon as he learned Autie was at the house he had returned, only to regret departing in such a hurry. General Custer moved his horse forward of his men, ready to battle such cavalry as Rosser was able to muster—few in number but yet capable of putting paid to the life of a lone rider slowly sweeping off his hat to hold it by his knee as he bowed his long-locked blond head in salute. No rebel discharged his weapon. It is said that bullets chase men who run from them; George Custer never did. "With Custer as leader we are all heroes and hankering for a fight," said one of his men.

"If I were to begin giving instances of his daring, brilliancy and skill," wrote *New York Times* reporter E. A. Paul, "I should never stop." But even accepting such viewpoint, while perhaps holding at a discount the reporter's declaration that young as he was, Autie had proved to be a second Napoléon, it must be said that the Union cavalry in the Valley held all the high cards. There came a moment of a fall day, in October 1864, when they massed seven thousand strong on a half-mile front. Their bands played as they moved forward at a walk. That changed into a trot and then, at Wesley Merritt's order, transmitted through dozens of bugles, a gallop.

Twenty-eight thousand hooves pounded as like what men compared to a monstrous thunderbolt, a thunderclap, a bursting storm. It was not a rhythmic gallop, but a hurricanelike rush three lines deep, guidons fluttering, the riders screaming, an unimaginable display of power. The horses avoided hitting one another as their riders fell upon the rebels to swing sabres and fire pistols, then to turn and come back to create more havoc. The Yankee artillery poured down shells over the cavalrymen's heads. In the lead was Colonel Charles

Russell Lowell, yelling at his men to take what rebel guns there were. Custer was always preoccupied with capturing regimental flags from the enemy to display as trophies, but Lowell never was, saying banners hurt nobody, while enemy cannons did. (He was also uninterested in publicity, referring to E. A. Paul of the *New York Times* as Autie's ridiculous little reporter.) His horse fell, fatally wounded. He grabbed another, and screaming, "Forward! Forward!" went on as the Confederate cavalry and infantry dissolved to be sabred down as they ran, hacked, slashed, stabbed. An attempt by the former vice president of the United States turned Confederate general John C. Breckinridge to set up a Wellington-at-Waterloo-like infantry square to hold off the Yankee riders utterly failed—it was simply overrun. Breckinridge had been the South's favorite son in the 1860 presidential election. He ran away with all the others, leaving behind a horse that was presented to Sheridan and given the name of his fled master. "We sent them whirling through Winchester," Sheridan was quoted as declaring, although the words actually came from his aide Major James Forsythe, the general actually having said that the triumph was "beyond my powers to describe." It was not, however, outside Autie Custer's scope of definition; he termed it "the bulliest day since Christ was born." The routed enemy did not halt in Winchester or any other place, but pounded down the Valley turnpike with the triumphant Federals in a pursuit that did not end for more than twenty miles, when Early's men splashed across Cedar Creek to huddle on its far side.

No victory—the "Woodstock Races" in the Northern press, the name deriving from a town along the route of flight—was ever more welcome. The following month would see the presidential election pitting Lincoln against the departed-from-service General George McClellan, who could as his first act of office be expected to call off the war. This would mean, Charlie Lowell had told friends, that the United States would become, like the countries of South America, a conglomeration of impoverished little entities, or another Mexico of perpetual revolution with caudillo's troops riding into the capital to take power from defeated generalissimo fleeing with what there was in the country's treasury. Union withdrawal from the war would bring that—"or worse," Lowell wrote. So it was everyone's duty to do everything possible to elect Lincoln. Lowell's viewpoint was not unique to him. It had come as a most unwelcome shock to the North that a year after being repulsed at Gettysburg the rebels retained the capacity to present Early at the very gates of Washington, there to menace the capital and actually endanger Lincoln's life. Grant had specifically told Sheridan that a setback in the Shenandoah Valley could mean the November election would go to McClellan. There was, after all, a limit to what the people of the North would endure, and with the horrendous losses of what was called the Overland Campaign, including the battles of the Wilderness, Spotsylvania Court House, North Anna, and, worst of all, Cold Harbor, where Union soldiers were fruitlessly slaughtered, all ending in the seemingly dead-end siege of Petersburg-Richmond, that limit was not far from being reached. He must be very careful, Grant had told Little Phil. Sheridan's response was the Woodstock Races, which deposited Early's seemingly whipped men on the southern side of Cedar Creek.

All seemed well in the Valley, Sheridan reasoned. His men lounged about on the northern banks of the creek, savoring what they had accomplished. Perhaps soon they would head for the Petersburg-Richmond line of siege to join in a drive to end the war's long agony. On October 18, 1864, the general entrained for Washington for discussions on the proposed troop transfer. He returned the following day to spend the night at Winchester in the home of a tobacco planter, where he was awakened before sunup by the faint sound of gunfire off in the distance. A minor outpost skirmish, he thought. But there was something more continuous and insistent about the rate of weapons discharge than could be expected from some trifling incident. He got up, took a hurried breakfast, told his staff officers Major George Forsyth and Captain Joseph O'Keefe to come along, and headed down the Valley Pike toward the sound of the firing. It was increasing in volume. Outside of town he picked up several dozen men of the 17th Pennsylvania Cavalry to ride behind him and the two other officers, who were positioned a length or two to his rear. At one point he halted, got down, and, Indian-style, put his ear to the ground. He knew Indian ways. As a junior officer serving on the West Coast he had had a relationship with a young Native American woman.

He arose with, Major Forsyth remembered, a "disconcerted" look on his face, and remounted. His horse was a jet-black Morgan of the Black Hawk line, a gelding of four or five years, more than sixteen hands high with, unusual for the breed, three white stockings. Such have always been taken as a fault, the color indicating weak-boned underpinnings. Additionally, the animal very frequently waved its tail, usually the sign of an unstable disposition. The apparent flaws did not offer correct warning signs in this case, for while the horse was so high-spirited as to make his former owner, a city-bred cavalry officer, wish to have done with him, he had never given Sheridan a bit of trouble and proved indefatigable, with a ground-devouring walk of five miles an hour and a very fast trot. Sheridan had taken him over in the hamlet of Rienzi in Mississippi when serving there prior to coming east to assume the duties of the commander of the Cavalry Corps of the Army of the Potomac. He named his new acquisition for the town.

Now aboard Rienzi going down the Valley Pike he saw what could never have been anticipated. Here before his eyes was the spectacle of his army flying before its enemy, half-dressed soldiers who had thrown their weapons away, abandoned supply wagons whose drivers had cut their traces so as to mount the draught animals for a run to safety, an infantry colonel shouting that all was lost. The previous night had been quiet and lovely with a full moon, and a large shipment of mail had been delivered to the camps of the Yankee soldiers at their ease along the banks of Cedar Creek. Buglers before a tent of one infantry regiment played "Home Sweet Home" and "The Girl I Left Behind Me" to announce that soldiers could come and see what the folks and the girls up north had written. Night fell and in their rows of white tents the soldiers slept.

They awoke at around five in the morning to what one half-asleep officer took for the sound of wood being chopped for breakfast fires. But interspersed was the "Yi! Yi! Yi!" of what was called the rebel yell, and along with rifle shots the banging down of artillery shells. It was very misty along Cedar Creek, and through those mists came lines of Confederates, great waves, Union men recalled, breaking upon their foes and sending them scattering away like leaves in rolling waters. Supposedly beaten, Jubal Early's men had silently come through the creek obedient to whispered orders and with canteens and sabres that might clank and announce their coming left behind. Now they fell upon Yankees literally caught with their pants down—many emerged from tents in their drawers. And wearing such, they ran. ("They jumped up runnin'," a Georgia private succinctly said.) Almost as one man, the Union force stampeded, bayonets and clubbed muskets assailing them on their way along with bullets. They were "one living sea of men and horses all fleeing for life and safety," remembered a Confederate officer. "Men shoeless and hatless went flying like mad, some with and some without their guns. Here and there loose horses galloped at will, some bridleless, others with traces whipping their flanks to a foam." "The stream of fugitives dazed by surprise acted like men who had forfeited their self-respect," wrote a Union officer. "They were chagrined, mortified, demoralized." There was no stopping them. The intense firing coming out of the mist was like a moaning wind sounding from a dense fog. Colonel Rutherford B. Hayes later made no bones about his actions. He managed to get aboard his horse to make a run. A shot took the animal and instantly killed it, Hayes hitting the ground to lie there insensible for a moment. He arose and sprinted off at best he could. A spent rebel bullet hit the future president of the United States in the head and stunned and staggered him, but he kept running with the others, who were casting "scared looks behind them," remembered a fellow Union officer. What was likened to a screaming tidal wave of rebels hurried on the bolting Yankee men and horses; but then, as General Early bitterly remembered, it halted—to loot from a hastily fled-from tent food, shoes, a nice hat or hats (one man grabbed a dozen, jammed them together into a pile a foot high, and stuck it on his head) or a frying pan or left-behind pistol: the temptations for the hungry and ill-equipped rebels were irresistible. As when with more drive and will to do and to be he might have taken Washington, Early proved unable or unwilling to take any action. But when above his pillaging men the mists vanished to reveal a blue sky, he harked back to Napoléon's Austerlitz victory and cried with reference to the little town overlooking Cedar Creek, "Ah, the Sun of Middletown! The Sun of Middletown!" Sated, his men got going again.

In the great wave of bewildered running Yankees, this "torrent," as it was described, some units, not many, tried to fight holding actions as eddies in the great tide. A mounted colonel of a Connecticut heavy artillery unit tried a rally. One of his officers shouted that adjoining units were going. "My God! I cannot!" the colonel cried. An instant later his horse was struck in the head to rise on its hind legs and spin about two or three times before falling dead with its rider, shot in the heel, going over its head. Three hundred yards away the rebels were coming on in a firm line. "Retreat!" the colonel shouted to those men who had not already done so. Within a very short time the northern side of the creek was almost entirely deserted by Union troops, save for very slight infantry displays and one cavalry unit that made sharp little disciplined charges with pistol and sabre, wheeled, and came back to dismount and take cover behind a stone wall before remounting to make another tightly controlled little stab at the enemy: the horse soldiers commanded by Charlie Lowell.

Miles off to the north, up on Rienzi along the Valley Pike, Sheridan was shouting. A lesser general beholding running-away sutlers' wagons, officers' servants, artillery battery forges, men singly and in groups wounded and unwounded, the first driftwood of the coming flood, might have thought to form a line, set up fortifications and dig trenches, and await the enemy with the hope of holding him. That never entered Sheridan's mind. "Come on back, boys!" he roared from the Morgan as he raced south. "Give them hell, God damn them! We'll make coffee out of Cedar Creek tonight!" Colonel Rutherford B. Hayes heard, "Boys, turn back; face the other way. I am going to sleep in that camp tonight or in hell." His legs were so short that his feet in hooded stirrups were in line with Rienzi's breast, but he nevertheless aboard the horse was commanding in presence beyond measure, screaming at men who cheered him, "God damn you, don't cheer me! There's lots of fight in you men yet. God damn you! Come up!" And they did. Pounding along behind him with Captain O'Keefe, Major Forsyth—Sandy to all who knew him—glanced back to see legions of soldiers turn in their tracks to head south behind their general. He did not see a single man do otherwise. There was a continual shout of "Sheridan! Sheridan!" from men come upon facing north who in a moment reversed to head south. "Turn back, men!" Sheridan kept screaming.

The three officers distanced themselves from their cavalry escort and kept going, sometimes abandoning for adjoining fields the macadamized Valley Pike of crushed limestone churned up and rutted by men and horses and wagon trains and artillery pieces during the advance south followed by the panicked rush north and now the of-an-instant-reversed turn south again. It was a golden sunny day of Indian summer, the road like a white dusty line through fenceless fields, with mountains to left and right enclosing the Valley ablaze with autumn foliage, and turning-about Billy Yank shouting, "Here's Phil Sheridan; we're going back" as, remembered one who was there, they threw their caps in the air, "leaping and dancing in wildest glee" even as their commander, on Rienzi, raced by screaming, "We're all right! We'll whip them yet!"

Within an hour Sheridan and his two subordinates were at the head of a great mass of Union soldiers. The three paused briefly now and then, once for Forsyth to obey his general's request that he cut him a switch to use on Rienzi—he had lost a rowel on one of his spurs. "Thanks, Sandy," Sheridan said when handed a tree branch. It was one of the very few times he said anything beyond the repeated shouted exhortations to fleeing men. He tapped the Morgan on the shoulder and got the immediate forward surge of a long swinging gallop effortlessly maintained. Rienzi seemed tireless. The same was not so for Forsyth's horse, and at one halt the major requisitioned another animal. This one was fresh and full of run, and Forsyth chased after his chief "with all the elation that a fresh mount after a weary one inspires in the heart of a cavalryman." They came to a field hospital hastily set up in a farmhouse by the road to see wagons bringing in wounded men from where they'd been hit along Cedar Creek, with stretcher bearers taking them inside, and dead men lying outside. Here was the result of the surprise the Confederates had sprung on Sheridan's army. "It was a gruesome sight to meet the eyes of a commanding officer who, three short days before, had left a triumphant host lying quietly in camp, resting securely on its victories." Sheridan kept going, yelling.

Up in front of him was Charlie Lowell, precariously holding out. He was on a requisitioned horse—as regimental commander he owned the immediate right to take from any soldier the man's mount. The Shenandoah fighting had seen him lose many horses. "How many does that make, Colonel?" an orderly had asked when the one previous to the one now ridden went down. "Thirteen, I believe," Lowell replied. "You see I am unlucky on horses," he had written a friend, adding that in light of the fact that he himself had never received a scratch "it is the best form in which ill luck could come." All through the war he had used for the most part animals privately purchased in preference to those issued by the great Giesboro Point government remount station near Washington. At Antietam he had ridden his chestnut, Berold, named for the horse in Browning's "The Flight of the Duchess" ("Mad with pride, Like fire to manage! / With the red eye slow consuming in fire,/And the thin stiff ear like an abbey-spire!"), but in the wake of the fighting in which Berold was hit with two bullets raising lumps as large as hens' eggs, the horse became what was called "corked"—unmanageable when hearing the sound of guns. So his owner sent him to Mrs. Lowell, who reported him as grazing happily while wearing a red blanket. Colonel Lowell's horses included Ruksh, the Gray, and Dick, upon some or all of whom, plus others, he regularly won informal races with men of his regiment, his natural riding ability merging with his advantageous lack of weight—for his attention to duty, which often caused him to rise two or three times in the course of a night, turned him almost skeletally thin. His favorite horse was Billy, who was on loan from the family of William Forbes, a friend who had been taken prisoner. The animal seemed indestructible. During the Valley fighting before the rebel retreat to Cedar Creek, Lowell wrote his wife, a bullet split Billy's halter ring and caused an ugly throat wound, which fortunately did not trouble his ability to swallow. Another hit through the point of the withers, piercing the blanket edge but striking no bones and "not troubling Billy in the least." He tried to spare Billy as much as he could, he told Mrs. Lowell—Effie. "I generally resolve to ride some other horse, and *do* ride one until the real time comes, and the other horse behaves so that I have to mount Billy in a hurry. I'm glad you mentioned Billy, for I don't want you to imagine for a moment that I was running him into danger inconsiderately." Two days later he had to tell Effie, "Poor Billy was shot in three places and is dead." He wrote the sister of the horse's imprisoned owner, "Poor Billy was mortally wounded in the fight of Monday. I know how badly you all will feel—I feel even worse than I did when Will was taken. The little fellow was shot in three places." Lowell had had his orderly put him down. He would, he told the owner's sister, get her brother a horse when he returned from captivity—"but of course he can never replace Billy."

Earlier that month, September 1864, Lowell had written his friend Henry Lee Higginson, remarking that it was a mistake to concern oneself overly with accumulating wealth: "All I now care about is to be a useful citizen with money enough to buy bread and firewood, and to teach my children how to ride on horseback and look strangers in the face, especially Southern strangers." Of children he had none, although Effie was due in two months; but now he sat a horse to face, if not strangers, for in a sense opposing soldiers know one another very well, then certainly Southerners, who, with looting done, were gathering to come forward against a greatly outnumbered Union force. He could not know that the screaming Little Phil was on the way, with behind him a massed horde growing in number with every step Rienzi took. Colonel James Kidd of Michigan came up to Lowell with a small force of cavalry that, like Lowell's, had stood fast. Off in the distance along a lateral line they heard the sound of firing from segmented Yankee infantry whose likely fate was to be overwhelmed within a few minutes. The two officers were on a field that might have been remembered as where the Union army lost for Abraham Lincoln the upcoming election, which was less than a month away. They had no orders from a higher authority and no guidance of any kind for the structure of military command had completely broken down in the panicked flight away. Kidd was not on the horse he had mounted when the rebels came pouring over Cedar Creek that morning, for it had been hit by a sharpshooter positioned on the roof of a house in nearby Middletown, the bullet burying itself in the horse's shoulder. Kidd had dismounted and gotten another, he remembered, sending the first to the rear, "much to the regret of the old hero"—so Kidd saw matters—"for he was a horse who loved the excitement of battle and relished its dangers."

They ought to move to the aid of the menaced infantry, Charlie Lowell said. He was going to do so. Kidd was hesitant, he wrote later. "I think you ought to go too," Lowell said. "Yes, I will take the responsibility to give you the order." They made for where Brigadier General William Dwight was frantically trying to keep elements of the 19th Corps in place. "They moved past me, that splendid cavalry. Lowell got past me before I could speak but I looked after him a long distance. Exquisitely mounted, the picture of a soldier, erect, confident, defiant, he moved at the head of the finest brigade of cavalry," Dwight wrote later. Across the lines Jubal Early took pause at the sight. Perhaps the Yankees were not so dispirited as they had seemed. Lowell had his men dismount and open fire. It was around ten in the morning, October 19, 1864.

Philip Sheridan arrived. Within a month the artist-writer T. Buchanan Read authored a poem that in an amazingly short time, days really, swept the North: "Sheridan's Ride." Its creation took him one hour, Read said. He could not have put much of that time into map study, for he located the departure point at Winchester twenty miles from the eventual destination along the banks of Cedar Creek, while in fact it was but a little more than half that. It hardly mattered. For decades into the future no child north of the Mason-Dixon Line got through grade school without hearing the poem recited at assemblies, or indeed being ordered by Teacher to memorize those beating-beating-beating stanzas telling of Rienzi's great run. ("The thing they liked best about it was the horse," Sheridan observed—as shown in the following excerpts.)

> And there, through the flush of the morning light,
> A steed as black as the steeds of night
> Was seen to pass, as with eagle flight;
> As if he knew the terrible need,
> He stretched away with his utmost speed.
> Hills rose and fell, but his heart was gay,
>   With Sheridan fifteen miles away.
>
> And the steed, like a barque fed with furnace ire,
> Swept on, with his wild eye full of fire;
> But, lo! he is nearing his heart's desire;

He is snuffing the smoke of the roaring fray,
  With Sheridan only five miles away.

And the wave of retreat checked its course there, because
The sight of the master compelled it to pause.
With foam and with dust the black charger was gray;
By the flash of his eye, and the red nostril's play,
He seemed to the whole great army to say:
"I have brought you Sheridan, all the way
  From Winchester, down to save the day."

Be it said, in letters both bold and bright:
"Here is the steed that saved the day
By carrying Sheridan into the fight,
  From Winchester—twenty miles away!"

The field of battle was completely open for Sheridan to view, almost treeless with but a few clumps and some slight dips in the ground. He took in everything—danger and opportunity both. His first order, wrote Sandy Forsyth, was that his aide go to Charlie Lowell.

"Is Sheridan here?"

"Yes."

"Thank goodness for that!"

"Can you hold on here for forty minutes?"

"Yes."

"Can you make it sixty?"

"It depends; you see what they are doing. I will if I can."

Forsyth rode to Sheridan, who was off Rienzi and standing with a group of officers whose number included Colonel Hayes and another future president, Lieutenant William McKinley. Forsyth told his general that Lowell estimated Federal losses at three to five thousand men killed, wounded, or missing, plus twenty artillery pieces, and that he felt he could hold for forty, possibly sixty minutes. Sheridan took in the information. "I can see him before me as I write," Forsyth recorded years later, "erect, looking intently into my eyes, his left hand resting, clinched savagely, on the top of the hilt of his sabre, the right nervously stroking his chin, his eyes with that strange red gleam in them, and his attenuated features set as if cast in bronze."

The general began ordering troop dispositions for the men who were pouring in from the rear, but thinking of the fragile lines of those in place, Forsyth urged that he show himself to them. They needed to know he was actually present. Sheridan demurred, but then complied with the suggestion. He mounted up and went off screaming, "We are going back to our camps, men, never fear! I'll get a twist on those people yet!" At the sight of him and the sound of his yelling, "We'll raise them out of their boots before the day is over!" Major Hazard Stevens remembered, "hope and confidence returned at a bound." He continued, "No longer did we merely hope that the worst was over, that we could hold our ground until night or make good an orderly retreat to Winchester. Now we all burned to attack the enemy, to drive him back, to retrieve our honor and sleep in our old camps that night, and every man knew that Sheridan would do it." A surgeon of the Medical Corps recalled how the beleaguered troops reacted: "The sight of that little man instantly inspired confidence, and threw them into a perfect frenzy of enthusiasm." The soldiers heard what they could hardly believe: cheering and shouting from men coming up at Little Phil's summons during his long gallop down the Valley Pike, first like a murmur on a far-off shore and then in time louder—a roar.

Jubal Early knew that every minute meant an increase in the opposing force. He put his all into volleys of heavy firing. Union lines wavered and then stiffened as men came running up singly or in groups to join the battle. In a short while a group of Yankees in one of the field's few patches of woodland took note that the volleyed patter of rebel bullets hitting the trees and knocking down twigs and leaves was decreasing in volume. But the Confederates were still in the fight, and one of their rifle rounds slammed into a rock to ricochet off and into the breast of Colonel Charles Russell Lowell. There was no penetration of the skin, but instead from the flattened round the effect of a blunt instrument striking with great force. Charlie could not speak as he was lifted from his horse and laid down behind a mound of dirt to protect him from incoming fire.

His people said he should be removed to the rear, but he managed to whisper that he did not want that. He asked for whiskey, and Wesley Merritt came to offer some from a flask. He indicated that he was cold and they covered him with an overcoat. Meanwhile the ever-growing Federal army strained at the leash with desire to go forward. Sandy Forsyth felt that with officers' continued cries of "Steady, men, *steady, steady!*" having held the line, and with indeed the rebel fire faltering away, it was time to go on the offensive. He had been sent to serve with the 19th Infantry Corps, but left his post to ride to Sheridan, who was found half lying down with his head on his right hand.

"Well, what is it?"

Their force should advance, Forsyth said. "I have come hoping for orders." He was impatient for them; he remembered, "as a cavalryman my first thought, after the repulse of the enemy, was a countercharge." His thinking was in conformity to all cavalry theory throughout history, the canon holding that no victory could be counted as accomplished without the victor's sabre-swinging devastation of the vanquished as they ran.

General Sheridan offered an amused look. "Not yet, not yet; go back and wait." Forsyth would return three times. It was more fearsome to wait than to do, he had always found. Finally, at a little past three, Sheridan was ready to order an advance. He had gone to sleep the previous night believing his army entirely safe in its position along Cedar Creek, awakened that morning to discover it faced catastrophe, and then ridden to its rescue in a manner for which history has no parallel—one man turning around in its tracks a routed mob and leading it to victory. Sheridan used to say that he never went into a fight wishing to emerge alive if the fight was lost. Jeb Stuart felt the same way, shouting even after sustaining his death wound that he'd rather die than be whipped. Now as he ordered the advance at Cedar Creek, Sheridan was in no danger of dying, for his force, he knew, was unstoppable. All along the line his infantrymen made sure their shoes were securely tied, pulled their trousers together at the ankles and drew socks over them, drew their cartridge boxes to their fronts, pulled their forage cap visors down over their eyes. From one end to the other across the field, ramrods rattled and gunlocks snapped as men made sure all was in order.

The cavalrymen saw to their horses, adjusting saddle blankets, tightening girths, looking to their sabres and seven-shot Spencer carbines. Wesley Merritt told Charlie Lowell that despite his injury, he would have the honor of leading the charge, and too weak to sit a horse unaided, he was lifted up and strapped into place. He was unable to raise his voice above a whisper, and when it came time to go forward his aides had to shout out his orders for him.

The Yankees went forward, those who had fled in the morning now the pursuers of an enemy quailing before them, shouting, Sandy Forsyth remembered, "Johnny Reb, we'll learn you to take a joke" and "Say, you Jeff Davis pimps, how do you like our style?" and "Surrender, you sons of bitches!" The forward move of the North's cavalry, remembered Confederate general John B. Gordon, produced "a dull, heavy, swelling sound like the roaring of a distant cyclone. As the sullen roar of the horses' hoofs beating the soft turf of the plain told of the near approach of the cavalry, all effort at an orderly retreat was abandoned."

And the rebels ran. Lying down and to the side, their heads below the level of those of their galloping horses, the Union riders emptied their Spencer carbines, shoved them into saddle buckets, drew pistols or sabres, and wrought carnage, havoc, and destruction upon a foe whose frenzied efforts to get away clogged the thin bridges over Cedar Creek and filled the waters with bloodied bodies. Rebel cannoneers deserted their field pieces and caissons, ambulance drivers deserted the wounded. Philip Sheridan shouted to his men, "Run! Go after them!" and when a soldier who had perhaps rushed in his wake all the way down from Winchester said, "We can't run; we're all tuckered out," Sheridan replied, "If you can't run, then shoot and holler. We've got the goddamndest twist on them you ever saw!" They had. All the Union artillery pieces taken in the morning were recovered, and all of Jubal Early's were taken, along with his ambulances and ammunition wagons, with great masses of his soldiers made prisoner. Autie Custer rode up to cry, "By God, Phil, we've cleaned them out of their guns and got ours back." Sheridan hauled him off his horse for an embrace, which Custer expanded by seizing Little Phil by the waist to whirl him round and round while planting a kiss on his commander's cheek—which he didn't much care for, Sheridan told his boyhood friend Henry Greiner years later.

There are military victories the effect of which can be if not shrugged off by a defeated force then at least taken in stride as a setback of limited import when seen in the larger view. Cedar Creek was not one. It meant denial to the Confederacy of its Shenandoah breadbasket—for in what was called the Burning, the Union troops put to the torch hundreds of barns and food-storage sheds, and slaughtered thousands of steers and hogs. Not a mill save one somehow spared was left functional. (Do what would force a crow flying over the Valley to carry its own provisions, Grant told Sheridan, whose obedience to the order created a twenty-mile swath between the mountains of a pillar of fire by night and smoke by day.) Cedar Creek meant that Lee had no room to maneuver, that he was pinned down on his thin line at Richmond-Petersburg in a siege whose end, he himself had privately said, must mean Confederate defeat. Really it was "criminal folly" for the South to go on with the war now, said Colonel James Kidd, who with Charlie Lowell had taken the Yankee cavalry along the line to hold until Sheridan galloped up.

That night a great bonfire was lit for Union officers to snake-dance about, and Lincoln's election the next month assured victory for the North. For more than a century later it was all attributed to . . . Rienzi. At least in certain quarters. "The Horse Who Elected a President," a recent *The Morgan Horse* magazine article is titled—not the first time those involved with the breed have so anointed the animal. (They also maintain that Sheridan was up on Rienzi for the entire duration of the great triumph as he rushed about shouting that his men had the goddamndest twist on the rebs they ever saw. He rode the black Morgan no less than seventy-five miles that day, they aver. Other sources record that he was for much of the fight that followed his ride down the Valley Pike mounted on Breckinridge, the horse captured from the former United States vice president and then 1860 presidential candidate turned Confederate general. The matter at this late date seems beyond being resolved.)

Years after the great run from Winchester, which along with his other achievements places him among the first soldiers of history,

Grant having defined him as the Civil War's greatest warrior and equal of Napoléon, Little Phil (no longer so little then, for he had grown very chubby, a portent of the heart attack that would kill him at fifty-seven) took note of the agitation attending the unveiling in Washington of an equestrian statue of Winfield Scott who, grown old, had given up the army command when the war came. The sculptor had seen fit to place the large, regal, always imposing General Scott aboard a mount who, in addition to being smallish, was—a mare. "Many poked fun. Scott's family complained bitterly about the humiliation." They forced a change in the "gender of the statue, although it was too late to change the size of the steed."

Sheridan told his wife—for he was married by then, the father of a son and three daughters—"Whatever you do after I'm gone, don't put me on a horse like that!" Says *The Morgan Horse* magazine: "He worried needlessly. In 1908, the soon-to-be-famous sculptor of Mount Rushmore fame, Gutzon Borglum, was commissioned to create a Washington statue of the general on his famous warhorse. It shows Sheridan in the moment he arrived at Cedar Creek, skidding Rienzi to a halt. It can still be seen today at Embassy Row where Massachusetts Avenue meets 23rd Street."

The stuffed Rienzi is in the Smithsonian, to be viewed by visitors the great majority of whom know nothing of T. Buchanan Read's once-famous poem detailing how the charger brought Sheridan down from Winchester to turn the tide, save the day, win the battle glorious, which—like all battles—came at a cost.

The wind accompanying a rainy day blew October's yellow leaves from Harvard's elms as soldiers in crisp blue overcoats bore the coffin from the family home to the new Appleton Chapel. Atop the casket was fresh bunting upon which rested a soiled cap and gauntlets and the worn hilt and battered scabbard of a cavalry sabre. As it came down the aisle the congregation rose, row by row. Longfellow was there, Emerson, Senator Charles Sumner, Oliver Wendell Holmes Sr. and the son named for him, thin and emaciated and invalided out of the service after suffering three wounds.

"Pleyel's Hymn," played for a fallen warrior, sounded; and the minister spoke of what the Bible had said of how the mighty are fallen. "Lament for a True Knight," headlined the Boston papers, and "Noble Death." Colonel Charles Russell Lowell, strapped to his saddle and unable to speak above a whisper for the ricocheting bullet that had taken him in the chest but given the honor nevertheless to lead the cavalry in the charge that broke the rebels at Cedar Creek, had gone forward at a trot and then a gallop only a very short distance before an enemy sharpshooter looked at him down a rifle sight from a rooftop at Middletown, adjoining the field of battle. The ball entered his right shoulder, passed through the second and third vertebrae to sever the spine, and exited behind his left shoulder blade.

He fell from the saddle to be caught by his adjutant, Lieutenant Henry E. Alvord. He was lifted into a blanket utilized as a sling, and for a few moments held up so as to see the Confederates run. Had he not held as he had, he and the horsemen under his command, the rebels would have been going in the opposite direction on the Valley Pike. There they would have met the oncoming Sheridan and perhaps overwhelmed him. History is full of ifs, of course, but had that occurred, the almost certain result would have been electoral defeat for Lincoln less than three weeks later, and immediately following the inauguration of President McClellan, an offer of peace to the South, two nations where there had been one, and likely what Charlie had written that he feared—a conglomeration of little countries sprouting up on what had been the territory of the United States of America. No one would ever have heard of Rienzi, and Philip Sheridan would be remembered as a general demolished by Jubal Early. That all that what-might-have-been "alternative history" never happened is due to Lowell.

He was unable to move his legs or even his chest. The rebels had run off from Middletown, so he was carried there and laid out on a table. In the room was one of his captains, wounded in no less mortal fashion than Charlie, but far less accepting of his fate. "I was always able to count on you; you were the bravest of the brave; now you must be strong, you must meet this as you have other trials," an attending doctor heard him tell the captain. "Be steady, I count on you." Lowell knew what he and the others had accomplished; he saw the picture and the future. They had held the rebels, the campaign was ended, Lincoln would be reelected, he told the captain as the man breathed his last. At least he had no family, Charlie said to the military surgeon Oscar DeWolf. As for himself, he went on, he had never discussed his possible death with Effie; but she would bear it better than one might fear. He smiled. (He was quite wrong. A month after his funeral she gave birth to a girl whom she named with a feminized form of her husband's first name, Carlotta. Dressed in black, she gave herself up to endlessly walking ghostlike about her home, the infant in her arms. In time Effie began a career in what today is called social work, devoting her family's fortune and, more important, her time and talents as a pioneering New York State official to improvements in the treatment of the insane, of conditions for working women, and in hospitals, jails, and orphanages. She never remarried. Many years after her young husband moved forward at Cedar Creek—he was twenty-nine then, she twenty-one—and when she lay on her deathbed, the noted social reformer Jacob Riis, with whom she had worked for decades, came to praise her eminent career. "Yes, yes; I know," she said. "But think of my waiting for my husband forty-one long years, forty-one years." Behind the main branch of the New York Public Library on Fifth Avenue, Bryant Park stretches to Sixth, and there near its outermost extension can be seen what was dedicated a century ago: the Josephine Shaw Lowell Fountain.)

Colonel Lowell lay on his table, twilight coming on. For the following day, October 20, 1864, the War Department had authorized the promotions from brigadier general to major general of Wesley Merritt and George Custer—the highest rank, two stars, held in the Union army by anyone save Grant, who had three. Charlie had been named for promotion to one-star, brigadier general's, rank. His pulse weak and breath shallow, he asked if his officers could not come in. "I am not very presentable but I should like to see you all," he got out, propped up by pillows, small and gaunt. Some took his hand and said a few words, others were silent. Enlisted men followed. He could barely speak, but whispered, "You did well."

He closed his eyes and fell asleep, DeWolf lying on the floor near the table. They had had a nice nap, Charlie said when he awoke. DeWolf went for some food into the next room, to which within a few minutes a sergeant came to say, "The colonel does not breathe."

He had been, Sheridan said, "the perfection of a man and a soldier," who had he lived would have risen to the command of all the cavalry of the Army of the Potomac, and "done better with it than I." A few days later the promotion papers for Custer, Merritt, and Charlie arrived from Washington. Merritt wept when he saw them. Custer also cried when he talked about her brother with Anne Lowell, who was performing nursing duties at Washington's Armory Square military hospital. The Union cavalry had suffered its greatest loss ever, Autie said.

According to army regulations, an officer was not actually promoted without signing the proffered commission, but Secretary of War Stanton waived the requirement, and so although he never actually served in the rank, the dead man was buried as, and is remembered as, Brigadier General Charles Russell Lowell. When he had written his friend Henry Lee Higginson that his main wish was to live to teach his children how to ride horses and look strangers in the face, Charlie had remarked that it was best not to think too much about money, adding that Higginson should never strive to become rich. The advice was not taken, and Higginson became very rich indeed, a banker of sufficient means to put up many years later the money to erect a Harvard Union building (since replaced by a more modern structure) and to donate thirty-one acres of land for the building of an early twentieth-century Harvard athletic complex, upon which stands to this day Soldiers Field, so named for Charlie; his brother, James, who died in McClellan's Peninsula campaign; Effie's brother Rob, who was buried with his soldiers of the 54th Volunteer Colored Infantry; and three other friends of Higginson's youth killed in the war. "Our hearts were touched by fire," Charlie's cousin United States Supreme Court Justice Oliver Wendell Holmes Jr. famously said of those in their circle who fought in the years from 1861 to 1865; and at the dedication ceremonies for the stadium, Higginson spoke of them, and particularly of the one who for all the passed years yet lived on in his heart and memory. "Although dead he is as alive to me as any of you," he said of Charlie.

The horseman memorialized at the dedication, a bust of whom by Daniel Chester French can be seen at Harvard today, was, like another great cavalryman, almost uniquely an anomaly. Alexander,

Attila, Genghis Khan, Seydlitz, Murat, Light-Horse Harry, Custer, Stuart, Sheridan—all had from earliest youth been intended for soldiers. Only Cromwell resembled Lowell in that not a soul knowing either man in the days before he became a soldier would have dreamed of predicting what military brilliance the future would reveal. What a Lowell biographer said of him was equally applicable to Cromwell: that Charlie found intense and deep pleasure in battle, clarity, stimulant, singleness of purpose. That here was his deepest realization of self. Where this came from and how it came is a mystery. It came. The war moved on.

"I know he is a hell of a damned fool, but I want just that sort of a man to command my cavalry on this expedition," William T. Sherman told General James Harrison Wilson. The individual referred to was Hugh Judson Kilpatrick, and the proposed expedition was what is remembered as Sherman's March to the Sea. After his appalling and inexplicable failure of nerve when Richmond with the cache of Union prisoners he had pledged to free lay almost defenseless before him, Kilpatrick was in very ill repute throughout the Army of the Potomac. He sought transfer farther south, and Sherman took him on to join in the fighting around Atlanta. "I wish to inspire cavalry with my conviction that caution and prudence should be but a very small element in their characters," Sherman once said—and Kilpatrick required no inspiring as regards those traits.

Lack of both was amply displayed on August 20, 1864, when Kill Cavalry, always signally noted for not clearly estimating a situation before jumping in with both feet, recklessly led a detachment of men into a Confederate ambush at Lovejoy's Station, Georgia, in an area bordering the plantation owned by Philip Fitzgerald, Margaret Mitchell's great-grandfather and the model for Gerald O'Hara, Scarlett's father, in the author's *Gone With the Wind*. Kilpatrick found himself closed in on three sides by the enemy. Then the rebels snapped the trap shut, closing off the fourth side. The rebel force consisted of some ten thousand infantrymen. The Northern contingent numbered around one thousand horsemen. Another commander might have elected for honorable surrender, but whatever

Hugh Judson Kilpatrick's fanciful version of his utterly failed raid upon Richmond. The *Harper's Weekly* artist was not the only person taken in by a cavalry officer of great talent mixed with a great lack of scruples and adherence to facts.

else he was, Kilpatrick was capable at times of proving himself a fighter. "Our only salvation is to cut our way out," he told two colonels, saying they would lead.

"General," replied Colonel Robert Minty, "I will form in any way you direct, but if it was up to me I would never charge in line over this ground." (It was cut up with deep gullies and two fences.) "When we strike the enemy, if we ever do so, it will be a thin, wavering blow that will amount to nothing."

"How, then, would you charge?"

"In column, sir. Our momentum would be like that of a railroad train. Where we strike, something has to break."

"Form in any way you please." The troops got ready, lightening the loads of their horses by throwing on the ground extra blankets, haversacks, cooking utensils, carbines, and ammunition. They retained only their sabres. There was an occasional jarring blast from rebel shells fused to detonate overhead, sending metal raining down. A Confederate rifle bullet dropped a soldier. Georgia's August heat was sweltering, and the air was hazy with gunfire smoke. Kilpatrick asked of a captain if he felt they could smash through; the captain replied in the affirmative. "Good! Drive the damn rebels to hell! Colonel Minty, are you ready?"

"All ready, sir."

"Then charge when you please."

Minty spurred his sorrel to the head of the line. "Attention! Draw sabres!" There was a sharp metallic rasp of cold steel coming from scabbards. Minty's bugler rang "Forward," the notes repeated by other instruments, and the colonel shouted, "Forward—trot, regulate by the center column! March!" Guidons unfurled as the riders got going. "Gallop!" Minty roared. "March! Charge!" Bugles sounded, and in three compact columns of fours, the one thousand horsemen shot on, boot to boot and stirrup to stirrup, Kilpatrick among them yelling at the top of his lungs and flailing his sabre as he put his spotted horse over one of the fences in the line of advance.

In front of them a rebel howitzer threw up canister shells that came down in a hail of round balls, but the soldiers dug in their spurs and thundered on. Kilpatrick's color bearer fell from his mount, the general's flag going with him. An Ohio private tumbled dead from his saddle, and when the boy's father dismounted to lean over the body, he too was shot dead. But the Yankee battering ram achieved what it was designed to do, slamming into and then piercing the Confederate infantry to roar past Confederate guns, whose men swiftly swung them around to fire at backs racing away. Half an hour later Lieutenant Sidney Champion of the 28th Mississippi Cavalry came too late with rebel reinforcements to look upon ground covered with guns, pistols, sacks of horse feed, cooking utensils, cups, buckets, and bullets the Yankees had discarded so as to make their run for safety as unimpeded as possible. "Horses, some trailing skewed saddles behind them, stood in suffering silence or struggled silently, crazed with pain and fear. Others sprawled glassy-eyed and still, the flies already swarming over torn bodies and protruding entrails. Nearby lay their riders, some in ashen-faced agony, others to rise no more."

It was all classic Kilpatrick, Kill Cavalry to a T, the getting into trouble by virtue of his own folly, then the thrilling and successful escape to boast of as a great triumph over foes enormously outnumbering him. ("His memory and his imagination were often in conflict," remarked General O. O. Howard. He might have added that it was others who paid the price so that Kilpatrick might tell and retell a glorious and glamorous story.) Nevertheless, it was Kilpatrick whom Sherman chose to lead the horsemen of what the South for a hundred years and more remembered as a moving orgy of destruction whose precedent and example could only be found in the Mongol horde, Attila the Hun, and the Visigoths and Vandals and other barbarian ravishers whose like, it was said, had thankfully vanished into the mists long ago but who now arose in what was formerly considered the enlightened nineteenth century as the demon William T. Sherman and his accompanying army of fiends.

"War is hell," the general is often quoted as saying, which he never actually did, though he declaimed something along the same lines; and to make the point, he decided to take his army, which had conquered Atlanta and gone on to destroy the enemy forces arrayed against him, and with it cut a sixty-mile-wide swath through the heart of Dixie, from Atlanta to the sea, so that no doubt could be left in Southern minds that to continue the war was a hopeless endeavor. He departed from Atlanta in November 1864, one month after the Battle of Cedar Creek, his situation precisely parallel to that of Sheridan's in the Shenandoah Valley when ordered by Grant to so devastate the region that a crow flying over would have to carry its own provisions—the Burning. Cavalrymen under George Custer and Wesley Merritt had executed the order in a limited geographical sphere, the Valley being not more than twenty miles in length and only a few across, with neither officer at all relishing the business. The premier horse soldier of the 60-mile-wide and 270-mile-long March to the Sea was of a different stripe. Kilpatrick's main assignment was to protect the sixty-two thousand infantry and artillerymen of Sherman's army, and the accompanying twenty-five hundred wagons pulled by fifteen thousand mules from any flank attacks the very weak Confederate opposition could muster up, and he performed it in exemplary fashion: not once were any of the moving Federal columns struck from the side. Neither did they meet any unexpected and unpleasant surprises in their front, their cavalry always keeping them apprised of what lay ahead.

But Kilpatrick added what was never before or after seen in America's wars. Certainly all conflicts know looting and pointless destruction, but in the case of American soldiers through history such have uniformly been on an individual basis, or coming from small groups temporarily banded together. Kilpatrick unleashed fifty-five hundred horsemen and gave them leave to run amok—which they did. Sherman intended for the South to be taught a harsh lesson (his march, he said, would be "one of the most horrible things in the history of the world"), but he issued orders that occupied dwellings be left intact and that his soldiers treat women with courtesy, that they avoid "abusive or threatening language." The concepts were in Kilpatrick's eyes laughable. Here was someone who had, as earlier mentioned, spent three months in prison for appropriating government horses, mules, and tobacco for his own gain, and who was in nineteenth-century terms known as a "sexual adventurer." Now the twenty-six-year-old was given a free hand to serve his country, increase his fame—and have a great time.

To a large extent Sherman turned a blind eye to what was going on. The provisioning of his foot-slogging army was the responsibility of groups of soldiers familiarly termed "bummers" who ranged about collecting cattle and hogs for slaughter, corn, potatoes, and certainly wines and liquor, in the age-old fashion of an invading army that lives off the land of its foe. The bummers had an assigned task to perform. They had quotas to fill, or at least expectations to meet, and can be seen as simply fulfilling quartermaster duties. In later years Sherman always was at pains to say that they performed those duties in an entirely professional and dispassionate fashion. But then there was his cavalry. It flitted about where it would, bivouacked where it might, adhered to no set schedule, and was accountable only to its chief. Because of its value under Kilpatrick's leadership, noted Major General Jacob D. Cox, who was there, Sherman became "willing to be ignorant of escapades which he could hardly condone." All bodies of troops take their tone from their leader. "A bad eminence in this respect was generally accorded to Kilpatrick," General Cox recorded, "whose notorious immoralities and rapacity set so demoralizing an example to his troops that the best disciplinarians among his subordinates could only mitigate its influence."

The best disciplinarians were outnumbered by officers taking their cue from the cavalry chieftain and "willing to wink at irregularities or to share the loot."

A horsed patrol bent on looting would appear at a plantation whose men were off with Lee in Virginia, or dead in the fighting around Atlanta. Armed with pistol and carbine, besworded, infinitely menacing, the riders would dismount. They were on what they called a "raid." Sometimes a slave or two was taken aside for inquiries as to where family treasures were. (General Kilpatrick was especially good at getting answers from frightened and intimidated blacks.) Meanwhile the ladies of the house were spoken with as the cavalrymen studied their eyes. Inevitably the women would glance at particular spots on their property. Bayonets and swords probed earth, featherbed mattress, corncrib, hayloft, and flower bed, pried open wooden chests, and ripped up carpets, and soon, wrote Lieutenant Thomas Myer to his wife, one had "fine gold watches, silver pitchers, cups, spoons and forks," adding that he had "about a quart of rings, earrings, breast pins" for her and their daughters.

Sometimes there was no need for investigatory subtleties: newly overturned earth could possibly indicate a recent burial, but far more likely where valuables had hastily been interred when word came that the Yankees were coming. And certain items were difficult to conceal. The usual army fare for horse soldiers on the march was a slab of bacon and some hardtack, plain or fried in bacon grease on a sheet-iron pan and eaten off tin plates. Now the men feasted on chicken, turkey, goose, and beef. A cow might be killed for a single steak, with the rest of the body left to the buzzards, which, it was said, turned the sky black with their coming when livestock was indiscriminately slaughtered (along with horses deemed of no use to the Union cause and dispatched with an ax striking between the ears). The men dined off fine plate, sometimes to the accompaniment of a command piano performance by the mistress of the house terrified that refusal would mean it would be put to the torch, and with blacks told to dance along. Even so she might well see her home go up in flames for her attitude, or for troops' carelessness, or for no reason at all. ("In after years," Kilpatrick told a dinner of his officers, "when travelers passing through shall see chimney stacks without houses, and the country desolate and shall ask, 'Who did this?' some Yankee will answer, 'Kilpatrick's cavalry.'")

It was a very common sight to see cavalrymen riding along in fur top hats or ancient three-corner ones over the wigs of a previous generation while wearing the dress coats seen at stylish balls of a century earlier. One man convulsed his fellows by lifting a dress mannequin up into his saddle to make what was described as "ardent love" to it as he rode along. That mannequin had been used, as had a thousand others, to create the long dresses of the period, which now were the property of the looting men, who offered them to the area's young black girls—"the finest silks belonging to the planters' ladies carried off to adorn Negro wenches around the camps," recorded the *New York Herald*, noting that the nocturnal visits of the girls to the troop tents soon became a part of every overnight camp. "A few months after the stalwart warriors had marched on to other adventures, many of those they had encountered were awaiting their progeny along the main routes of Sherman's army."

In this regard—to reference General Cox's allusion to "irregularities"—Kilpatrick was in the forefront, his tent rarely lacking an after-hours visitor. There came a moment when he was literally caught with his pants down. A rebel patrol swarmed down on a cavalry encampment, with a Confederate rider beholding a man rushing out of a tent wearing some sort of garment covering his upper body, a nightcap, and very little else. The rider demanded to know where General Kilpatrick was, and was told, "There he goes on that black horse." A pursuit was immediately launched as simultaneously the largely naked man grabbed another mount and rushed off on its bare back in an opposite direction, leaving behind his uniform, two ivory-handled revolvers, a gold-mounted sword, and that night's female companion. The incident became known as Kilpatrick's Shirt-Tail Skedaddle. Sometimes the cavalry leader took along on raids a concubine or, in a particular case, several. He arrived at one manse with three in tow to make the elegant ladies of the house prepare him a meal enjoyed as with his companions, said the *Macon Telegraph*, he carried on "the most familiar and indecent conversation." The women were "vulgar, rude, and indecent," said a doctor whose home Kilpatrick took over, "but fitting companions for a man of General Kilpatrick's character."

Such opposition as the South could muster against what the Federals called the Army of Invasion was led by the cavalry brigadier general Joseph Wheeler. (There was effectively no rebel infantry, still less artillery.) He was known as Fighting Joe, a designation earned in different fashion than the same appellation applied to the Union's Joseph Hooker, who got the title when a newspaper typesetter at work on a headline describing a battle, "Fighting: Joe Hooker," inadvertently dropped the colon. Wheeler and Kilpatrick had been West Point classmates of the class of 1861. After graduation the former had been posted to the West. As part of an escort for a wagon train leaving Missouri for the New Mexico Territory, he had stayed with one when it dropped out so that a surgeon could assist a woman giving birth. The wagon with the woman and the two men was alone in an emptied prairie when Indians appeared. Lieutenant Wheeler fired a musket and then charged with a pistol. The Indians ran, and the surgeon's telling of the story created the title. At the academy, Fighting Joe had been called "Point" for his lack of physical substance; he was five foot five and weighed no more than 120 pounds "with his spurs on." He was the same age as Kilpatrick, so youthful looking that his men—behind his back to be sure, for he was a humorless West Point martinet—called him "the War Child" and "That Boy." His assignment to oppose the March to the Sea was thankless and his situation dire; his outnumbered cavalrymen rode worn-out jades and carried weapons far inferior to the seven-shot Spencer carbines of their Yankee foes.

The Army of Invasion soldiers went southeast, their destination Savannah, and arrived where the legislature had been holding its sessions after fleeing the state capital of Atlanta when Sherman occupied that city. Now the legislature had departed Milledgeville in turn, and the troops settled into the chamber where they had met, appointed themselves the new lawmakers to repeal the order of secession, pass resolutions denouncing the leaders of the Confederacy, and hold a debate as to the virtues and deficiencies of various types of whiskey. A state arsenal had proved to contain a large supply of long knives, which were waved in the air as denunciation and praise of various alcoholic beverages were offered. Kilpatrick went to the podium.

"Though I am a very modest man that never blows his own horn," he declaimed, "unlike some other gentlemen I might name, I must honestly tell you that I am the Old Harry on raids. My men, too, have strongly imbibed the spirit and are always full of it." His remarks if transcribed in the records of an actual legislative session would certainly have indicated at this point [laughter] and [applause]. "I must confess that my fellows are very inquisitive. Having come so far to visit the good people of Georgia, who are famed for their hospitality, they live in free and easy style among them; and if, perchance, they discover a deserted cellar, believing it was kindly left to their use by the considerate owner, they take charge of it. It sometimes happens, too, that they look after the place and other little matters. Coming to my own particular raid, it was one of the handsomest and most brilliant assaults of the war. I—"

We cannot know exactly to what he referred, for he was interrupted by a soldier raising a point of order: "I believe it is always the custom to treat the speaker." Agreement was voiced by all, and Kilpatrick said, "Yes, I beg to inform this honorable body that I am going to treat the speaker," and raised a bottle to his lips. There followed a generalized shout from many throats of "Order! Order!" mixed with group singing of "We Won't Get Home Until Morning" and other songs. The concert concluded when someone stuck his head in the door and bellowed, "The Yankees are coming!" at which in imagined imitation of the real Georgia legislators, the men charged out of the building. In the morning Kilpatrick looked at a great collection of horses taken from around the Milledgeville area, and ordered a proportion to be retained and the rest given ax blows between the ears. If he couldn't use them, he remarked, neither would Wheeler. What was described as "a mountain" of dead animals was the result.

The army came to Savannah and for the first time since leaving Atlanta established contact with Washington. Standing off the coast as part of the blockading force strangling the Confederacy was the USS *Philadelphia*, Rear Admiral John A. Dahlgren commanding. (It was purest coincidence that he was the father of "Ulric the Hun," the officer assigned by Kilpatrick to lead half of the two-pronged raid upon Richmond that had so signally failed.) The admiral got word to President Lincoln that it was General Sherman's pleasure to offer the city as a present for New Year's Day 1865, and the army stayed in Savannah for a time to rest and refit and for Secretary of War Edwin M. Stanton to sail down to attend a grand review honoring Kilpatrick upon his promotion to brevet major general. "We will do more, dare more than ever," he proclaimed to his troops, "to have General Sherman say, 'I am satisfied with my cavalry.'"

Just north of Savannah, over the river of the same name, lay South Carolina. It held a particular place in the North's perception. It had been the first state to secede from the union, and in its harbor at Charleston the first shots of the war had been fired, at Fort Sumter. Here was the birthplace of the war and the heart of the Confederacy. "We will let her know," one soldier grimly swore, "that it isn't so sweet to secede."

"The march through Georgia," a historian says, "had been somewhat restrained, the destruction (excepting Kilpatrick's activities) directed only against properties of military importance to the enemy. South Carolina, however, would be treated differently." The way of the infantry was strewn with things stolen and then tossed away, decayed vegetables, shot mules, cattle, and horses. Pianos were demolished and molasses poured into what was left of their works; old family bibles were taken for use as saddles; sabres were thrust through ancestors' portraits; carpets were cut up for service as tent rugs; crockery was smashed; bureaus, trunks, wardrobes, and furniture were overturned and broken into bits; watches and jewelry were demanded at pistol point. The uproar and stamping and cursing was remembered by victims as a horrible nightmare.

The cavalry continued as it had before, with an added intensity that, says one chronicler, left foot soldiers "appalled by the degeneracy" of the horsemen. Even before reaching South Carolina, Kilpatrick bivouacked in an old Congregationalist church near Savannah whose walled graveyard he used as a corral for appropriated livestock awaiting slaughter, with the organ made a butcher's block, and dressed carcasses hung from the balcony, and wooden grave markers used for the cooking fires. In South Carolina he lit far greater flames. It was said that upon crossing the state line he ordered that each cavalryman's saddlebag be filled with matches, an overdone allegation as rhetorical as the charge made by one historian that he was "too busy bedding women of ill repute to attempt any control of his outrageous troopers." In actuality he was entirely prominent in the incendiary activities, leading the chaplain of an Indiana regiment to say that "the whole world seemed on fire."

"I changed its name to Burnwell," Kilpatrick joked after leaving Barnwell, like Columbia, practically a mass of smoldering cinders. (Before putting the town to the torch he stabled his horses in the Church of the Holy Apostles, where the Baptistry was used as a watering trough, and then held a ball at one spared manse, with as guests local girls intimidated into regarding their invitations as orders and who "like sad ghosts went through the whirling mazes of the dance while their dwellings were in flames." It was the "bitterest satire" he ever witnessed, said the Union officer Smith Atkins.) Regarding his relations with women, whether of ill repute or not, at least one was a splendid specimen. As his ranged-out columns approached the North Carolina border, he took up with a certain Marie Boozer, described as "the most beautiful piece of flesh and blood" one observer had ever beheld. The Bright's disease that would eventually kill him at forty-five was already manifesting itself in the form of severe back pain, and so he traveled in an appropriated carriage with his head in her lap, she swathed in white blankets. The onset of the illness had perhaps commenced even earlier, for one who knew him said of his bent-forward seat on a horse—perhaps due to the severe kidney pain associated with Bright's disease—that he was "a very ungraceful rider, looking more like a monkey than a man on horseback." But then, that observer was hardly a Kill Cavalry admirer: "Kilpatrick is the most vain, conceited, egotistical little popinjay I ever saw."

In front of him, Joe Wheeler had no choice but to drift back before the greatly superior opposing forces, his only recourse to send bitter letters across the lines: "The history of no war, however barbarous, can tell of atrocities equal to those daily and hourly committed by your command." The opinions of his onetime West Point classmate disturbed Major General Kilpatrick no more than the tears of the mayor of North Carolina's capital when the Yankee cavalry entered Raleigh. The mayor had an attendant with him who carried a stick to which was attached a white handkerchief representing surrender. It was raining. The Stars and Stripes were raised over the state capitol.

Kilpatrick would leave the army to seek the governorship of New Jersey as furtherance of his long-held plan for the presidency, but failing to receive the Republican nomination he instead got himself named ambassador to Chile. There he married the daughter of an eminent family. Their descendants are interesting. Before her husband's death, within the year of their wedding, Mrs. Kilpatrick gave birth to a daughter, Laura. The baby grew up, married, and had twin girls. One, Thelma, married Lord Marmaduke Furness, and mixed in the highest social circles of London between the two world wars. For several years Kill Cavalry's granddaughter was the acknowledged mistress of Edward, Prince of Wales, heir to England's throne. Lady Furness had a friend from Baltimore who was married to an Englishman. When she had to travel to America for a brief time, she asked the friend to entertain His Royal Highness during her absence. Upon her return she found herself unable to get through to the prince on telephone calls to his varied residences. Wallis Warfield Simpson had entertained Edward very well, and after becoming king upon the death of his father, he gave up the throne in order to marry her. They lived out their lives as the Duke and Duchess of Windsor.

The second twin, Gloria, married Reginald Claypoole Vanderbilt, great-grandson of Commodore Vanderbilt, whose activities created the basis of one of America's greatest fortunes. The bridegroom lived long enough to give his wife a girl named for her, and then drank himself to death. The money left to his daughter and the three-way battles regarding it and the relationships between Kilpatrick's daughter Laura, Laura's daughter Gloria, and Gertrude Vanderbilt Whitney, aunt of the inevitably titled Little Gloria, became for years a staple of innumerable newspaper stories accompanying endless photos of a solemn-faced child stepping from a limousine to enter yet another courthouse. The Poor Little Rich Girl, Little Gloria, Kilpatrick's great-granddaughter, survived to see the day when her name was emblazoned upon untold pairs of designer blue jeans and her son was nationally known as television's Anderson Cooper.

Palace romance, tabloid headlines, and TV newscasts were long for the future when Ambassador Kilpatrick died in Chile. He was buried in the cemetery on the grounds of his alma mater high above the Hudson. Then as now, it was the custom for every deceased West Pointer to be eulogized in print for a graduate publication, the task to be performed by someone who had been at the academy with the late departed. To write on Kilpatrick was not an easy assignment. It fell upon Eugene B. Beaumont, who, pointing out that one should never speak ill of the dead, told of his classmate's financial generosity to friends fallen upon hard times, including those who served in Confederate gray, his vivacity and zeal, and his undoubted contributions to the eventual triumph of the Union cause.

But, Beaumont wrote, other aspects of the man's life needed mention. Kilpatrick, he wrote, accorded his troops such "license" during the March to the Sea as permitted acts that others "shrank from with disgust as unbecoming American officers." Attila's name was for comparison purposes mentioned in the obituary, and "the deadly Apache," and reference made to "wanton outrage, the sea of flame, the destruction of the home treasures of the defenseless." Yes, all true. Yet who remembers Kill Cavalry today? It is Sherman who is remembered as ruthless wrecker, despoiler of the South, not his cavalry leader who did far worse.

There was another horse soldier of those days whose name is known to everyone. Less recognized is how very brilliantly George A. Custer performed in the final moments of the drama that was the Civil War. When at long last Robert E. Lee went to sit in the parlor of a home in Appomattox Court House, Virginia, to surrender to Ulysses S. Grant the Army of Northern Virginia, there followed a frantic scrum for souvenirs by members of Grant's force after the two generals left the house. Sheridan had from the beginning of the war carried in his pocket two ten-dollar gold pieces likely to be of value should he ever be captured by the enemy. He parted with both to purchase the table Grant used when drafting the capitulation terms and handed it to Custer to present to Libbie along with a note the contents of which make clear Little Phil's estimation of Autie as Autie was in those days: "Permit me to say, Madam, that there is scarcely an individual in our service who has contributed more to bring about this desirable result than your gallant husband." Custer jumped on his horse, balanced the table on his head, and raced away. He and the other cavalrymen of what had become the Union's premier fighting force had come down from Cedar Creek to join in breaking Lee's long Petersburg-Richmond line, whose piercing, they and everyone else knew, must end the war. Their thrusting moment had come on April 1, 1865. "I tell you," Sheridan cried the preceding day, "I'm ready to strike out tomorrow and go to smashing things!" He shot forward with ten thousand cavalrymen upon a little crossroads dot on the map called Five Forks. He pushed the rebels back upon the Southside Railroad, Lee's last link for supplies from what was left of the Confederacy. Fitz Lee was in command of what remained of Stuart's cavalry there, but he and the infantry leader George Pickett of the doomed charge at Gettysburg were not present. The first shad of the season had been plucked from the Virginia rivers, and they were at a shadbake.

In action like Mars himself, so it was said, Sheridan plunged Rienzi among his riders as he waved a flag, shook his fist, entreated, encouraged, threatened. "I want you men to understand we have a record to make, before that sun goes down, that will make hell tremble!" he roared, standing up in his stirrups. "You understand?" he demanded of Custer. "I want you to *give* it to them!"

"Yes, yes," Autie cried. "I'll give it to them!" An officer rode up saying he had captured three rebel artillery pieces, and Sheridan shouted, "I don't care a damn for their guns, or you either! Go back to your business, where you belong! What I want is that Southside Road!" The position that was the buttress of the left wing of Lee's army was being overrun. "Hold Five Forks at all hazards," he had telegraphed, but the rebel formations began to disintegrate. Sheridan spurred Rienzi up to a breastwork, cleared it with a bound, and landed in the midst of a huddle of Confederates. "Go right over there," he cried, pointing to his lines. "Get right along, now. Oh, drop your guns; you'll never need them any more." Yankee cavalrymen right and left were going over the works with a hurrah, the blue tide sweeping on to put the railroad in Union hands; and Lee had no choice but to pull his men from the lines they had held for nine months and run. Of necessity he could not take a route south, for Sheridan was there and coming on. So the rebel army poured through Richmond and headed west. Behind them came the Federals, including black men wearing the uniform of the United States Cavalry, who bared their sabres and sang as they rode up Broad Street's hill.

To become entangled with the rear elements of his retreating foe was the last thing Grant wanted, and so as the rebels ran for it, a parallel Union force traveled at their side. Sometimes the two were so close that the evening's campfires of the one were discernible through the woods to the other. Ahead of both raced the Union cavalry, deviating from its course now and then to strike at the flanks of Lee's columns. Eight days after the cavalry took the Southside Road, the exhausted and battered rebels made camp in Appomattox Court House. In the morning they hoped to press on, but when they looked to the west they saw rows of horsemen in blue. "I wish you were here," Sheridan had written Grant days earlier from Amelia Court House, the message wrapped in chewing tobacco tinfoil and carried by a scout masquerading as a rebel soldier. Grant had been in the saddle all day, but he had a fresh mount saddled and rode more than fifteen miles to be with his commander of horse. No cavalry was available for an escort, all of that arm being up front with Sheridan, so the lieutenant general gathered a dozen officers as a guard. The group struck Sheridan's pickets late at night and was directed to a tobacco patch log cabin in whose loft Little Phil was sleeping. He came down to offer a meal of beef, cold chicken, and coffee.

"Lee is in a bad way," Grant said. "It will be difficult for him to get away."

"Damn him," Sheridan replied. "He *can't* get away. We'll have his whole army; we'll have every —— of them." So it proved to be, and blocking the farthest point of the fleeing rebel army there appeared on the morning of April 9, 1865, a screen of Union cavalry commanded by Wesley Merritt. The Confederates made as to brush it aside, but then like a curtain in a theater, it parted to reveal what was behind: Yankee infantrymen hurrying up to bolster the horse-men, their number increasing every minute. It was the end for Lee. The rush to get in front of him, with the cavalry going on through the hours of darkness, the infantry to follow, had achieved what had been sought for four years. "The night of despair fell with the 8th of April," Merritt wrote, "darkly and terribly on the Army of Northern Virginia." (Sheridan had not been completely right when he told Grant they'd bag "every —— of them," for a small force of Confederate riders under Tex Rosser broke through the Yankee lines and got away. That they had done so was his premier feat of the war, Rosser said in later years, proclaiming, "The cavalry never surrenders.") At Washington's grand two-day review of the armies of Grant's of the east and Sherman's of the west, the two generals sat with President Andrew Johnson on a Pennsylvania Avenue review-ing stand, flags everywhere and the city draped with bunting. Just before the march-past began, a lone horseman shot past the wait-ing troops, the hundreds of schoolgirls all in white, the hundreds of thousands of citizens of the victorious North. Blond curls streamed from under the rider's wide-brimmed cavalier hat, and his long red tie floated behind as he rushed along to scatter Merritt's staff officers as they got out of the way. He had lost control of his charger, the former racehorse Don Juan, Autie explained—something that never happened to him on any mount before or later. Merritt, and others, were intensely annoyed, but what really did it matter? The last war in which cavalry played a dominant role was over.

13

"For this are we soldiers"

A few years after the Civil War a young woman left America to board with the family of a German general in Hanover. She found enchanting the atmosphere in which she now moved, the elegance and glitter of uniforms at the balls she attended. At the theater the parquet was filled with officers, who as soon as the curtain fell between acts rose, turned around, and raised their opera glasses to look upward at the ladies seated in the boxes of the tiers. Then they came to visit, their attire lending tone to the theater visit as it did to all other affairs. "I used to say, 'Oh, Frau General, how fascinating it all is!' 'Hush, Martha,' she would say; 'life in the army is not always so brilliant as it looks. In fact we often call it, over here, *glänzendes Elend*' "—glittering misery.

The visitor returned home to marry a U.S. Army officer, who was assigned in 1874 to Fort Russell, Wyoming Territory. She often remembered there what her hostess had said. "Those bitter words," Martha Summerhayes wrote, "made a great impression on my mind, and in after years, on the American frontier, I seemed to hear them over and over again."

One understands. There was glitter in the postwar United States Army shrunken to fewer than thirty thousand men. On each of the two hundred posts sprinkled across the country, mainly in the West, the most rigid military formality was sedulously adhered to,

Indians, as portrayed in the *Police Gazette*.

with proscribed procedure and much "circumstance" to attend the leaving of cards and the paying of calls and the precise details of uniform—leather sword knot decreed by army regulations for this occasion, gold for that—the order of entrance to dinner, the form of address of subordinate to superior. Cavalry regiments comprised a third of the total army strength, and dominated in the Military Division of the Missouri, with four departments each larger than New England and totaling one million square miles reaching from Chicago to Utah and from Canada to Mexico. Infantry in that measureless region was of little use save for guarding fixed posts, and artillery less, for Indians rarely attacked fortified positions and never massed in such fashion that a bursting shell could do damage—even assuming you could get guns up for a barrage, which in a vast trackless domain you likely could not. Indians fought on horseback, with no saddle save a blanket strapped on, no stirrups, no bit but instead a rope around a pony's muzzle. To combat them, to protect the railroad builders across the prairie and desert, and the ranchers, and miners, and woodsmen, and the settlers coming into a tiny town that one day would be a major American metropolis—three dusty or alternately depthless muddy wood-sidewalk streets, one for houses of prostitution; one for banks, saloons and shops; one for residences— only cavalry would serve. Its officers were uniformly Civil War veterans of the Northern side, save for the raw shavetails coming west fresh from the Point and feeling more than a little abashed at being put in the position of giving orders to enlisted men who in the war, sometimes, had commanded Southern regiments.

The army's veteran officers had held high brevet rank, been acting brigadier or major general before in many cases reaching their twenty-fifth birthdays, had commanded tens and indeed hundreds of thousands of men seen as the country's saviors. Now they who had put up stars on their shoulders, so the expression had it, served in drastically lowered rank, but with form of former address carefully adhered to: the man superintending a company of seventy riders— the term "troop" for cavalry did not come into use until 1881—was called the general in memory of what he had once been, back in the great days. For many their lives out on the great lonely frontier were and would always be a paltry echo of the past, with the Indians they dealt with a degradation to war against, bestial savages unworthy of the military attention of an officer and a gentleman. They grew old in their modest rank, the one-time high officer turning gray, reaching fifty and even sixty as he remained in a tiny army still a captain. So they constructed a perception of themselves as heirs to the knights of the Middle Ages and earlier who stood against chaos and fought off the barbarian hordes assaulting civilization and then as Crusaders went up against those at the outer fringes of Christendom.

They and their wives held theatrical performances and costume parties with people dressed as Mother Goose, or the Jack of Spades, or a babe in swaddling clothes, or the Evil Eye. They danced the polka, the mazurka, the schottische, the quadrille, and the cotillion to the music of the band that every post had, the players uniformly German or Italian enlisted men who for the occasion put away the brasses and drums used for formal guard mount and flag-raising in favor of stringed instruments. Officers were in dress uniform of gold lace and white gloves, double-breasted frock coat, standing white collar, patent leather shoes, and heavy gold-ornamented headgear, and their ladies in elaborate ball gowns created in sewing circles from patterns and material ordered from back east. There were other entertainments. Libbie Custer remembered an elaborately arranged race in Fort Leavenworth, Kansas, in June 1868 for which each officer of her husband the lieutenant colonel's 7th Cavalry selected the most recalcitrant animal he could find in the quartermaster's corral of mules for pulling supply wagons to outlying posts.

The object of the race, Libbie recorded, was to have your mule come in last. He would be ridden by one of the other contestants, you doing your best to get someone else's to the finish line first. Her husband defined his mule's age as threescore years and ten; a lieutenant offered the lineage of his Break-Neck as by Runaway out of Wouldn't Go, the second dam being Contusion by Collision out of Accident. Another was Slow by Tardy out of Late, the second dam Lazy by Inactive. Riders wore jockey silks described as "uncommonly blue" and "queer." The contest to be last was unusual, certainly, but so were other types of races for people whose entire focus was on horses: soldiers competed in what they called the Roman style, standing with one foot on the back of each of a pair of mounts, or Cossack style, standing erect on a single one. When the Leavenworth display of mulish slowness and bucking and stubborn refusal to move was over, the participants and the spectators returned to their quarters through rich river bottomland, the flowers and blossoms of wild grape perfuming the air as the crowd of laughing and shouting officers, wives, and jolly soldiers went along. "It is seldom that so light-hearted and joyous a company of people is gathered together," Libbie Custer wrote. "The cavalcade was something to rejoice in, and as the long line wound through the wood, the days of knight-errantry might seem, in the dim twilight, to have returned again in the nineteenth century." Once at a hunting party a guest turned in his saddle to look back at the groomed horses with sunlight glittering off shining bits and burnished spurs and the polished firearms of officers and men sitting their mounts with such ease, and said, Libbie remembered, that "nothing in our prosaic nineteenth century was so like the days of chivalry when some feudal lord went out to war or to the chase, followed by his retainers."

From such hunts one garnered for a feast a rib roast of buffalo to be well larded with bacon, deer and antelope steaks, fish, mallard, and quail, cooked over an open fire or baked in Dutch ovens standing in a coal bed and with the cover holding more coals. Lanterns hung from trees to illuminate dancing couples. There was beautiful scenery to view on riding expeditions, such being one of the chief benefits of army life, one woman wrote, with a wagon going along filled with provisions. Gallantry, form, procedure, a code, the knowledge of one's place in the world, and a certain gaiety and even uplift accompanying acceptance of that place, response to the sound of the drawn-out cadence of the bugle's tenor and the trumpet's baritone floating out over the prairie, and contact with nature and a increased feeling of matters spiritual—yes. But the earth-floor quarters hastily built as the frontier moved west were of unseasoned wood that contracted so that mud was used to bar entrance through gaps, not so successfully as to keep out dust in summer and snow in winter, nor to preclude sharing a room with fleas, gnats, wasps, flies, scorpions, centipedes falling from the thatched-roof ceiling onto the bed, mosquitoes, and rodents. One lit a match when entering at night to make sure no rattlesnake was in a corner.

There was nothing approaching education beyond the most basic fundamentals, and so the children were sent back east for schooling, not to be seen, sometimes, for years on end. A military surgeon, who would inevitably prescribe Epsom salts, iodine, or quinine for all ailments and injuries, could pull an aching tooth; beyond that there was no dental care unless an itinerant practitioner stopped by in a tour of the far-flung one- or two-company posts. In Arizona the temperature reached such heights in summer that silverware was hot to the touch, and it was said that one's shadow sweated. No book about that place in that time omits telling, often in the first chapter, the story of the soldier who died at Fort Yuma and went to hell. Soon he was back seeking his blankets. It was cold down there, he complained. On the Plains in winter the drifts blocked out the world. Eggs, butter, fresh fruits, and vegetables were difficult to obtain and, if found, prohibitively expensive, and when on rare occasion the commissary got in luxuries like chocolates, macaroni, prunes, raisins, or dried apples, they had to be partaken of with care for fear of indigestion, as was the case when spring brought the emergence of wild strawberries, an event greeted with more excitement than any news in any newspaper. Available water was often alkali in composition, always unpleasant and sometimes impossible to drink. Milk in Texas had the flavor of wild garlic.

Yet one carried on—or at least most did, although many men spent too much time in the sutler's store, where in addition to blankets, bridles, lariats, molasses, hairpins, and calico there was liquor for drinking the hours away by the officers' section billiard table. Some women found intolerable the isolation, the smells, the routine, the obligations, and went back to Boston or New York. But for others married to the commissioned soldier sworn to his duty there was meaning in an existence entirely different from that envisioned when vows were exchanged with the officer fighting to put down the beastly rebels, or when at the wedding to a newly minted second lieutenant she passed under a canopy of raised sabres at the Point chapel. The dashing cavalry officer, in his blue uniform with yellow stripes down his breeches to his shining high boots, went with his lady on a long railroad trek though empty vastness and then by rattling and swaying stagecoach, sometimes for days, to the windswept little world within itself in which they would make their home and find their destiny. In winter there would be ice skating and then, around a bonfire, group singing led by wives playing guitars. There were almost no single women. A girl coming out to visit her cavalry brother or cousin was almost instantly besieged with offers of marriage from lonely young officers. (It was virtually impossible to retain a serving girl imported from back east for more than a very short time; a noncom would swiftly scoop her up for marriage and she would go to work as a laundress on Suds Row, which was more agreeable and companionable a labor than housework. It also offered opportunities, in some cases, for the garnering, away from an officer and his lady's eyes, of monies enlisted men were willing to part with following their once-every-two-months payday of thirteen dollars a month for a private, down from the Civil War's sixteen. For men unable to arrange the services of accommodating laundresses, there was outside of every post a settlement of huts referred to as the Hog Ranch.)

For what other diversions were available for the youth who, it was said, had enlisted for what "penny dreadful" pulps, cheaply printed and illustrated, portrayed as the swashbuckling life of a swaggering cavalryman adventuresomely serving his country out on the great frontier of the Plains and the desert? He gambled with his fellows and he drank. Along with the Hog Ranch there was the Blind Tiger with a little turntable built into its outer wall to receive your money and spin back a glass of rotgut.

Those activities were for when the regiment was in garrison, absence from which could last for weeks and even months. The column moved out to the sound of the band playing "The Girl I Left Behind Me," the women of the post, laundress and officer's lady alike, watching as the men and their horses became as dots in the distance and then vanished. There was an element of danger for those from whom the horsemen departed. With the cavalry gone and only a small contingent of infantry in residence, there was always the chance that Indians might storm in. Should that occur, standing orders dictated that the women be shot by such soldiers who for the moment survived the onslaught, or gathered in the powder magazine to be blown to bits. Anything was better than being taken captive, with serial rape their fate, and being repeatedly traded for a pony or a rifle by one brave to another. A fate worse than death, the expression had it. Such certainly also awaited any cavalryman knocked off his horse and captured. He and any of his comrades equally unfortunate were hamstrung with cords through their legs and marched to the Indians' camp, where the teepees and wickiups emptied of inhabitants so that all could watch the men slowly burned to death, an arm or a leg first, then the face or the heart. Or they were buried to the neck in the ground near a hill of biting red ants and scalped, the blood and ripped flesh attracting the swarming insects. They were staked out with eyelids sliced off while positioned so as to look up at the unforgiving sun and with a trail of sugar attracting insects to a mouth pried open with sharp sticks.

Sometimes after long torture a man was loosely tied in a sitting posture, with inches away a rattlesnake staked to the ground by an arrow through its tail. Sooner or later the soldier would sag down, to be struck by poisonous fangs. "The only good Indian is a dead Indian," Sheridan was famously quoted as saying, to which he responded that he never had. His actual declamation was, he explained, that the only good Indians he ever saw were dead. Young Theodore Roosevelt, out in the West for his health and for adventure, seemed to agree with either concept, saying that nine out of ten Indians were better off dead, "and I shouldn't like to inquire too closely in the case of the tenth." For a time Sherman, promoted to head of the army when Grant assumed the presidency, pooh-poohed the menace of those universally referred to as "the savages." Then on an 1871 inspection tour, escorted by a handful of cavalry making for Fort Richardson some 450 miles northwest of San Antonio, he came under the eye of an unseen hundred-man Kiowa war party deterred from attacking by the proclamation of the seer Mamanti—a "medicine man" to whites—that he had a presentiment that a better target would soon be along. Mamanti's vision proved correct. The men of a long wagon train that soon appeared were annihilated to the last one before the Indians looted the shipment's contents and took away the mules. General Sherman readjusted his thinking.

It was not pleasant to deal with the remains of those who died. The results of what was called the Fetterman Massacre were indicative of what a relief party found. Captain William Fetterman, ex–brevet lieutenant colonel, had been known to say that with eighty cavalrymen he could cut his way through the entire Sioux nation. It was while leading almost precisely that number of riders in 1866 near Fort Phil Kearney in Wyoming that he spotted a small group of Indians, who raised themselves on their horses contemptuously to waggle their bare buttocks before fleeing at the soldiers' sabres-out, hell-for-leather forward run. The Indians vanished and Fetterman and his men followed—to find themselves in an instantly closed-off cul-de-sac surrounded by vast numbers of warriors who knew how to use every knoll, rock, tree, and tuft of grass to conceal themselves before springing up. Fetterman's death wound and that of his subordinate Captain Frederick Brown showed the manner in which they had died: they had counted down and simultaneously fired their pistols into each other's temples. It was preferable to be a murderer than a suicide. Of course, effort was required to deduce the manner of their deaths from the powder burns and exact placement of the shots, for like all of the command, they had had their eyes torn out; their arms, chins, and ears cut off; the muscles of their calves, thighs, stomachs, breasts removed, all lain on rocks beside what was left of their bodies—"teeth chopped out, private parts severed and indecently placed on the person, ribs slashed to separation with knives, punctures upon every sensitive part of the body, even to the soles of the feet and palms of the hand," reported the colonel of Fetterman's regiment. Those of the troop horses who survived were gone to new owners, as were all unbroken arrows of the estimated forty thousand discharged in the affair.

A similar destiny to that of Captain Fetterman awaited a contingent of the 7th Cavalry force that Lieutenant Colonel Custer unleashed upon an encampment along Indian Territory's Washita River, present-day Oklahoma, as retribution for what had befallen the wagon train trailing the escaped-from-disaster General Sherman. The years after the war had greatly changed Autie. At West Point he had been a slovenly cadet who got a plentitude of demerits and graduated last in his class. Then as a serving officer he received leaps in rank perhaps the swiftest in the history of any army, rising from first lieutenant in July 1862 to brigadier general, soon to be major general, in July 1863. He was twenty-five years old when the fighting stopped. Reduced to lieutenant colonel of the tiny Regular army, he reversed the familiar concept of the man promoted above his abilities, for while brilliant in high rank he was quite otherwise serving in a lower capacity. During the war he had been popular, but now he was disliked by his men and hated by several of his subordinate officers. For manifest deficiencies he was suspended from the service for several months. A brutal disciplinarian whose always-filled guardhouse was a giant hole in the ground with a trapdoor above that closed out all light, he practiced the most obvious favoritism, filling his regiment with relatives serving in military and civilian capacities. Irritable, bullheaded, prickly, unwilling to hear opinions contrary to his own, terribly quick to take offense in almost childish fashion, he presided over an outfit with evocative desertion

George Armstrong Custer with
his wife and brother Tom. Two
of the trio will die at the Battle of
the Little Big Horn.

rates. (During a twelve-month period of 1867–68, Wesley Merritt's
black 9th Cavalry, the Buffalo Soldiers, had 48 desertions. Custer's
7th had 456.) Autie had avidly sought publicity during the war, and
continued to do so out on the Plains, courting any newspaper or
magazine writer who came by, and sending his own articles to publishing outlets back east. (It is a question who wrote them. People
noted that Libbie was always with the lieutenant colonel at his desk
when he allegedly penned his pieces, and was if not his ghostwriter
then a signally active collaborator.)

His attack along the Washita was conducted in frigid weather,
the men in buffalo or bearskin greatcoats, knee-length lamb's-wool
socks, thick fur hats, and woolen gloves over gauntlets of musk-
rat or beaver fur. (Winter was harder on cavalry than infantry, for
the men of the latter could at least stamp their feet and clap their
hands, while the former had to sit straight and hold the reins.) The
command arrived at night. For hours soldiers stood silently and by

direct order motionless by their horses waiting for sunrise. One of the commanding officer's greyhounds barked, and when muzzling failed to quiet the dog, it was garroted with a lariat. At daylight Custer ordered his band to break into "Garryowen," the regimental song. The first notes sounded before spittle froze in the horns and the music halted save for rolling drums as the horsemen charged forward to shoot up the camp, kill Indian ponies, and burn habitations. Without making any kind of reconnaissance, Custer ordered Major Joel Elliott to detach a dozen and a half men and find new avenues of conquest. Instead catastrophe awaited. There were outlying camps near the original point of attack, and from them poured warriors to annihilate the major and all of his men. The bodies were later found in the usual mutilated fashion, feet, heads, and penises cut off. Additionally, "wolves," an officer remembered, "must have held high carnival over them." Custer departed without making any attempt to check on their progress, come to their rescue if it was not too late, or at least recover their bodies before they were shot, arrowed, hacked, and then bitten to shreds. He was never again trusted by anyone.

Custer made much over his supposed triumph along the Washita, but really it was only one of hundreds of such encounters larger and smaller between whites and Indians in those years after the war as the frontier moved west. Yet intermittently, relations between the two races were almost companionable, despite the army's saying that every native had been, was now, or soon would be what was called "a hostile." Indians were always around the little one-troop posts, hired for scouting duties against tribal enemies, or trading goods they had made—moccasins were far preferable to the army boots produced at Fort Leavenworth's military prison for long-term offenders and were frequently worn on field expeditions, when all clothing codes were abandoned, the men putting on what they wanted, including straw hats and fringed buckskin shirts, with officers not bothering to don shoulder straps. After a long absence from base, the band sounding as they came in "When Johnny Comes Marching Home" in counterpoint to the departure rendition of "The Girl I Left Behind Me," returning men resembled wandering gypsies from some impoverished Eastern Europe backwater province—thin, unshaven, with hair down to the shoulders, equipment battered and scratched, and filthy clothing patched with swatches of material used for wagon-train bags holding grain for the horses. They, too, were thin and worn. Indian ponies existed during the cold months exclusively on bark gnawed off cottonwood trees and whatever tufts of grass could be uncovered in the snow, and at times in the field the army's mounts were hardly better fed. Finding water for man and beast was always a problem. Maps indicated where water holes were reputed to be, but frequently when reached they were found dry or of undrinkable alkali nature. There were some nine million buffaloes out there in what those back east viewed as the romantic West of iconic cow-boy and dashing cavalryman, and when the latter came to a buffalo wallow, they lay flat, their horses' noses alongside, to gulp what the wallow had. Your tongue pushed the buffalo hairs from your teeth.

Sometimes the rations of hardtack, salt, coffee, beans, bacon, and a little flour ran out, and when the command made camp, two or three worn horses were shot. "It seemed like cannibalism" to eat what men called their "long-faced friends," one officer wrote; another remembered the unpleasant task of knocking them in the head with an ax and then cutting their throats: "It was pathetic to hear the dismal trumpeting (I can find no other word to express my meaning) of the dying creatures as the breath of life rushed through severed windpipes. Prejudice to one side, the meat is sweet and nourishing."

Life for the cavalry horses periodically issued by the quartermas-ter was not easy. In addition to the soldier, whose average weight in 1873 was 140 pounds, the animal bore a 14-pound, 13½-ounce saddle; rations of canned soup, pressed tongue, and corned beef; a watering bridle; socks, drawers, shirts, and an overcoat; forty rounds of pistol ammunition; a forage sack; 15 pounds of oats; a lariat with tethering pin, curry comb and brush; replacement horseshoes fitted out by the farrier for each individual mount; fifteen shoe nails; two blankets; a saddle cover; a surcingle; a sabre with sling; a holstered pistol; and a carbine with sling and swivel and box holding twenty-four rounds, the total weight according to an army estimate 240 pounds, 12½ ounces. The horses arrived at their posts unbroken. At Camp Grant, Arizona, those who would serve in the 3rd Cavalry were "first thrown and blindfolded," wrote Captain John G. Bourke, "and then the bridle and saddle were put on, the latter girthed so tightly the horse's eyes would start from their sockets. Then, armed with a pair of spurs the diameter of a soup-plate and a mesquite club big enough to fell an ox, the Mexican vaquero would get into the saddle, the blinds would be cast off, and the circus begin." All was accompanied by "squealing and struggling and biting and kicking and rolling in the dust and getting up again." Civilian horses of the time and place hardly fared better. A cowboy purchasing an unbroken animal starved it for a few days before roping and then throwing it down for saddling, following this immediately with an all-out run, leaving the mount exhausted and with spirit broken. The cowboy used a Mexican saddle with high pommel and cantle and immense wooden stirrups. Sweat leathers protected legs whose boots had great spurs with rowels two inches wide, the spikes revolving. There was a powerful, cruel bit. Like Indian mounts, cow ponies subsisted solely on grass (in winter, bark). Usually they showed backs sore or festering.

Their owners generally hated the army, for it represented law and order to desperadoes given in off-duty hours to drinking, fighting, whoring, and shooting up towns. And while soldiers were hardly choirboys, being instead usually semiliterate roughnecks, at least a tinge of devotion to something noble—to fidelity, bravery, discipline, esprit de corps, the regiment, something above themselves—lived in all but the most degraded. They had, after all, the Flag out there in their tiny remote posts of a vast nothingness not unlike what surrounds a ship at sea as at retreat they stood to attention in their starched uniforms, white-gloved hands smartly smacking carbines in manual-of-arms salute, wearing strapped-on polished-leather ammunition boxes, and, for a time, high-spiked headgear, the most elaborate of United States Cavalry history, imitations of the *Pickelstaub* of the Prussian army. They loved their horses, speaking of them almost as long-married people did of their mates, Libbie Custer noted. It was tremendously resented when her husband decreed that each troop of his regiment ride horses of the same color, bays for one, blacks for another, each branded with a "United States" on the left shoulder and on the left thigh a designation of their company of the 7th. In theory the distribution by color meant that the commander could of an instant see where his riders were deployed, but troopers mourned the separation from the horses they had ridden and soldiered with for years.

The duties that they and their horses performed were of two natures. The cavalry were involved with protecting the stagecoach line, the paymaster traversing the Plains or the desert, the miners' camp or expedition, steamers on rivers traversing dangerous points, woodsmen, land surveyors, cattle ranchers, the railroad workers putting in the lines uniting New York and San Francisco, the settlers' wagons moving west to colonize, indeed create, a new nation. Desperadoes, outlaws, train robbers, cattle rustlers, and highwaymen constituted a portion of those the army combated, but of course the Indians counted for far more. It was government policy that they be confined to reservations as government wards, to be issued there food, clothing, firearms, seeds, and implements, the hope being that they would in time become farmers, ranchers, good citizens. Nothing was more out of line with the thinking and traditions of a nomadic people who had always ranged freely. Here was the ineradicable contradiction between two cultures. It was the task of the cavalry to force the one to the other's will: the Indian must get out of the way of the nineteenth century and get to and stay where the white man decreed he must be.

In the spring of 1876, as the United States prepared for a nationwide gala July Fourth celebration of the hundredth year since its founding, three formations of cavalry set out to corral a great mass of Indians for installation in reservations. If the Indians elected to fight this tri-pronged force, soldiers said, the last great battle of the red man and the white man would find its result. Former brevet major general, now lieutenant colonel, George Armstrong Custer led one of the columns.

He departed Fort Abraham Lincoln, Dakota Territory, on May 17. "My husband rode to the top of a promontory," Libbie wrote, "and turned around, stood up in his stirrups and waved his hat. Then they all started forward again and in a few seconds they had disappeared, horses, flags, men." Yellow Hair, as he was to the Indians, rode with a flag bearer carrying a yellow-fringed blue silk regimental standard a little larger than two feet square showing an eagle with below on a scroll the number 7. Autie did not wear his uniform, but instead a suit of buckskin and a broad-brimmed hat. Behind him fluttered the swallow-tailed guidons showing the twelve troop numbers of the 600 cavalrymen accompanied by some 50 Indian scouts and, in the rear, a beef herd and a long pack train of 150 mules pulling wagons of supplies, including bridge-building materials. His brother Boston Custer was in the back, serving in civilian capacity as a pack master; up front with the troops were Autie's brother Tom, recipient of two Medals of Honor for gallantry during the Civil War, and their nephew Armstrong Reed. The reserve herd of led horses included two of Custer's. He hurried his force on, rejecting suggestions that he take along a battery of Gatlings, early machine guns capable of firing six hundred rounds a minute, for they were cumbersome and would slow his progress. The plan was for the three columns, of which his was one, simultaneously to arrive at the point of destination, but in his headstrong way he appears to have decided that he and he alone would garner the trophies awaiting the final great meeting of two races. Custer saw himself as a future president of the United States. The day was coming when he would be in Washington as the Great Father, he had upon several occasions predicted to Indians. At the very least he would be someone whose name would feature in history. "I want my name to resound with future generations," he once said.

At a supply depot at the confluence of the Yellowstone and Powder Rivers he had the men's sabres put away for storage—they became dulled on long rides as they jolted about in their scabbards and additionally produced noise as they clanked against saddle equipment and spurs. He seemed oddly fixated on the need for silence, ordering as the trek went on a "silent reveille"—no bugles. But could he have thought that his prey would be unaware of an advance raising clouds of dust so dense as completely to obscure the view of the rear of his two columns from each one's front? His reaction to signs of recent movements along the route was equally unfathomable. Normally one strained to discern the slightest signs that someone had earlier traversed the path one was taking: a tiny tree branch deflection, a broken twig, a grass stem pressed in an unnatural direction.

But on the trip to the Little Big Horn River there was a recent trail no one could miss seeing, for it was more than half a mile wide. An enormous band had recently come this way, its members from varied tribes comprising the largest gathering of Indians in history.

Custer did not care. The greater the enemy, the more glory in defeating it. He pressed on, right arm rising smartly to order advancement from walk to trot, with officers in line behind duplicating the signal. (The army-decreed walk was at four miles an hour and the trot at nine, with the slow trot at seven felt to tire horses less than a constant walk.) The force passed from Dakota to Montana Territory, its leader as evening approached going ahead with an advance party to select the night's campsite. It was if possible by a stream along which officers' tents were pitched, the furnishings a cracker box covered with a rubber blanket serving as tablecloth, a tin washbasin, and a looking glass. Horses were rubbed down and then put to grazing on thirty-foot picket lariats planted in outlying area ground, mounted guards attending them. A number of nearby animals were saddled and loosely girthed so as to be ready for mounting by quickly summoned soldiers if hostiles appeared. Should that occur, the consequences could be dire. An onslaught of whooping and screaming Indians could spook the tethered horses into rearing, jumping, and plunging, to snap their lines with a crack like a pistol report, or to pull the picket from the ground to hurtle swishing through the air as a missile more dangerous than a bullet.

As sunset came on the troopers were marched to the herd to pull out picket pins, coil lariats, and move horses to the water source, which ideally did not have boggy banks or mire beds. Feed was issued and the horses curried and combed, an officer silently observing the noncoms checking the work. It was a part of the cavalry canon that an officer avoided speaking directly to a private, and did so as little as possible to a noncom, often riding side by side for hours with his sergeant–flag bearer without uttering a word. Such was the tradition perhaps inherited from the British. The cavalry officer General Sir Douglas, later Field Marshal Lord Haig, was known never in his life to have spoken with a private.

The horses brought in to be repicketed within camp limits and able to graze on grass earlier untouched, soldiers ate their hardtack fried in bacon grease or mixed with condensed milk, had meat from butchered steers of the herd, drank coffee from beans ground on a flat rock with revolver butts, and then sat around a campfire singing along with harmonica music and smoking pipes. They slept to arise a little after four in the morning for stable call, inspection, breakfast, and then the trail. They were precisely one month away from Fort Abraham Lincoln when on June 17 George Crook, commanding one of the other two converging forces, ran into trouble along the Rosebud Creek. Crook was the antithesis of George Custer or any other cavalry officer of flair and display, undemonstrative and so dismissive of panoply and pomp that he had absented himself from the war's-end Grand Review during which Custer flew down Pennsylvania Avenue aboard his allegedly out-of-control horse. Phil Sheridan's West Point roommate, Crook in the West devoted his off hours to solitary hunting and fishing trips, for which his only companions were his dog and his horse, and when on duty he pursued the decidedly unglamorous task of designing gear that would enable mules to carry greater loads than the regulations-stipulated 175 pounds. "Granddaddy of the Pack Mule," his innovations so distributed weight that an animal could comfortably bear 350.

His progress along the Rosebud was halted by an Oglala Sioux attack. Among his subordinates was Captain Guy Vernor Henry, whose son of the same name would in time become, like his father, a legendary figure of the United States Cavalry; between them they garnered major generalships, designations such as Chief Instructor of Horsemanship at Fort Riley's Cavalry School, captain of the 1912 Olympics equestrian team, and Chief of Cavalry during the conversion of the horse cavalry into the army branch now called Armor. The senior Henry, winner of a Civil War Medal of Honor, took at the Rosebud a Sioux bullet that destroyed one eye before veering into his mouth to shatter most of his teeth. For moments he remained in his saddle trying to go on, and then he tumbled to the ground. Sioux warriors came to finish him right there or, worse, bring him to their camp for torture, but Captain Henry's Shoshone scouts fought them off, the hooves of their horses and those of the Sioux striking the ground about him and on him, and took him to the rear. He was put on a litter slung between two in-line mules for removal to where he could be given medical treatment, two hundred miles distant, a trip of seven or eight days, and then transferred to a mule-drawn travois with a square of material draped over his broken face to spare him from flies. A brother officer approached to offer sympathies. "It is nothing," Henry said. "For this are we soldiers."

One week after the events along the Rosebud, the 7th Cavalry reached the Little Big Horn, a meandering shallow stream. The area was one of low foothills. Custer could see from atop one of them an Indian camp. He ordered his command partitioned into three elements, two to take up positions calculated to block Indian flight from the charge of the third and largest segment, which he would lead. One of his officers asked if it was wise to divide their force in the face of the enemy.

"You have your orders."

The two supporting forces rode to their assigned posts, and he placed his group of 272 men in two lines. What then occurred is known a century and a quarter and more years on to millions, who if asked to itemize famed soldiers of the nineteenth century will come up with Lee and Grant, Stuart maybe, possibly Sherman and Sheridan—but Custer certainly. What was in his mind that long-ago hour on a windswept Montana hilltop has been the subject of book, thesis, psychological study, movie, and speculation by drinkers viewing reproductions of the famed painting *Custer's Last Stand* hanging behind the bar of untold pre-Prohibition saloons. "I regard Custer's massacre as a sacrifice of troops brought on by Custer himself that was wholly unnecessary—wholly unnecessary," President Grant said.

Yes, of course, no one can argue with that. But why did he do what he did? Libbie had always seen Autie, she made clear in the long years of her widowhood, as a figure out of time, a knight in shining armor. Perhaps he also took himself as one. ("Custer was," Sheridan said, "the embodiment of gallantry. If there was any poetry or romance in war he could develop it.") Perhaps he saw himself as the Christian standing off the heathen, civilization's champion opposing the barbarian. His actions were suicide, some theorize, a Wagnerian desire to go to Valhalla surrounded with his loyal retainers and men-at-arms, soldierly accoutrements, noble warhorses.

The bugles sounded and the men—boys, really, teenagers save for the noncoms and officers—shouted and hurrahed as the horses of the 7th went forward in the style of a thousand years' projection of unstoppable force.

But here they rode against not the formed lines that Alexander on Bucephalus broke, nor the fleeing enemies Seydlitz annihilated, nor the Imperial Guard Wellington's Scots Grays scattered at Waterloo, nor the rebels that Custer's own charge prevented from coming in behind the Yankee lines at Gettysburg. For Indians had neither lineal formations nor emplaced fortifications and no defensive artillery, but fought as individuals—there were no rigid lines the breaking of whose discipline meant disaster. Sitting Bull and Crazy Horse were there at the Little Big Horn, great chiefs both, and Rain in the Face and White Bear and Flat Hip and Brave Bear, but they did not function as what the white man called leaders of cavalry for their tribesmen, all of whom were mounted—they did not have any footed personnel—but flitted about as bees or flies, circling and darting and coming in from all angles, the best light cavalry, as oft repeated, the world ever saw. They hung off the sides of their mounts with head and body obscured, nothing for the soldiers to shoot at, and like the Assyrians of old previously referred to, sent off flocks of arrows. They had rifles provided by a government reasoning that such issuance would make it easier for them to garner game and thereby constrict the territory they patrolled, thus making the lands they had occupied for millennia available for the onrush of the Gilded Age. From their rifles they had direct fire into the ranks of the 7th, and if their high-aimed arrows arcing down did not kill, then at least they wounded and discomfited.

It cannot have taken but a moment for Lieutenant Colonel Custer to understand the situation. As with his Washita assault, he had gone forward without making any kind of reconnaissance. He got away with it then, but now he found his force surrounded by a completely elusive, circling enemy perhaps ten times its number, two to three thousand warriors with faces smeared with war paint, headdresses of eagle feathers spreading from rider's forehead to pony's tail, necklaces of bear claws adorning throats, hair braided with otter fur. Behind were women voicing high-pitched ululating screams and bringing replacement horses and ammunition for their men. He fell back seeking high ground, found it, and ordered soldiers off their horses to get down and make a stand. It must have been terrible for him and his men, for all experience shows that a cavalryman off his mount is instantly demoralized, accustomed as he is to relying on the strength and courage of his horse. Custer and his men became like an island amid swirling waters rising by the minute. Shouting and whooping Indians swooped in, and the horses of Troops I and L stampeded away into swirling dust, each bearing saddlebags with 150 rounds of ammunition their dismounted riders would never use.

Soldiers crouched for protection behind shot horses, and also shot comrades. The two detached elements, unable to see the main force and under attack themselves, huddled in menaced defensive stance, expecting that at any moment their triumphant leader would come to their rescue. They were still waiting when two days later an advance party of one of the other columns sent to join with the 7th Cavalry in ending the Indian problem out there in the West arrived at the Little Big Horn. A strange sight met their eyes. Seemingly they beheld a meadow containing an outcropping of white boulders, with dark motionless shapes spotted all around. They came closer to find that the dark forms were dead horses, and the supposed stones the naked bodies of those who had followed the doomed leader in the most disastrous charge of American history. Not an Indian was to be seen anywhere. Off in the distance, the main scene of battle blocked by hills and wood from their view, cowered the two supporting forces, with no idea of what had occurred. Among the naked bodies on the field of battle at the Little Big Horn a soldier found a friend whose leg had been hacked off and thrown over his shoulder. Under a triangle of teepee sticks were three severed heads with open eyes sightlessly staring at one another. A soldier lay with "an iron picket thrusted through his testicles," a report said, "penis cut off and stuffed into his mouth. Bodies were set up on their knees and elbows and their hind parts shot full of arrows" so they appeared almost like porcupines. The abdomen of Autie's brother Tom had been cut open so that his entrails spilled out on the ground. Once, in those many soldier-Indian meetings leading to nothing, Tom's brother

Yellow Hair had smoked a peace pipe with Medicine Arrows, Keeper of the Cheyenne Sacred Arrows, after which the latter had emptied the ashes over his fellow smoker's boots. This meant, he said, that if the lieutenant colonel ever menaced any Cheyenne he would pay a terrible price. Two women of the tribe came to Autie as he lay dead. They jammed sewing awls deep into his ears. Perhaps he had not earlier heard what Medicine Arrows told him. Now he would be able to hear better.

One living creature stood surrounded by dead bodies of horses and men on the silent field. Captain Myles Keogh was the son of an officer of the Royal Irish Lancers. Like his father, he became a soldier. He served in the Vatican's Papal Guard, then went to America and joined the Union army. After the war he was sent West. A competent-enough military man, he was a drinker who knowing his weakness for liquor gave his orderly his pay along with instructions that it be doled out to him in such slight amounts as to preclude his going on a monumental binge. In the spring of 1868 some forty horses purchased by the army quartermaster at Saint Louis, average price $40, were delivered to the 7th Cavalry. Captain Keogh took one, a light bay. When the horse suffered a slight arrow wound in a skirmish against the Comanches, Keogh named him for the tribe. Now, far more grievously injured, hit seven times by bullets and arrows, his bridle slipped from place and with saddle dangling loose, left behind to die by the Indians who took away some hundred sound troop horses (including Vic, the one Custer rode), Comanche became nationally celebrated as the sole survivor of the Massacre of the Little Big Horn. (It took nearly a century for the United States public to take note of the survival of the other hundred horses, plus thousands of Indians, and additionally to amend the term "massacre," previously an inevitably used description of Indian victories, to "battle.") Comanche was taken back to Fort Abraham Lincoln to be given medical care such as few horses ever had, including for months every other day mash containing almost a full bottle of Hennessy brandy. When he recovered his health he was by regimental orders never ridden again. He lived in a stall whose door was always open so that he could come and go as he pleased, to be described as "panhandling" for bottles of beer, and never impeded as he kicked over garbage cans "to make food selections." When bugles sounded for troop formations, he galloped to the head of his old unit to take up his place, almost as if Captain Keogh were on his back. Each June 25, when the 7th memorialized its great loss, he was draped in black net and saddled, with empty boots placed reversed in the stirrups. Comanche died in 1891, aged twenty-nine, and his stuffed form can be seen today at the University of Kansas in Lawrence.

Over the years relics taken from the field by the victors of the affair turned up. In 1906 an Indian sold to a Montana saloon keeper a Civil War–era watch from the days when its owner was to the newspapers the Boy General with Golden Locks. On its back, below a representation of the Michigan state seal and two crossed sabres, was engraved *To General Custer from the Michigan Brigade. "Ride, You Wolverines."* The saloon keeper lost the watch in a dice game to a traveling salesman. It went to a California antique dealer and ended up in a Montana museum. Its former owner's map case can be seen in the United States Military Academy museum. One of his replacement horses, Dandy, alternately ridden with Vic, was back with the wagon train and so escaped capture at the Little Big Horn, although he was slightly wounded in the neck by a long-range stray arrow. Libbie sent him to her husband's family in Michigan, and Father Custer, as she always called him, rode him in local parades, shows, and fairs.

She herself, beneficiary of a $30-a-month government pension, returned east to write books about the army, her husband, and herself, and magazine articles on public affairs, ballet, opera, vandalism at Mount Vernon, children, and the economic status of women. A shrewd investor, she became increasingly prosperous, able to travel extensively in Europe and the Far East and to spend winters in Daytona Beach. "It's really rather suspicious of me to be living on Park Avenue, don't you think?" she said. Successful and strong and making her way unassisted at a time when there were very few assertive women such as she, Libbie was yet the quintessential professional widow, living out her long years speaking and writing of her late husband as innocent of any wrongdoing. The Little Big Horn catastrophe, she held, was the fault of the officers commanding the outlying detachments, or the original orders sending Autie on his way. "She was blind, deaf and dumb to any shortcomings of her husband. To her, Custer was a god, a saint, an immaculate hero, a knight without stain or reproach." When his body was removed to the West Point cemetery, she took violent offense at the statue erected over it, saying it portrayed him as a roughneck instead of as a sensitive intellectual. Her complaints were so persistent and vocal that the statue was dismantled and another erected in its place.

She developed a strange hatred for Wesley Merritt, her husband's fellow in the Shenandoah Valley during the war—"I owe it all to the brave boys Merritt and Custer," Sheridan had said—and then out in the West. She took him as deficient in endorsing her view that her husband's subordinate and superior officers were responsible for his death, and also laid the offensive statue at his door. Her disdain notwithstanding, in October 1879 Merritt exemplified almost too perfectly that familiar characterization of the Cavalry to the Rescue when some thirty men of a mixed cavalry and infantry formation found themselves surrounded by a force of White River Ute Indians along the Milk River in Colorado. The soldiers circled their wagons and shot their horses and mules as additional protective fortifications and for food. The first of these strategies proved effective; the second after five days turned rank. Entrenched men put gunpowder on the meat to kill the stench. The encircling enemy set fire to the grass, and so the soldiers had to battle smoke and flames. All day long as the Indians waited to starve them out, the death wail was heard, the death chant. Drums sounded and the troopers heard the long howl of wolves attracted to the smell of carrion. One man broke through the Indians and raced to Rawlings Station along the Union Pacific tracks to telegraph word of their plight. Merritt arose from a sickbed at Fort D. A. Russell in Wyoming to order his black 9th Cavalry onto a train. The tracks were cleared of all other traffic. Newsboys in the streets of a hundred cities shouted "Extra!" as their papers breathlessly detailed the soldiers' progress.

Merritt offloaded at the railhead nearest the scene of the siege and set out in the rigidly disciplined manner he had learned from Philip St. George Cooke at the commencement of the Civil War taking cavalry from Utah to Washington, intent upon not "winding" or "pumping out" the horses. Along the way there was nothing to be heard save the tramp of hooves and the rattle and jingle of riders' equipment, but a great deal to be seen: heaps of ashes with fragments of iron and chains and harness and rubbish—and the bodies of settlers and the officials of the Indian Agency slaughtered by the Utes. When within earshot of the embattled men, he had his buglers sound Officers' Call. At the notes—"the sweetest sound we had ever heard," a soldier remembered—and the sight of more than five hundred galloping troopers coming up in straight lines on fresh horses, the Indians scattered; and soldiers weeping with joy for being saved from death and worse swept up to surround their savior.

Merritt went on to be superintendent at West Point and then to command the American forces occupying the Philippine Islands in the wake of the Spanish-American War. That conflict was held as finally ending the lingering divisions between North and South, and to emphasize America's unity, ex-Confederates were given high place in the ranks of the army against which they had fought in the sixties. The rebel infantry commanders of the conflict were mature men when they made their wartime names, and therefore dead or too old for new service, but cavalry officers who, like Merritt, had been young back then were seen as eligible for military duties. Fighting Joe Wheeler, who opposed Kilpatrick as best he could during the March to the Sea, and Stuart's subordinate Fitz Lee were given major generalships, with Custer's West Point friend and wartime opponent Tex Rosser made a brigadier. None of the old soldiers had a chance to display for a new age the cavalry skills shown in the long ago, as was true for the young riders who unborn then now served under them. America's naval shipment of troops to assault the Spanish holding Cuba was a horror of mismanagement, with too few vessels to accommodate the horses of cavalry units, which were therefore forced to serve unmounted.

The single ship used to transport officers' mounts approached shore to find that there were no piers, and so the animals were simply pushed overboard with the expectation that they would swim to land. Instead they headed in the wrong direction, out to sea, and were never seen again.

Libbie Custer grew very old, her tendril curls yet worn in the manner of the 1880s, her wedding ring on her finger. Like Jeb's widow and Little Phil's, who said she would rather be the wife of the dead General Sheridan than married to any living man, and Charlie Lowell's also, she never remarried. She died in 1933, four days short of her ninety-first birthday. "Autie lies in such a lovely spot," she had said of his West Point grave with the new statue above it, and there fifty-seven years after the Little Big Horn she joined him, the old lady put with her young hero, a military band playing "Garryowen" as she went to his side.

"I regarded Mackenzie as the most promising young officer of the army," Grant wrote in his memoirs. "No man better understood the use of horses in war," says a modern historian. Few they are who remember him today, although Ronald Reagan in his Hollywood days long sought to portray him in a movie, and he was the subject of a one-season television series starring Richard Carlson, *Mackenzie's Raiders*. Ranald Slidell Mackenzie was the son of a naval officer who wrote books on the side and moved in literary circles, Longfellow his close friend. He was in command of the USS *Somers* when a mutiny was raised under the leadership of a cadet who was the son of the secretary of war. Apparently a severely disturbed young man, Philip Spencer had it in mind to make of the *Somers* a pirate ship. Captain Mackenzie had him hanged from the yardarm, illustrious parentage notwithstanding. The incident led to the creation of the United States Naval Academy at Annapolis—previously Navy officer aspirants underwent training with the Fleet, an educational process that the Spencer matter brought into question. The senior Mackenzie died young; his son Ranald, to spare his widowed mother difficult-to-meet expense, withdrew from Williams College and enrolled at the free West Point. A premier student there, he graduated first in his class of 1862. The elite Engineers took him, but he found wartime bridge construction a "bore," he wrote home, and got himself transferred to a Connecticut heavy artillery regiment essentially acting as infantry. A brevet colonel at twenty-three, he proved hardly less a severe disciplinarian than his late father, capable among other things of replying to a call for coffee from the ranks when the men took a brief rest on a testing route march by not only denying issuance of the beverage but making the soldiers stand at attention for the entire period before they got back on the road. Deserters of his unit were strung up by the thumbs, and anyone who straggled on a march had a heavy log attached to his pack.

Taking him for the very model of a rigid by-the-numbers and by-the-book West Point martinet, the soldiers detested Mackenzie. "The men hated him with the hate of hell," the regimental history frankly says. A group of them decided to get rid of this despot when the enemy was engaged. It would be easy enough in the smoke and confusion to put a round through him. But when they went up against the rebs they found their leader alone of all their number declining to lie flat on the ground to protect against flying bullets and bursting shells. Instead he put his cap on the tip of his raised sabre and cantered up and down his lines, exhorting soldiers to hold fast and then come on. To kill so brave a man was an impossibility, soldiers told one another.

Ranald Mackenzie was a strange mixture of cold brute and frail little 145-pound shy boy. He was never known to have anything approaching a close friend, and was seemingly terrified of women, his mother and sister Harriet the only ones he ever knew well. He never touched liquor, he never caroused, he was the last officer to swashbuckle about. In the years of the war he took six wounds. A bullet knocked off two fingers; he was back in the saddle within days. At Cedar Creek he was hit when the Confederates surged forward to catch the Federals napping, and then temporarily paralyzed when struck again as, such was the expression, General Sheridan aboard Rienzi returned the call. Like Charlie Lowell at that affair, he had himself strapped into his saddle, refusing the suggestion of Sheridan himself that he retire from the field. Grant perceived him, very late on in the war, March 1865, as a cavalry leader, and he was given command of the horsed contingents of the Army of the James, a force subsidiary to the Army of the Potomac. (Union armies were usually named for rivers.) Like Merritt and Custer, he was at Appomattox when the Yankee cavalry drew back like the curtain in a theater to reveal to Robert E. Lee an impenetrable mass of infantry.

Afterward came the swift reduction to a scattered few of what had been the great Union army, and with it a drop to a captaincy for former brevet major general Ranald Mackenzie. He labored at this and that and then took on the colonelcy of one of the new black cavalry regiments. It was a position many officers disdained, but in his harsh and determined yet fair manner he took a mass of ignorant field hands formerly beaten-down slaves and made of them smart Buffalo Soldiers. He was given the colonelcy of the white 4th Cavalry Regiment, and it became the premier mounted force in the West. Legislatures appealed to the War Department for assignment to their area of Mackenzie's Raiders, the sole outfit identified by the name of its leader. Wesley Merritt's great 1879 run over the Continental Divide and into the Rocky Mountains to save trapped soldiers from rampaging White River Utes had captured the country's attention and admiration while oddly emptying the leader of desire to go on in the West; and so when a great demand arose that the Utes be sent elsewhere from their lands, Mackenzie and the 4th were given the dispossession assignment.

Bad Hand, so the Indians dubbed him for the two fingers lost to a reb bullet during the war (he was Three-Finger Jack to his soldiers behind his back), met with Ute chiefs. They must go, Mackenzie told the Utes. The Great Father in Washington desired it. He, Bad Hand, ordered it. There was nothing to discuss. They would depart the Colorado they had always known and go to Utah. The next morning they were herded away by cavalrymen. Within three days their rich former lands were occupied by whites, towns laid out and lots selling for high prices in what would be one of the prime garden spots of Colorado. "Poor things!" wrote an officer, writing also that Mackenzie felt pity for them. Yet it was best, he held, that they go without attempting a fruitless and bloody fight in which they could not possibly prevail. And to harry them away, to have them gone, was his duty.

Once, at Fort Sill, Indian Territory, in present-day Oklahoma, Mackenzie sat with the lean and parchment-faced interpreter Horace Jones, who had married a Comanche girl and lived much as her people did. (He would like someday to go to Fort Riley, he told people, "and see what those machines called railroads looked like.") A group of Indian renegades had been raiding in the area and then sheltering themselves on a nearby

Mackenzie, the most brilliant of
all Indian fighters.

reservation among their more peaceful fellows, who were situated
there with their wives and children. This must stop, Mackenzie
told the tribal leaders, Jones interpreting. These renegades
must be brought to him for punishment. The leaders protested,
explained, remonstrated. Mackenzie heard them out for a while.
Then he said, "Jones! Tell these Indians I have listened to their
talk long enough." The renegades must be in his presence in the
next twenty minutes. If not, he said, "I will go out to their
camps and kill them all. Repeat that, Jones, just as I have said it.
I—will—go—out—to—their—camps—and—kill—them—all."

An officer recorded: "This he said without the least appearance
of excitement, in a quiet, deliberative voice. He then left the room."
The renegades were brought in as prisoners within the stipulated
time. Mackenzie was not always so calm as on that occasion. He was
subject to sudden fits of temper, during which he decreed in what
others took for irrational fashion draconian punishments for relatively minor transgressions: putting officers under arrest for failing

to submit properly filled-out reports, making men stand outside in deadly cold weather saluting tree stumps over and over for an hour and a half because they had addressed him in what he considered an insufficiently respectful manner. He took desertion from the 4th Cavalry as a personal affront, raging that men who went over the hill must be traced to New Orleans, Galveston, or even New York. Yet when upon occasion he felt himself to have been unjust in a matter, he was capable of apologizing, even to a private. He had a curious way of loudly snapping the stubs of his amputated fingers, the action indicating he was irritated. His men heard the sound frequently. Perhaps his irascibility and the fact that he was a notably ungraceful rider was due to his always being in pain—about which he never complained—from his many wounds, and a generally run-down condition deriving from his inclination to sleep very little, prowling about at night to check things with the intent that the 4th be the best it could be. It was difficult for anyone to have warm feelings for a commanding officer capable of sitting through an entire meal with his officers while never uttering a word; but when he learned that one of his people had financial difficulties, he freely made loans, saying there was no need to hurry in repayment—let the money be returned at the borrower's convenience. He seems to have been comfortable within himself only as the harsh disciplinarian, and appeared awkward and shy as he encouraged the enlisted men to play sports, and got them equipment. It was all done on his own, the army taking no interest in such entertainments.

Mackenzie was the first soldier of America's army thoroughly to analyze what that army and the people it served faced in the West. The Indians were nomads. They had no cities. In their temporary camps were their women and children and their old, all vulnerable to attack—save when, as with Custer's doomed one at the Little Big Horn, the troops went in facing odds of ten to one. There was no point in simply shooting up their camps, Mackenzie reasoned. What was needed was complete destruction. He went in 1876's Wyoming winter, with temperatures on Christmas Day at Fort Sanders registering fifty-eight degrees below zero, to a Cheyenne encampment along the Powder River. The approach march was desperately difficult,

with steep slopes and narrow ravines and gullies slippery and dangerously capable of wrenching fetlocks and pasterns. The horses'
bits had to be run through hot water or ashes before being put in
to prevent their taking off the skin of the animals' mouths. But
Mackenzie arrived to drive off the tribe's warriors and then put to
the torch everything that could be burned: the teepees, tons of buffalo meat, blankets, stored clothing (including robes of delicately
tanned antelope skin decorated with beadwork, porcupine quills,
and elk teeth), bridles, cooking utensils, which were smashed before
being committed to the flames, artifacts. (Relics of what befell
Custer six months earlier were found and preserved. They included
silk guidons, the roster of Company "G" of the 7th Cavalry and
the memo books of several company first sergeants, canteens and
nose bags, a buckskin jacket lined with taffeta that had belonged to
Autie's brother Tom, a gold pencil case, letters with stamps affixed
and ready for mailing, pocketbooks with photographs, and paper
currency and coins.)

Mackenzie went away leaving more than four thousand men,
women, and children either to perish of the cold, which many did,
or go into reservations, which the survivors did, the chiefs Dull
Knife and Little Wolf knowing their people had no other choice.
Army casualties amounted to one lieutenant and half a dozen
enlisted men. Swiftly frozen stiff, the bodies were lashed to mules
and taken back to post, the officer per army policy for embalming
and dispatch home, the men put into wooden packing cases originally utilized for food or rifle or clothing shipments but now doing
duty as coffins. The stenciled description of a case's earlier contents
could be read as it and its contents were lowered into the post cemetery. The officer's wife Frances Boyd once wandered through one
looking at the grave markers. No one in the lonely last resting place
out past the barracks, stables, and parade ground and on the edge of
the vast prairie was more than twenty-three years of age.

When not in their camps, Mackenzie knew, Indian men were
likely to be on their ponies. Sometimes, to be sure, they were simply hunting game. But on other occasions they were out to do what
it was his duty to prevent. His solution was to kill the animals. That
was not a completely original concept—as we have seen, Generals

Kilpatrick and Sheridan freely slaughtered horses to keep them from serving the Confederates. But Mackenzie, in coldly logical fashion, raised the matter to new dimensions. The horse to the South's rebel forces was a tool of war. To the Indian it was as indispensable as the buffalo he hunted when mounted on its back, the prey furnishing food, clothing, and shelter from its hide and fur, tools and adornments made from its bone and horn, validation of prowess in a warrior.

Without a horse, the Indian could never harvest what he wanted and needed from the buffalo herds. Without the buffalo, the Indian was doomed. (Each of the buffalo should be killed, all the estimated nine million of them, Sheridan said. Any white man shooting one for its tongue, a delicacy upon which to dine while the rest of the creature was left to rot; or for its fur, to fashion into a coat, a blanket, or a robe; or simply for sport from a passing train, should be given a medal. The award, the general said, would show a buffalo on one side and a "discouraged-looking Indian" on the other.) Man for man, an Indian had far more horses than did the members of the Union or Confederate or any other army; he traveled in a group as had the Huns, with a mass of replacement animals following. It was said of the Comanche that he could take a mount discarded by a white man as utterly played out and get a hundred miles out of it before stopping for a rest. Even so, no tribe had enough horses. They were the be-all and end-all of survival, as they had been for the Hun and the Mongol. This Ranald Mackenzie of the 4th United States Cavalry Regiment knew. To destroy an Indian camp, as he had done along the Powder River in Wyoming, was to annihilate a sanctuary. To slay their horses was to deprive them of mobility and of freedom. From atop the heights of the Palo Duro Canyon in the west Texas panhandle near Amarillo he looked down on a camp so far below that the ponies of the herd appeared as small as chickens or turkeys. He sent his men down to the valley floor to scatter the warriors he had sought during a twenty-five-mile ride into uncharted territory through blinding sandstorms, at night.

He blocked any escape for the ponies as his troops formed to hold off their masters. It was said that horses maintained by whites were terrified by Indians, Libbie Custer recording that she had hard work getting a mount to approach even entirely peaceful Indian women. The reverse was true, with Native American animals fearful of whites. In the case of the Palo Duro matter, the Indian horses' instincts were correct, for after Mackenzie had more than fourteen hundred of them pushed up to the canyon rim, he ordered them shot, their carcasses to be shoved over to plummet down. "The massacre of good horseflesh sickened many of our troops," wrote the regimental adjutant, Captain T. S. Parker, "but they continued to fire into the herd and shut out the sound of animals in agony. After we returned to the post, many of the youngest troopers had nightmares about the slaughter for many months after." But Lone Wolf led his people into a reservation.

In April 1873 the 4th was ordered to Fort Clark, about 140 miles west of San Antonio, the assignment personally ordered by President Grant. Its commander was told to precede the troops for a meeting with Secretary of War William Belknap and General Philip Sheridan. For years the border area had been one of the most lawless places on earth. Much of what produced the Wild West was due to white desperadoes, but a portion was traceable to Kickapoo and Lipan warriors who came over the Rio Grande from Mexico, raided, burned, ran off livestock, and went back over the river to be safe from United States retribution. The Mexican authorities looked the other way.

"Mackenzie," Sheridan said, "you have been ordered down here because I want something done to stop these conditions of banditry, killing, et cetera, by those people across the river. I want you to control and hold down the situation, and do it in your own way. I want you to be bold, enterprising, and at all times full of energy. When you begin, let it be a campaign of annihilation, obliteration, and complete destruction." There was no need to read between the lines. Sheridan was calling upon his subordinate to invade a neighboring country and there conduct combat operations.

"Sir, under whose orders am I to act?" Mackenzie asked. The war with Mexico was precisely a quarter of a century past, and now a colonel of cavalry was apparently being told to risk a new one. "Will you issue the necessary orders for my action?"

"Damn the orders! Damn the authority!" Sheridan pounded his fist on a table. "Your authority and backing shall be Grant and myself." And so Mackenzie sent civilian spies into Mexico to look for Indian encampments. He dispersed six troops of the 4th to varying locations distant from Fort Clark, thinking that word of large-scale, united training might reach across the border. He had his dispersed troops issued large amounts of carbine ammunition for target practice, had them endlessly drilled in columns of four at all gaits, ratcheted up their already stringent discipline, studied maps and spies' reports.

Near the village of Remolino, near Piedras Negras in Mexico, just south of Eagle Pass in Texas, there was a large Kickapoo encampment. Its inhabitants were quite accepted by the Mexicans there, for the tribe offered protection from other Indians, and traded in things stolen from the Americans. The camp was some sixty miles from Fort Clark. Mackenzie gathered his dispersed troopers at the Las Moras Creek in the early morning hours of May 17, 1873, and splashed over the Rio Grande with 360 enlisted men, 17 officers, 14 civilian guides, and a mule-drawn wagon train. With no infantry and no artillery, he was conducting an invasion of a neighboring country with which his own was not at war. It was boiling hot. Tremendous clouds of choking dust rose in the air. His column went along trails and cattle paths through dense canebrake and low chaparral, with always the possibility that an aroused citizenry, or Indians, or the *rurales* or *federales* of the Mexican military might fall upon the detested gringos. The 4th became dangerously strung out, with the overhanging chaparral clutching the loads of, and so impeding, the progress of the mules. Up at the front of his men, Mackenzie was not aware of the situation. No one wanted to tell him.

After hours on the march, mostly at a slow gallop or lope, through mesquite, prickly pear, cacti, and Spanish bayonet, he ordered a brief rest along a little stream. He was informed of the mule situation, that the pack train had been unable to keep up and was far behind. Three-Fingered Jack "exploded with a burst of profanity," one of his officers remembered, cursing his quartermaster for the "unworthy mules." He ordered that their loads be taken off and thrown away, but that first every man should fill his pockets with hard bread, while stuffing more in his shirt. He was about upon the Kickapoo village. The men were reminded to hold their horses well in hand and not to scatter out. "Mr. McLaughlin," he told a lieutenant, "you have the honor of opening the ball." The platoon galloped forward to discharge a carbine volley, then wheel out of the way for the next following while the men reloaded to go in again. "Left front into line!" Mackenzie shouted. "Gallop! March! Charge!" The Kickapoos, never expecting such an attack, ran off over corn and pumpkin fields, the firing American horsemen following as the rear troops set aflame the tribe's grass huts. Screams of Indian women and children mingled with the "yells of cheering troopers," an officer remembered, and the crack of carbines and the drumming of horse hooves. Captain R. G. Carter had been through the Civil War and had seen many charges, but this remained in his memory as the most disciplined and precise and successful one he ever knew.

The 4th's troopers slashed about, finding other outlying camps upon which to inflict the annihilation and destruction that Sheridan had ordered, their own casualties one soldier who would die, one whose arm a surgeon would amputate, and another who sustained a wound to the face. Dozens of warriors perished. The invaders went about their business for some six hours, using lit pampa plumes as torches to burn every habitation, and then in the afternoon gathered up forty Indian women with infants in their arms and put them on ponies to be taken away as hostages. They headed north from the scene of their assault. "Ruin and destruction marked the spot—a cyclone could not have made more havoc or a cleaner sweep up," Captain Carter wrote.

They rode all day and into the night, bright moonlight producing shadows frightening to half-asleep men's imaginations. Fatigued Indian women began to fall from ponies, and so Mackenzie had them lashed on with lariats, with their babies lashed to the women. From sleeplessness and strain, Carter remembered, the haggard and dust-covered faces of the soldiers took on a look "pallid and corpselike." The sun rose and brought stifling heat, and so when the riders came to water they soaked sponges in it for putting under their hats. Some who had gone without sleep for three nights "had hallucinations and showed signs of incipient insanity," becoming "depressed, excitable, irritable, morose and quarrelsome."

They got over the Rio Grande and to American soil and Fort Clark, having covered 160 miles with no sleep and only bread and water. From then on and for a long time it was said things were so quiet along the border that you could hear a pin drop. Mackenzie produced a peace that over the span of hundreds of years had eluded five nations: Spain, Mexico, the Republic of Texas, the Confederate States of America, and, until him, the United States. Editorials fulsomely praised the colonel, and the Texas Legislature formally tendered its thanks. "One of the most remarkable feats of arms in the history of our army," one historian has called his mission. The Kickapoo men came in to enter reservations, and their women and infants were restored to them. As late as 1958, Kickapoo mothers frightened stubborn children into obedience by threatening that if they were not good, Mackenzie would come and get them.

Mackenzie became a brigadier general, his services so in demand by local authorities all along the frontier that General Sherman, chief of the army, had to point out that he could not be everywhere. He served in New Mexico, Oklahoma, Utah, Wyoming, Arizona, Nebraska, and Colorado, commanding the 4th for twelve years. When in the wake of the disputed Hayes-Tilden presidential election it appeared that fighting might break out in Washington, the outgoing President Grant sent for Mackenzie to come east and take command of all troops in the capitol. In 1883 he was assigned to the command of the Department of Texas, with headquarters at San Antonio. His return to the scene of the great raid into Mexico was greeted with joy by the governing authorities and all of the population.

But he was not the man he had been. He complained of physical ills that seemed imaginary, and spoke in a bitterly wild manner of the War Department authorities in Washington who were unappreciative of his showings, saying he was persecuted if not indeed martyred. His outbursts of temper became more frequent: when his foxhound pack, which was trained to run wildcats and bears, instead attacked wild hogs, "the rage of the general was frightful! In the end the hounds suffered almost as much as the pigs," wrote Lieutenant James Parker. The erectness of carriage that had always characterized him despite his many old wounds vanished, and he seemed physically depleted. He told people that he had degenerated as a soldier, and said that if he had the courage he would blow his brains out. "He talked more like a crazy man than the commander of a splendid body of cavalry."

Someone who had always been a teetotaler began to drink, and declared himself a failure and a coward—"He was so worked up that he could hardly talk and had often to stop and collect himself," one of his officers, Richard Dodge, told his diary. Mackenzie had taken command of the Department of Texas in October 1883, and through November and early December was in such a state that his subordinates debated if it was liquor or insanity that afflicted him. On December 18 a man entered a San Antonio saloon, became violent, and when evicted went to a closed shop loudly to demand that he be sold a watch. When the proprietors refused to open the door, he went away threatening to get even. It was past midnight when he returned, banging on the shop walls so violently that crockery fell off shelves. One of the brothers who ran the place went out a back door and then around to the front and was confronted by a wild man holding a broken chair leg that he slammed into the shopkeeper's chest. Another brother came out to be joined by neighbors in beating the intruder into submission. Bleeding and with his clothing ripped, he was tied to a cart wheel. A gag was put in his mouth to halt his shouting.

The police were called. They instantly recognized Brigadier General Ranald Slidell Mackenzie, Commander of the Department of Texas. He was taken to his quarters, where he alternated rational speech with grandiose declarations that he was going to reorganize the country's armed forces. Telegrams to Washington described the situation to General Sheridan, chief of the army in succession to General Sherman, who replied that Mackenzie should be told the War Department wished to hear of his plans and that he should come east. He left San Antonio aboard a private railroad car in the company of a medical officer, two aides, an orderly, a civilian doctor who seemed able to control him, and his sister Harriet, who had been in charge of his household arrangements after the death of their mother.

He was taken to New York's Bloomingdale Asylum for the Insane at the Boulevard—now Broadway—and 117th Street. After observing him for two months, its superintendent, Dr. Charles H. Nichols, wrote Sheridan that the prognosis of recovery for the patient was "altogether unfavorable." A military retiring board was convened at the asylum on March 5, 1883, five months after Mackenzie's assignment to his high Texas post, some three months after his breakdown. Its presiding officer indicated the importance of the matter, for he was General Winfield Scott Hancock, Gettysburg hero, director of the execution of John Wilkes Booth's fellow conspirators, director of Grant's great funeral procession, former Democratic Party candidate for the presidency.

Mackenzie said, "I think that I am not insane. I think that I have served as faithfully as anybody in the army. I would rather die than go on the retired list. The army is all I have got to care for. I don't wish to stay here. I am treated very kindly by Dr. Nichols and Mrs. Nichols and many others." The board ruled him "lunatic and of unsound mind," and he was discharged from service, although he did not seem to realize it, faithfully writing the War Department of his future plans to go back to Texas and providing a current address, which was first in Morristown, New Jersey, and then at the home of a cousin in New Brighton, Staten Island, New York, where he was looked after by two attendants and his sister. He became very gentle, with neighborhood children "adoring him" as he turned no less childish than they. He was suffering from tertiary paresis, the final stages of syphilis. Unable to walk, oblivious to his surroundings, he died in January 1889. He was buried at the West Point cemetery just next to Hugh Judson Kilpatrick, Custer not far away. He was the exemplar of the Indian-fighting soldier, the perfect frontier cavalryman. Years later, during the Philippine Insurrection, the eminent General Henry W. Lawton, remembering earlier military days in the West, said, "Whenever I am in a tight place, whenever I am uncertain of what to do, I say to myself, 'What would Mackenzie do?'" One of Lawton's subordinates passing on his orders was known to say, "Mackenzie wants me to do this; I mean, Lawton."

In the year following his death, 1890, the government let it be known that the frontier had been closed, that now the hold of the United States reached from the Atlantic to the Pacific. That meant Indians had been driven back and hemmed in by gun and telegraph and railroad and barbed wire, and that now it was upon dreams, trances, and visions that they had to rely. The Paiute mystic Wovoka proclaimed that he had traveled to the next world to be told there that if the native peoples began to dance, and danced long enough, all would be as once it was, that their dead would return to life, the lost buffalo herds brought back and the whites sent away.

Across thousands of miles of vast space, tens and hundreds of thousands of Indians chanted, sang, and danced for hours and days, on and on. The Ghost Dance, whites called it. Newspapers back east erupted with headlines, and the army's horsed regiments were called upon to halt this terrifying display, with the 6th Cavalry's Second Lieutenant John J. Pershing, West Point 1886, among the junior officers called upon to do the job. From the moment of his arrival, after an endless swaying and bouncing trip along the rickety tracks of the Atchison, Topeka, and Santa Fe into what he called in letters home "the land of the burro, cactus, and tarantula," at his assigned destination of New Mexico's Fort Bayard of dusty parade ground, enlisted men's barracks, officers' quarters, flagpole, commissary, quartermaster's storehouse, and adjutant's office, reached by deposit at the railhead and then a day and a night sitting erect in a jolting stagecoach, Pershing loved the Western deserts and the army itself. He adapted at once to reveille, and stable call after breakfast, drills, garrison courts, general courts, guard mounting, rifle and pistol and sabre practice, jumping hurdles, dismounting to fight on foot, troop patrols with seeing to the "points," the flanks scouting to left and right in front of the column, trumpets sounding, bugles calling. Of course it came as a shock to a spit-and-polish former First Captain of the Corps of Cadets back at the Point to find one month after taking up his duties that every member of a before-daylight patrol he was to lead in a search for renegade Apaches under Chief Mangus was drunk, including the company first sergeant. But once away, the men turned earnest and soberly efficient. That night, in the Mongollon Mountains, the horses and the mules for the accompanying pack train stampeded and ran away. Perhaps coyotes frightened them; perhaps it was Indians. The cavalrymen were on foot in Indian country. They rounded up the animals and thereafter put on hobbles before loosing them to graze in the darkness. Not long afterward, the lieutenant came afoul of a mounted Indian, who clubbed him off his horse. Pershing's revolver flew to the ground when he fell unconscious. The Indian dismounted with the choice of seizing the weapon or dispatching with another blow or blows the future commander of America's forces in World War I. He opted to retrieve the weapon, remounted, and was gone. Yet what the government had done to the red man, Pershing wrote home, was a disgrace to a Christian nation. But he had his sworn duty to fulfill, and set about to join in herding those who performed the Ghost Dance into reservations where their ceremonies could be halted and they disarmed.

A detachment of the 7th Cavalry took charge of a band of Lakota Sioux under Big Foot and escorted them to the Pine Ridge Reservation and a camp at Wounded Knee Creek. The night of December 29, 1890, was intensely cold. Some of the soldiers had liquor with them. Some of the older ones had been with the elements of the 7th that were told to take up blocking positions while Custer charged with the main body fourteen years earlier, and Indians were asked if they had been there on that occasion, at the Little Big Horn. Chief Big Foot was very ill with pneumonia, and Custer's successor, Colonel James W. Forsyth, put him in a tent with a portable oven that would keep him warm, and sent an army surgeon to offer aid.

The soldiers were ordered to take all firearms from the captives. Disarmed, they would then in the next days be sent by rail to Omaha. There were some 350 Indians, men, women, and children. The 500 cavalrymen off their horses began prodding warriors to see if they had guns under their blankets. A deaf Indian did not understand their demands that he surrender his rifle, but asked payment for it. A fracas broke out. No one knows who fired the first shot, but at its report the soldiers opened up with their carbines and pistols. On slight rises above Wounded Knee Creek were four Hotchkiss guns, light artillery technological marvels for the times that discharged two-pound rounds bursting into fragments upon hitting the ground. They were capable of getting off shells at a rate of fifty per minute. Their gunners opened fire.

The masses of Indians ran, and the soldiers mounted up to chase them, some shouting, "Remember the Little Big Horn!" The 7th Cavalry chased Big Foot's people for up to five miles across the prairie, the Hotchkiss guns continuing to sound. Bodies lay everywhere. Some three hundred Lakota Sioux perished, and twenty-five soldiers, many taken by ordnance fired by their fellows. A blizzard descended upon what at the time was called the Battle of Wounded Knee but more latterly has been described as the massacre there, the term previously reserved for Indian doings now applied to those of the 7th Cavalry. The temperature dropped to forty below.

Several days passed before civilian burial parties hired by the army could extract from under snow the bodies of the Sioux dead. Many were frozen in their death throes, arms outflung or legs akimbo. Before being dropped into a mass grave, some were photographed, their grotesque appearances bringing grins to the observing soldiers seen in the background. Wounded Knee marked the end of the hundreds of years of warfare between the red man and the white. Only once thereafter were the army's horsemen called upon to deal with Indians. Seventeen years later, in 1907, a group of Ute children refused to go to school, and the 6th Cavalry, Pershing's old outfit, which he had long departed, was called to act as glorified truant officers enforcing attendance.

As the burial parties went about their work, they heard, four days and three nights after the shooting commenced, the cries of an infant. By a little hollow of rolling hill in prairie grasslands, a trooper had put two bullets into the breast of an Indian mother. She burrowed into the hollow to die there, her body shielding and sheltering her tiny daughter. The baby had on her wrist a bracelet, and wore moccasins. On her head was a hide cap decorated in beads with the American flag. An old woman of the Lakotas named her Zintkala Nuni, Lost Bird. An officer took away what the papers described as the "little heroine," the "little dusky maid" who was an "Indian princess," this "Ghost Dance baby." Adoption papers were filled out. She was raised according to the standards of middle-class Victorian life. But it was typical of her childhood that when her adoptive mother took her for a visit to the adoptive mother's hometown in Illinois, the local paper reported that "a dark little stranger" had come to town, her hair and features showing the "unmistakable traces of her race." When children jeered that her real mother was a dirty squaw, she attacked them with such ferocity that it was said she had reverted to savagery. She always loved to look at and handle her bracelet, cap, and moccasins, and as she grew up wanted to learn about Indians while never coming closer to one than the wooden statues commonly found in front of cigar stores. She liked to ride the circling painted carousel horses in the park for hours and had to be removed from them at the end of the day by force.

She did badly at school and was expelled from several. At sixteen she ran away and got work at a Wild West show. She made her way to reservations, but knowing nothing of the food, the manners, the music, the culture, she was unintentionally offensive. She talked at mealtimes, laughed too loudly, seemed pushy, forward, too forceful—like a white, the people said. Once at a reservation she stood in rain and mud screaming, "It's me, Lost Bird! Zintka Lanuni! Please help me!" When she said her name she mispronounced it, the Indian listeners noted. At seventeen she became pregnant and was sent to a reformatory. The baby was stillborn. At the Wounded Knee mass grave in which, somewhere, her mother lay, she flung herself down with arms outstretched, weeping. In Hollywood she played bit parts in silent Westerns depicting what had been, what had created her situation and that of all the others of her place and of her day—*The Round-Up, The Battle of the Red Men, War on the Plains.* She was married at various times to men who gave her a sexually transmitted disease and administered drunken beatings; she performed in Indian or cowgirl attire in saloons and dance-hall dives of San Francisco's Barbary Coast, lived in cheap places among the cribs of the red-light district, and was dead in 1920 at twenty-nine of heart problems complicated by venereal disease. She was buried in California. Seventy-one years later her decayed redwood coffin and its contents were taken from the ground and interred near the mass grave holding her mother, her relatives, the friends she would have had if all had been different. Hundreds came to the funeral on foot, in cars and pickups, on horses. Eighteen years before, in 1973, members of the American Indian Movement seeking national attention to what they saw as government mistreatment of those coming to be known as Native Americans had occupied for more than two months the site of what occurred when the 7th Cavalry dealt as it did with Big Foot's people. The occupiers were forced out by armed U.S. Marshals and National Guard contingents.

"Lost Bird has returned today to the same place she was taken from," the people at the funeral were told by Marie Not Help Him, great-granddaughter of Iron Hail, the last survivor of the Battle of the Little Big Horn, and a survivor of the massacre at Wounded Knee. Lost Bird was put into the ground with an eagle plume attached to a cherry tree by the coffin, hers the last interment of all those who lived the Cavalry versus the Indians, and died, too. The trill for bravery rose in the air: *Li-li-li-li-li!* Then the Indians performed the ceremony of the Releasing of the Spirit for one who had a foot in two camps but never a place to stand. By then, of course, in 1991, all were gone who for decades maintained their Order of the Indian Wars with get-togethers, publications, and the telling and retelling of their stories about their days out there in the West, the old soldiers, on their horses.

14

"No one ever came to grief—except honorable grief—through riding horses"

Just before the end of the American civil war, and during a few years afterward, the Europe that had been at peace since Waterloo witnessed three armed conflicts. King William I of Prussia had a brilliant chancellor, Bismarck, and a brilliant army leader, Moltke. In his service they rearranged the map of the Continent, and its political situation, amalgamating conquered territory into a Prussia become the German Empire. Denmark fell, Austria, and then France. The first two opponents presented little military challenge to the Prussians, and the third was dispatched with but moderate difficulty in the Franco-Prussian War of 1870–71.

The France of Napoléon III, "the nephew of the uncle," son of the Great Emperor's brother Louis, dreamed that it was heir to and incarnation of the country that had conquered half the world. There was a cult of worship for its former leader and for his stepdaughter, Hortense, Joséphine's child and Napoléon III's mother. The uniforms of France's army were virtually unchanged from those of the soldiers who had done so wondrously, nor were their tactics. That heavy cavalry had been ineffective in Russia was seen as an anomaly, with cadets at the cavalry school at Saumur instructed, so a visiting magazine writer noted, not only in the fashion of their predecessors serving in the Grande Armée, but in a manner that "savors of the romantic, for it is to a certain extent a connecting link between the era of the knight-errant, the cavalryman of medieval times, and the modern equestrian man-at-arms." Students replicated the tourney jousts of long before as part of their training, and felt quite at home in doing so: "The personnel of the cadets includes not a few whose ancestors wore the coat of mail and wielded the lance."

The young future officers of horse drilled with straight sword, curved sabre, carbine, pistol, and lance, putting the last at the gallop through a series of suspended discs with openings less than two inches in diameter, three of them in a run of one hundred yards. They practiced charging in such close formation that riders' boots touched one another, recorded the magazine writer. "The same precision is noted also in wheeling and oblique movements. One of the most picturesque features of the carousel is the charge of the entire command from end to end of the grounds, at the order bringing their horses instantly to a full stop within a foot or two of spectators' enclosure." The quoted description of cavalry doings at Saumur was written early in the twentieth century; but as late as 1917 West Point's cadets were taken on what were called staff rides, on horseback, to study the scenes of the events of the Battle of Gettysburg, while the trench warfare going on along World War I's Western Front received no mention in class.

Whatever the perfection of training for France's horsed soldiery, the riders were no match for Prussia's quick-firing field artillery and new infantry rifle, the breech-loading "needle gun." The French certainly cannot have studied anything that America had to teach, for they displayed nothing resembling Stuart-like delicacy in darting in and out, and even less the decoying and swirling tactics of Indians, but simply ploughed forward in mass formations reminiscent of the doomed Light Brigade charge at Balaklava and, even farther back, what had been seen in medieval days. A Prussian officer's reaction to what happened at Vionville was that although he was seeing the enemy's destruction, "as a cavalryman his heart bled at the sight of the absolute powerlessness of the brave French cavalry against the calm and stubborn infantry. The French Cuirassiers of the Guard, well mounted, well equipped, and capitally led, charged in excellent order and with the greatest possible exactness and courage.

"But their splendid horses fell in masses under the well-aimed fire. In a few minutes nothing remained of this magnificent regiment of cavalry but a few scattered troopers, who had scarcely succeeded in cutting down a single infantry soldier." At Gravelotte a similar scene brought from the watching King William of Prussia a cry of "Oh! The brave men!" At Sedan the French horsed contingents were annihilated: "de Galliffet's cavalry saved their honor, but had no influence whatever on the course of the battle."

Once and only once during the ten months' Franco-Prussian War was a cavalry move of importance, but that in the highest degree. The events at Mars-la-Tour are remembered as directly leading to victory for the Prussians, and for decades into the future were harked back to as an example of the immeasurable value of horsed operations. Early in the fighting a small Prussian contingent found itself in a position whose topography of blocking rivers and heights had the potential to create great problems for the French. If reinforced, Moltke's troops could divide France's main force and drive its segments into fortresses that could be surrounded and starved into submission. But the nearest Prussian reinforcements were a hard four hours' march away, and the French were present in overwhelming force.

The Prussians decided to brazen it out, and what artillery they had on the field at Mars-la-Tour opened upon the French as their bluffing infantry went in. The response to their effort was devastating. In tribute to the gunner who became the Great Emperor, France had always stressed artillery, and now their batteries poured down fire. An unstoppable infantry assault routing the slight Prussian force could be expected to follow. A holding action must inevitably fail, but perhaps a further bluff might succeed in buying time. There was a hard decision to be made, but the highest officer present took it. The plentitude of French guns, supported by massed footmen, were placed before a line of woods. "You must break through to the trees, Herr General!" a staff officer transmitting the orders of the Prussian field commander told the ranking cavalry officer.

"Break through to the trees?" asked Major General Frederick von Bredow in a tone described as "incredulous."

"The day's fortunes depend upon it," replied the officer. Some eight hundred riders were available to go in against greatly superior French infantry and artillery. Their support would be only what slight barrage could be mustered up from horse artillery devastated by the enemy. Bredow had served nearly forty years in his country's horsed units. He looked "like the stereotypical cavalry officer grown old in harness," and "glared out at the world from behind a formidably thick snow-white mustache," wrote the military historian Steven Eden. "He had no illusions as to the inevitable result of an unsupported cavalry charge against artillery and infantry in good order. But if he and his regiments were to be deliberately sacrificed, he was determined that they would not be lost in vain." Accompanied by a small escort, the general reconnoitered the terrain as far forward as he could while keeping out of sight of the French. He saw the possibility of using slight changes in elevation to deploy his riders while keeping them hidden from his enemy—there was a depression free of any significant obstacles where he could form up unobserved. Yet to get to his objective he must emerge from the hiding place to cover a mile of open ground while exposed to cannon and rifle fire.

He positioned his men with himself at their head and ordered a forward movement at the trot for the white-coated 7th Magdeburg Cuirassiers, who wore spiked helmets and thigh-length jackboots, and the 16th Altmark Uhlans, who wore dark-blue tunics, with black and white pennons fluttering from a forest of upraised lances. His few horse artillerymen raised a ragged cheer as he crested the protecting ridge. He went forward fifteen hundred yards to a slight embankment, took it, and put his riders into a gallop across level ground. It was a hot, sultry day. His firing batteries kicked up dust. It was difficult for the French to see what was approaching, but when the Prussians were some six hundred yards off, a French subaltern perceived the situation and told his section batteries to open fire. But a superior officer, convinced that the horsemen were French, immediately countermanded the order.

The riders crashed into the gun line. The battery commander died beneath a Prussian sabre; the artillerymen, unable to bring their guns to bear on the riders, were reduced to firing revolvers and swinging ramming staffs. Beyond the wreckage of the French line, the Prussians ran into batteries moving up in column. There was no time for unlimbering, and the Prussians plunged into the wagon train, soldiers using their lances as clubs. Some drivers whipped up their horses to get away and rushed into their own infantry, throwing the footmen into disarray. The fighting became entirely disordered, with soldiers fighting one on one with sabres, lances, and revolvers. The ground was covered with dead and wounded men and horses. French soldiers crouched behind artillery pieces to snipe at the Prussian horsemen. The commander of the 16th Uhlans lay wounded and pinned beneath his dead horse, ringed by the corpses of his lancers.

General von Bredow had accomplished his mission: he had forestalled, preempted, any devastating French blow, and soon Prussian reinforcements would be arriving, their coming to hold the line bound to force the splitting of France's armies and their dispersal into untenable positions. When he saw French cavalry approaching, he knew his force faced complete annihilation, and frantically searched for a trumpeter to sound the recall. For a time he could not find one, for they all seemed dead or disabled. When finally he got one, the man's horn had a bullet hole in it and could produce no sound other than a wail remembered as sounding "like the shriek of a banshee." But of their own accord, horsemen began disengaging to head back to where they had begun their charge. As they went away, French rifles and cannons poured fire into their backs. General von Bredow's horse was done in after the charge followed by the frenzied melee, and he "was barely able to goad his exhausted beast forward." A French cuirassier took in the situation and rode forward with a raised sabre, "prepared to deliver a killing blow." But a Prussian dropped to one knee, raised his rifle, and toppled the cuirassier with a single shot.

The fight at Mars-la-Tour saw casualties for Prussian riders of fifty percent, with nearly sixty percent of the horses dead. It is remembered as Von Bredow's Death Ride. And yet: "It is no exaggeration to say that the resolute charge of eight hundred horsemen not only altered the outcome of a battle and a war, but also the course of European history."

For soon the Prussian army was marching down the Champs-Élysées, and in the Palace of Versailles the German Empire came into being. Napoléon III, released from detention by Bismarck, went to join his wife the empress in English exile. Eugénie had run away half a mile, through the halls of the Tuileries and the Louvre, past statues of Egyptian pharaohs and Louis XIV paintings, to a waiting cab for hire and a Channel ship, terrified that the Parisian mobs revolting against her husband and the lost war would do to her what they had done to Marie Antoinette, a fate she had always strangely feared as likely even during the greatest days of the Second Empire. That her skirts would be pulled up and everybody would see everything was her nightmare. When her husband died, in 1873, their son, Louis-Napoléon, the Prince Imperial, whose riding lessons began at eighteen months so that he was able in miniature uniform to sit a pony at reviews when he was three, was named Napoléon IV. The former empress was more than excessively strict with her son in matters financial, doling out so little money that he could not accept invitations for stays at friends' country houses for lack of funds to tip the servants, and when in 1879 he joined a British force operating along the Blood River in Zululand, the privately owned saddle on his horse was of the cheapest make. (Prime Minister Disraeli was against letting him go, but Eugénie appealed to Queen Victoria, who approved, and Disraeli gave in, saying no man could oppose two women.) The potential heir to France's throne and the members of a mounted patrol were off their horses and lounging about on the ground, discussing the campaigns of the Great Emperor, when from six-foot-high grasses a band of natives burst upon them.

Spears flashed. The British officer in command leaped into the saddle, clapped spurs into his horse, and ran for it. The patrol followed. The Prince Imperial had one foot in a stirrup when his horse panicked and shied. He ran alongside, clinging to a leather. A trooper rode by, yelling, "Sir, for God's sake get mounted!"

His horse, Fate, was bolting. He grabbed the pommel with his left hand and vaulted up. He was nearly aboard when the pommel broke. It was hardly more than paper. He went down on his face, grass filling his mouth. The horse ran after the vanishing patrol. He got up, his right arm useless. Zulu war cries sounded. He ran a few

Lieutenant Churchill of the 4th Hussars.

steps, turned to face the natives, pulled out his revolver with his left hand, and walked toward them slowly, firing. A spear lodged in his leg. He pulled it out and attacked. The next day the British found Napoléon IV lying naked on his back. He was twenty-three.

A gallant and glorious death—for all seventeen spear wounds were in the front. Most regrettable, of course, but of a nature to be taken as constituting "only a sporting element in a splendid game," remembered a subaltern of a few years later serving with England's 4th Hussars in India. These things would happen, the former junior officer wrote long afterward, "in the little wars of Britain in those vanished light hearted days," "this kind of war filled with fascinating thrills" that saw an officer of Her Majesty's Forces in a sola topee doing his bit against the Fuzzy Wuzzies or the Wogs under a tropical sun and in exotic places so that more and more of the map would show the red indicating the Empire's domains—a third of the world eventually. One scattered the natives with a volley and an *arme blanche* charge which would add another faraway name to the regimental colors.

As a Royal Military College cadet the subaltern had yearned to be a cavalry officer: "Horses were the greatest of my pleasures at

Sandhurst. I and the group in which I moved spent all our money in hiring horses from the very excellent local livery stables. We organized point-to-points and even a steeplechase in the park of a friendly grandee, and bucketed gaily about the countryside.

"And here I say to parents, especially to wealthy parents, 'Don't give your son money. As far as you can afford it, give him horses.' No one ever came to grief—except honorable grief—through riding horses. No hour of life is lost that is spent in the saddle." And if, he went on, you break your neck at a gallop, it "is a very good death to die." He got his queen's commission and an assignment to India in 1895. His father was on his deathbed. The last words of Lord Randolph Churchill, son of the Duke of Marlborough, were a question regarding his son Winston's imminent dispatch out to the Raj, the jewel in the Empire's crown: "Have you got your horses yet?"

The young man about to turn twenty-two sailed through the Mediterranean and the Canal and out to the East and a "gay and lordly life," dining at the 4th Hussar mess of twenty or thirty officers off a table bearing plate and trophies gathered by the unit's two hundred years of sport and campaigning. "In an all-pervading air of glitter, affluence, ceremony and veiled discipline, an excellent and lengthy dinner was served to the strains of the regimental string band," Churchill remembered. Officers wore uniforms adorned with gold cord and gold-braided epaulets, feathers on the headgear, choker collars, sashes, buttons, sword with gold braided knot and heavily filigreed guard, elaborately done-up sleeves, shining boots, gleaming spurs and smart gauntlets, the scarlet jacket featuring facings of the regiment's colors. They were serving in the heyday of the British race. The Queen-Empress was head of the family to half the world's monarchs, the British pound the world's standard for currency, the City of London the world's banker and insurer, the iron and coal and railroads unchallenged anywhere. At the very top of the imperial social structure, above any manufacturer or anyone "in trade," stood the officers of Her Majesty's Forces, which had won and now kept secure the Empire. Each regiment of the army had a defined and recognized position, and those of the cavalry ranked with and sometimes even above those of the Guards. Cavalry officers affected an inability to pronounce the letter r. It was always the "wegiment." Their pass-by of blue and gold and scarlet and steel showed "a broad and scintillating flood" in exercises and reviews, which Lieutenant Churchill loved: "There is a thrill and a charm of its own in the glittering jingle of a cavalry squadron maneuvering at the trot; and this deepens into joyous excitement when the same evolutions are performed at a gallop. The stir of the horses, the clank of their equipment, the thrill of motion, the tossing plumes, the sense of incorporation in a living machine, the suave dignity of the uniform—all combine to make cavalry drill a fine thing in itself."

He remembered always in later years the "beautiful intricacy of archaic maneuvers" when shifting from column into line, with at the divisional level thirty or forty squadrons wheeling to form a front through clouds of dust to commit to the charge. One could hardly help letting off a joyous shout. His salary was 120 pounds a year, and his mother settled upon him another 500, the total almost but not quite sufficient—for yearly he ran up new debts—to live in a splendid bungalow on a luxurious cantonment with a garden and magnificent flowers while seen to by squads of people overseen by butler in the house and head groom in the stables. Servants pulling ceiling fans, palms in brass urns, silver candelabra, fire jugglers in the garden, pig sticking and cricket and race meets—"Princes could live no better than we," said Churchill. (It is recorded of an officer of higher rank than Churchill, and greater finances as son of the founder of the Scotch whiskey firm still bearing the family name, Major Douglas Haig of the 7th Hussars, that on field exercises he moved about followed by a dozen to a score of bearers, grass cutters, sweepers, cooks, stable boys, launderers, water boys—plus two or three generations of their families riding in his bullock-drawn wagons, with strings of elephants to carry gear, including tables and chairs, wines, carpets, and lounge chairs.)

Each day in camp, Churchill wrote, the evening shadow, indicating that the murderous sun was become less potent, proclaimed the Hour of Polo. "The prince of games. Of emperors." Major Haig certainly would have agreed, for he excelled at that, with his 7th Hussars fielding the crack team of the British army, winners of the Inter-Regimental Cup four years running. Offered as a lieutenant a place on a British team scheduled to play against an American contingent at Newport, Rhode Island, he joined in a slaughter, the visitors winning by scores of 10–4 and 14–2. No one was ever more the cavalry officer than Douglas Haig. Undisturbed by any interest in art, the theater, food, liquor, cards, or reading unconnected with his studies, he was the outstanding Sandhurst cadet of his day, the number one man in his class and Senior Under-Officer, the highest honor the school offered. "A Scottish lad, Douglas Haig, is tops in almost everything," an instructor said, "books, drill, riding and sports; he is to go into the cavalry and before he is finished he will be top of the army." Horses had always been his main interest in life. Before going to Sandhurst he had for a time matriculated at Oxford, arriving with a string of polo ponies. On the evening of his first day there he discussed with another entering student what the longtime head of Brasenose College had said to each when first meeting him. "Drink plenty of port, sir," the other boy was told. "You want port in this damp climate." To young Douglas, the man said, "Ride, sir, ride. I like to see the gentlemen of Brasenose in top boots."

Reserved, controlled, entirely self-contained, and never in his life possessing anything approaching a close friend, never going about in society and never dancing, solitary, aloof, alone, an unflinching look on his extremely handsome face, always polite and always a gentleman while unconcerned with the views of others, Douglas Haig was esteemed by all who met him as the most inarticulate person they had ever met, the complete meaning of his mumbled half-sentences begun and never finished intelligible only to those who had been long in his company. (His was not a type unfamiliar to those acquainted with persons deeply involved with horses. Such often do better with animals than with people.) Haig seemed almost the exemplar of the laugh-producing stage version of the fumbling British aristocrat. That others saw him so would have meant less than nothing to him, preoccupied with his work as he was and enrolling himself in Camberley's Staff College back in England, a move unusual for England's cavalry officers of the period, who almost to a man took dash and daring as quite sufficient for success. In the officers' mess it was forbidden to discuss women, religion, and politics. But the supreme prohibition was against talking "shop."

There must be no mention of anything relating to work, such as it was. To do so was to identify oneself as kin to the scrubs, swats, and smugs who spent their free time back in boarding school discussing geometry or irregular verbs. What was important was to have what was called the Cavalry Spirit that had proved decisive on the Indian plains at Gujarat and Shabkard, and in a hundred other fights. That spirit was expressed by being of course good at polo, and doing well at horse shows and in the hunting field. One had to be a fellow who would never let the regiment down and who was willing to die, if that proved necessary, like a gentleman, with sabre in hand and face to the enemy. Queen's Commissioned Officers, and for Britain's separate Indian Army, Viceroy's Commissioned ones, knew about billiards, tennis, making a good showing at steeplechases at the Turf Club, winning as if they were used to it and losing as if it did not matter. Playing the game. The day's work was usually concluded by eleven o'clock in the morning. Officers had almost no direct contact with the enlisted personnel—"other ranks" in British parlance—who were seen to by the sergeants. In fact, the officer could hardly speak to a private, for they shared not the slightest bond of experience. (Whatever his shortcomings, Haig was astute enough to comprehend that apart from his inarticulate manner of speech he possessed an utter inability to communicate with troopers who were the sweepings of British life, slum dwellers and the sons of rural poverty: it is recorded that never in his life did he say a single word to an other rank.)

In 1898 both Major Haig and Lieutenant Churchill were gazetted to the Anglo-Egyptian force outfitting for service against the Khalifa's forces in Sudan, the River War along the Nile in which Great Britain would paint the area red on the world's maps and avenge the death of General Charles "Chinese" Gordon at the hands of the fanatical Khalifa's predecessor, Allah's Servant the Mahdi, who had hung his vanquished opponent's severed head above the palace at Khartoum. The lieutenant was attached to the 21st Lancers, and as Bimbashi Haig Bey temporarily in Egyptian service, the major to the command of a squadron of conscripted fellahin cavalrymen more used to camels and donkeys than horses. Instructing them as best he could in the Cavalry Spirit, he joined with them and the others in going up against the Khalifa's vast horde of robed warriors, who in tone, weapons, outlook, and hatred for the infidel differed little from those who had opposed the Crusaders. Rows of gorgeous white-and-yellow standards danced above the dervishes, and sunlight glinted off their waving swords while their elephant-tusk trumpets sounded and their war drums rolled.

The contending forces met at Omdurman, across the Nile from Khartoum. The Khalifa had sixty thousand men whose glittering spears and upraised banners reminded Churchill of what he had seen when viewing the Bayeux Tapestry. The British had twenty thousand soldiers backed up against the river, which held some gunboats able to join with the field artillery in shelling the enemy, white balls of smoke rising from where a round hit with, after a pause, the dull thud of a distant explosion. Churchill sat his horse near the 32nd Field Battery, whose officers were standing on biscuit boxes to study with field glasses the effect of their work. The dervishes came on, their tremendous yelling like the tumult, he thought, of the rising wind and sea before a storm, and as a troop commander the lieutenant moved forward with his regiment at a walk to meet them, speeding up when trumpets sounded the trot. The sound of artillery rounds screaming overhead mingled with the jingling and clattering of the riders, he remembered, who when the trumpets called for right wheel into line broke into a gallop. The officers of all sixteen troops of the 21st Lancers unsheathed their swords, but Churchill was nursing an injured shoulder, and when he tried to raise his, he knew he couldn't use it. He returned it to its scabbard—"not the easiest thing to do at a gallop"—and drew a Mauser automatic pistol from its holster.

The regiment locked up into a long galloping line, the polish of peace missing from the horses hung all over with water bottles and extra saddlebags, and the men bent over to protect their eyes from the dust. They came within 250 yards of the dervishes. To these the British were enemies of God, infidels, the accursed; to the British their opponents were barbarians and savages—a division of views seen for a thousand and more years. The 21st Lancers and the others rocketed forward, their large-scale and full-gallop and close-order rush to Churchill's memory magnificent: "Nothing like the Battle of

Omdurman will ever be seen again. It was the last link in the long chain of all those spectacular conflicts whose vivid and majestic splendor has done so much to invest war with glamour."

The riders were what the lieutenant described as "a half polo field" away from a band of crouching enemies, the long dancing lances of the other ranks lowered. (A polo analogy quite expectedly also came into the mind of Douglas Haig: the whole business at Omdurman, he remarked, was very like a prolonged chukker, the plunging horses and dust.) Of a sudden from a depression similar to a sunken road, new masses of dervishes rose up to confront the 21st Lancers. From this crease in the ground, a dry watercourse, a *khor*, they sprang up twelve deep "like magic."

The Lancers increased their speed, knowing that they must crash into and then through, to pull up, turn about and come again. Churchill felt no fear. Ordinary life, he said in later days, reflecting upon a career of extraordinary ups and downs, was much like a cavalry charge. "So long as you are all right, firmly in your saddle, your horse in hand, and well armed, lots of enemies will give you a wide berth. But as soon as you have lost a stirrup, have a rein cut, have dropped your weapon, are wounded, or your horse is wounded, then is the moment when from all quarters enemies rush upon you.

"Such was the fate of not a few of my comrades in the troops immediately on my left. Brought to an actual standstill in the enemy's mass, clutched at from every side, stabbed at and hacked at by spear and sword, they were dragged from their horses and cut to pieces by the infuriated foe." He himself with some other Lancers got through to halt and then turn. Suddenly a dervish sprang up among the riders. "How he got there I do not know. He must have leaped out of some scrub or hole.

"All the troopers turned upon him thrusting with their lances, but he darted to and fro causing for the moment a frantic commotion. Wounded several times, he staggered towards me raising his spear. I shot him at less than a yard. He fell on the sand, and lay there dead. How easy to kill a man!" The victim of Churchill's Mauser was one of the eleven thousand of the Khalifa's men slain when, with all the pride and might of the Dervish Empire on display for the last great day of its existence, it went to its doom against the weaponry of the Industrial Age. British-Egyptian losses amounted to a few hundred. The Highlanders' pipes sounded, and the drums and fifes, as the infantry went in to mop up: a thrilling sight, ensigns up, sunlight on the bayonets. Yet Lieutenant Churchill did not forget the men and horses of his troop slightly wounded from spear thrusts or sword cuts, and, worse, "horses spouting blood, struggling on three legs, men staggering on foot, men bleeding from terrible wounds, fish-hook spears stuck right through them, arms and faces cut to pieces, men gasping, crying, collapsing, expiring." But the Union Jack floated where once the desert hawks had circled the decapitated head of General Gordon; and the maps were colored red.

Both Haig and Churchill in a little while went out to South Africa, where those of Dutch background contended with the British in what would be called the Boer War. The fighting brought Churchill fame for the adventures he chronicled, first in newspaper articles and then in books. Haig drew from it a great sense of disquiet. He realized that the British had been fortunate at Omdurman for having enemies so ill armed, and officered not by logic but by religious faith. In South Africa he saw Boer farmers running rings around those who thought that British pluck and what was good enough for Wellington would serve in the modern world. One embarrassment after another darkened London until General Sir John French, commanding the Cavalry Division, came with a dashing rush to the relief of the besieged town of Kimberley in one of the great moments of Victorian England. As cavalry chief of staff, Haig issued concise outlines for the movement and disposition of the horsemen, as quick and accurate with his written orders as he was fumbling and inarticulate when called upon to speak. Sir John French was acclaimed as the greatest British cavalryman since Cromwell, but even then Haig esteemed him as something other than that, and even then perhaps foresaw that Sir John's star would never again burn so brightly. In the winding-down of the far from glorious war, Haig oversaw the work of six mounted columns rounding up rebellious Boers in Cape Colony, and then was given the colonelcy of the 17th Lancers, the Death or Glory Boys for their skull-and-bones insignia, among whose battle streamers was one for the doomed charge at Balakclava: men of the regiment had been among the brave six hundred.

Haig went to India with the rank of acting major general accompanying the post of Inspector of Indian Cavalry. Traveling in a special railroad car attached to regular trains, he had himself dropped off at cavalry posts he then toured on one of his several mounts, Knight of the Deccan being his favorite, whose comfort he always assured at the end of each day before seeing to his own. He studied in the most methodical manner the disputed issues of the cavalry of the day: whether the rifle was superior to the carbine, the lance to the sword, whether it was better to cut with the latter or to thrust. The most hotly contested question was the ancient and never-ending one of whether horsemen should be swiftly brought to a point of contact with the enemy and then dismounted to fight on foot, or if they should stay horsed and deliver the classic shock-action blow. In short, should they be dragoons or not. No army ever completely decided the matter, but the tendency in all European forces was to favor the all-out mounted charge. The eminent cavalry authority Sir Evelyn Wood certainly held that view. The year before Omdurman, in a book on his subject he asked readers to imagine the effect upon themselves if they saw a runaway horse coming at them. Two summers earlier, he wrote, a horse pulling a hansom cab without a driver ran down Pall Mall and collided with the lamppost at the foot of St. James Street. It was a cast-iron pole sunk two or three feet in earth, and protected by four short pedestals of solid stone. The lamppost was broken off, and half the pedestals uprooted. If such drive and power could be inspired by a cab banging at its heels in a horse one step removed from those pulling a plough, what could be expected of a trained cavalry mount who had a trained soldier on board with a fearsome weapon in hand? No matter the defense, Sir Evelyn said, the gathered charge does not fail.

Additionally, cavalrymen largely felt, it was absurd even to think of a brilliantly garbed rider off-mounting to crawl along the ground infantry-style in his high boots, elaborate headgear, and protective cuirass, his sabre on its sword-belt dragging in the dust or mud behind him. No. The place of the horseman was on top of a horse. Leaders rode horses, the king, the emperor, the tsar. They dressed the part. Save for country shooting parties in plus fours and Norfolk jacket, with gamekeepers driving the game into range of their guns, or perhaps a yacht outing in blue blazer, white slacks, and naval cap, they rarely wore anything but military uniform. Germany's emperor, William—Kaiser Wilhelm II—had four hundred uniforms from his own regiments and other countries of whose units he was honorary colonel, those of his cousin Nicky, Nicholas II, the tsar, and his cousin Georgie, the king of England, George V, both of whom had available for ceremonial occasions the attire of cousin Willy's regiments dating back to deployment by Seydlitz and the Great King. And, of course, the most glorious were those worn by mounted units.

Wearing such, one million horsemen were among those taking the field when the Great War, the World War, came in 1914. Field Marshal Sir John French led Britain's army over the Channel, with Douglas Haig serving under him as one of the British Expeditionary Force's two corps commanders. In its earliest stages along the Western Front, the deployed cavalry units of the Germans skirmished against those of the French and the British, the latter shocked at the lack of what was called horsemastership, care of the animals, by their ally's riders. It was a matter for court-martial proceedings in the Empire's forces if a man was found to have sat his horse for more than ten minutes during a march break. Their horses were not easy chairs, troopers were forcibly informed. Girths must be loosened. If the break looked as if it was going to take a while, doctrine decreed that saddles be removed so that mounts could roll if so they desired, and freely graze if grass was available. The French seemed less painstaking, and it was said one could smell their mounted units' approach for the horses' galled backs.

But such issues became academic after a matter of weeks, for the contending forces of the opponents each sidestepped head-on conflict so that for four hundred miles, from the Swiss border to the North Sea, lines of trenches, barbed wire, and concrete-fortification machine-gun nests formed. Untold tons of artillery rounds exploded down to make of the no man's-land between the enemies a pockmarked surface of great holes and depressions seen to resemble those of the moon shining down, if the clouds of gas and detonations permitted. Horses could never get through that. They lingered behind the lines, in time one hundred thousand of them for Great Britain

according to one account, as for four and a half years the allies
sought to break a hole in Germany's defenses so that they could gallop forward, quickly spread out to attack the enemy's supply lines
and devastate his rear areas, sabre down his artillerymen, dislocate
him, do, in short, on a grand scale what Bredow did at Mars-la-Tour
on a small one.

The occasion never arose, although Douglas Haig, raised to
command in place of the pushed-aside John French, never ceased
hoping that it would. He oversaw the muddy death and destruction that lives in our thoughts as typifying and defining World War
I while maintaining the demeanor of the coolly competent officer
of horse, steady, unexcited. He wore flared riding breeches, boots
with spurs, and a shining leather Sam Browne belt, as did his officers, and went about with a cane or a swagger stick. When in 1917
the Americans came, their leader, John J. Pershing, once of the 6th
Cavalry back in New Mexico, and of the 10th in Cuba, appeared to
the eye almost Haig's mirror image, complete with carefully tended-
to brush mustache, although actually their personalities were quite
different, Pershing being far more human, capable of displays of
humor and deep emotion. He brought no cavalry to Europe. The
very dangerous shipping problems attendant to crossing the U-boat-
infested Atlantic precluded doing so, for every vessel departing the
States required destroyer escorts, and every inch of space for cargo,
human or materiel, was precious. Horses would have required too
much room. American purchasing agents spent fabulous sums to buy
them from European sellers for pulling guns and supply and equipment wagons, and General Pershing was almost fanatically attentive
to their care, saying each was worth its weight in gold. He personally put out money for two he could ride on inspection tours behind
the lines or even up to them, and if he found a stable sergeant of his
field artillery deficient in grooming, feeding, watering, or bedding
duties, the repercussions were severe.

After the initial weeks preceding the stalemate in France and
Belgium, horses were never again involved in cavalry deployment,
but losses among draft animals were dreadful in the long days of
those red years, as Churchill called them, likening Haig to a surgeon
intent upon the operation while removed in his professional capacity

from the agony of the patient or the anguish of the patient's relations. At Verdun, where for ten months the lifeblood of the Teuton and the Gaul poured out as the enmity from centuries past found its ultimate expression, a single German artillery round killed ninety-four corralled French horses. Cavalry did nothing along the Western Front, and played but a subsidiary role in another theater of operations of the Great War, out in the limitless reaches where Imperial Russia confronted the Germans and the Austro-Hungarians.

Dismally backward, corrupt, short of money, and with supply systems incapable of doing anything approaching competent work, the tsar's army yet had a vast force of cavalry, more than a quarter of a million riders and horses. Many were stationed along the flat, wet, dreary, impoverished, thinly settled frontier in what had been and would be again an independent country but now was partitioned Poland. Within half an hour of the declaration of war, mounted units crossed the border. Many of the enlisted personnel were from Russia's easternmost provinces, descendants of the Mongols, whose horsed expeditions had once terrified the world. When they put their horses into a charge, they emitted an eerie scream reminiscent of what their ancestors' victims likely heard: *Urii! Urii!*

Their officers were of European and not Asiatic background and, as almost uniformly of noble birth, adhered to the viewpoints of their similarly titled counterparts in the armies of all the great powers of the day, disdaining involvement in the study of explosives or communications devices such as field telephones, the telegraph, and the heliograph. Such matters were beneath them. "A good cavalry officer," they believed, remembered Vladimir S. Littauer, who in 1913 was commissioned a cornet in the Sumsky Hussars, a regiment dating back to 1651, "should be a good rider and swordsman, be smartly turned out and be able, above all, to lead a charge and die for Faith, Tsar and Country if necessary. We believed that we would charge bravely when the time came, and that nothing else would matter very much." Russia maintained three instruction centers for future horse officers. Boys entered cadet school at the age of ten or eleven, stayed there until they were seventeen or eighteen, then went to one of the three centers for a two-year course. Littauer's was the Nicholas Cavalry School in Saint Petersburg, known as the Glorious

School, or just the School. Its sergeant major was alluded to as the God of the Earth of the Glorious School. Under his tutelage officer-aspirants went through such drills as the one requiring that while mounted and moving, they unbuckle their girth, pull off the saddle to hold in their left arms, and then jump fences, a class required to do so in perfect uniformity, as one man. For individual display of riding prowess, special eight-inch-long heavy iron spurs were awarded, great ceremony attending the presentation. The uniform had a black jacket with two rows of brass buttons, wide apart near the shoulder epaulets and close together at the red-and-black striped belt. For parade occasions a plastron—breastplate—was buttoned on. The breeches were dark blue with red piping; the boots were black. In warm months students wore red caps with no visors, and in winter black leather-and-metal shakos, with tall plumes added for parades.

The younker—student—found physical exercise stressed, with no indulgence in any sport that was not of a purely military nature. (An attempt to introduce football, what Americans call soccer, failed. No one would play, Littauer remembered.) Littauer and his fellows were schooled in riding of what was called the menege type—dressage—with horses moving in high elegant steps, neck arched and head brought in. They also worked at what was called the Italian method, with shortened stirrups and the body inclined forward and out of the saddle when jumping hurdles. The most rigid discipline was enforced when a unit performed evolutions, for otherwise a troop's horses might end up as scattered as a handful of dried peas dropped to the floor. "A romantic attitude towards the picturesque battles of the past still prevailed among us. The stress was still on fighting in the saddle," Littauer wrote.

Graduated and commissioned, the cornet reported to the Sumsky Hussars. Its enlisted personnel, like all the Russian army's mounted men, were issued a sword, a lance, and a rifle, its officers a sword and a revolver. The latter's most important status symbol was the epaulet. Tsarist code decreed that anybody tearing one from an officer's shoulder must be killed to protect the honor of the uniform, and if this was not done it was incumbent upon the officer to kill himself. So besides his sabre, Littauer always carried a small

Browning pistol. (He could not have foreseen, in those last waning days of the old order soon to give way to war and revolt, that the day would come when in the streets of Saint Petersburg, and Berlin also, those of the lower classes, known in Russia as the Dark People, would seize officers and with metal nails hammer their epaulets into their shoulders.) The young hussar had an orderly and a batman. He dined with his fellows at the officers' mess from a table with a silver punch bowl decorated with enameled medallions showing mounted soldiers of the regiment in actions of the past. The bar offered vodka, hors d'oeuvres, ham, *pirozhkies*—varied appetizers— smoked fish, hot and cold meats. "Keeping up of what one believed to be the prestige of the regiment was a full-time occupation," he remembered. "To look and act like a hussar from the ballads was my consuming ambition. The hussars of the songs and verses charged with drawn swords all day and drank all night sitting around the campfire."

Kaiser Wilhelm once proclaimed that he would hold innocent an officer seeing fit to cut down with his sabre a civilian deemed insufficiently respectful of rank and uniform, and a similar viewpoint reigned in the world Littauer now inhabited. To punish an enlisted-man hussar who misbehaved in a civilian situation "was not the business of the silly police and the yet sillier courts," for the regiment would take care of the matter in its own manner. August 1914 and the war came, and the Russian cavalry went forward, odd-numbered hussar regiments riding blacks, evens aboard grays, dragoons on chestnuts, and uhlans on bays. Littauer's enlisted soldiers had blue dolmans with yellow braid (gold for officers), brick-red breeches, and red-blue-and-yellow pennons fluttering from lance tips. Their mounts had entered active service at around five years of age, after two years of training. The early days of the war saw them showing in the fashion depicted in paintings of the previous century, hussars beginning a charge at the trot with lances resting on their thighs at an upward angle of forty-five degrees, gun batteries advancing to take up position. "Swords out, slope lances, gallop, march!" Half the men, those in front, lowered their lances parallel to the ground. Once used on an enemy, they were to be dropped as riders drew swords to join with the men behind them who from the first had unsheathed theirs.

But war proved very different from the drills of peacetime. The Sumsky Hussars got rid of curb bits and rode on snaffles, and abandoned the practice of riding with rifles across their backs, attaching them to saddles instead. The horses hardly ate as they had in the past, for the wretched Russian supply system almost entirely failed to provide feed, and so men fed them barley, sawdust cakes, heather, twigs, pieces of trees, and the thatching of Polish and Lithuanian peasant cottages, which brought on stomach and intestinal problems because of the fungus and mold ingested. There was a shortage of iron, caulks, and coal for the field forges, so animals were shod poorly or not at all. And time had left behind the classic notions of war with which the soldiers had been brought up, for they faced rapid-firing artillery and machine guns, against which no charge could succeed. Littauer remembered his unit dismounted and pinned down by German fire and the regimental commander shaking his fists at the enemy, exclaiming, "If only we could get *to* you!"

So as with the Western Front, the fighting in the East found cavalry use impractical. It was quite different in a third area of operations.

15
The Desert Mounted Corps

Edmund Allenby was a descendant of Oliver Cromwell, and like his ancestor, an officer of British cavalry. Yet it was a calling for which he seemed unsuited. His main interest all his life was the study of birds and plants. He liked poetry and travel. He himself said that his "martial ardor" was never very intense but instead "a somewhat feeble flicker." Tall and bulky, his lifelong nickname the Bull, he did not show well on horseback, his weight and physical characteristics making him something other than a lithe, stylish rider. He would have been better cast as a reclusive scholar, said those who knew him.

Yet this aesthete possessed a temper that made him when aroused seem almost insane. A subordinate dithering or hesitating in answering a question produced in a moment a roaring Allenby, who waved his cane or swagger stick and threatened to hit the man. Officers actually fainted as he screamed at them, and there are recorded instances of their becoming sick to their stomachs from his verbal assaults. The Bull was as unpopular with enlisted men as with commissioned ones, not least for his mania about troopers using the chinstraps of their headgear. Up to the beginning of the twentieth century, the line of a chinstrap on a sunburned face was the mark of a soldier, but fashions change, and men found them tiresome. That held no water with Allenby. God Himself could not protect the

Lord Allenby of the Seventh
Crusade.

trooper who, holding a sabre, additionally used his hand to keep his
cap from flying off his head.

For all his mad rages, Allenby was seen as an outstanding
and far-seeing cavalry leader for whom no detail was unimportant. Like Haig, he rose to high positions in India and in South
Africa, and went to the European War as commander of the British
Expeditionary Force's six thousand riders. During the short weeks
before the Western Front solidified into trench warfare, he cleverly
screened the retreat of the infantry and the artillery giving way to
the far greater numbers of the German right wing. Then the cavalry permanently went to the rear, and it seemed to Allenby as he
viewed the quagmire of wire and machine guns that characterized
modern war in France and Belgium that perhaps the role of the
horse in battle was finished. That was a viewpoint with which Haig
did not concur, holding as he did that "the role of cavalry on the
battlefield will always go on increasing" and that bullets had "little

stopping power against the horse." The opposing concepts caused, along with other disagreements, a perceptible coolness between the two men. But the War Office back in London esteemed Allenby, and he was named commander of Britain's Third Army, showing general-ship of a much higher order than usual in a stalemated situation where such was rarely found. His temper remained as it had always been. An up-front high officer in a war featuring "château gener-als," he once went into an instant fury when on a trench inspection tour he came across the body of a slain soldier wearing a cap, not a helmet. Someone offered the opinion that it was wrong to speak ill of the dead—"which did not help matters." The incident became widely known all through the BEF and was taken as definitive proof that Sir Edmund, as now he was, was a rigid martinet, a Thud and Blunder brass hat. Nobody was sorry when he was transferred out of the French-Belgian theater of operations.

General Allenby's new posting was to Cairo, where British inter-ests required protection of the Suez Canal from Germany's allies of the Ottoman Empire, and, if possible, conclusion of Sublime Porte participation in the war. If the sultan threw in the towel, Bulgaria could immediately be expected to follow suit, and then Austria-Hungary. That would leave Germany exposed and friendless. Turkey's forces, as befitted what was called the Sick Man of Europe, were but intermittently formidable, and were stiffened with German and Austrian detachments, with Berlin's officers entirely dominating the higher echelons—the number of German staff officers sixty-nine, and Turks, nine. Upon his arrival at Ismailia station in June 1917, as he walked along the platform, Allenby came under the gaze of Britain's liaison officer with Arabs opposing the Turks. Lawrence of Arabia perceived "a very large and superior general, this heavy, rubicund man." When the new commander entered his office for the first time, he was handed a sheaf of written reports. He glanced at them for a moment and then pitched the pile into a far corner of the room. His time was not to be wasted on matters better dealt with by a junior, he raved—he could not be involved in details of dress, discipline, martial law.

Allenby had matters of far greater import on his mind. He saw his job as clearing Palestine's sandy and waterless wastelands of the

Turk, German, and Austrian. He was going to have to do it with animals, not machines. No automobile or truck could traverse a desert whose best roads were little more than goat trails and that had in places steep and rocky mountains. It would be up to the Imperial Camel Corps, his mules, and, primarily, his horses. It wasn't going to be easy. The scattered wells of the region were sufficient to service the occasional Arab caravan, but a massive cavalry army would require a more plentiful drinking supply. He ordered a pipeline installed to carry chlorinated water from Egypt two hundred miles across the Sinai Desert and Gaza. To an extent, that would deal with his water needs, but he faced other equally daunting problems. For there was the everlasting dust that caked his men's faces yellow and burned the nostrils of the horses. At times the khamsin blew for days, a hot dry wind raising blinding clouds. Eyes turned blood-shot from the blinding glare of the sun, and tongues swelled to fill dry mouths so that it was difficult to speak as lips turned a purplish black to burst open, with quick attention from swarming flies that bid to drive soldiers mad.

The flies of course horribly tormented the horses, as did afflictions familiar and otherwise, glanders, anthrax, mange, piroplasmosis (tick fever), and epizootic lymphangitis. How different and how difficult it was for those "descended from the English stock that had furnished chargers for King Richard and his knights and warriors," mused a sympathetic British officer, now "transported from cozy thatched barns and rich lush meadows" to the burning sands and waterless plains. It was not only affiliation with the ancestors of the Egyptian Expeditionary Force horses that brought Richard the Lion-Hearted to mind just then and in that place. In the twelfth century's Third Crusade he had reached the outskirts of the well-defended Jerusalem, the Holy City in the Holy Land, but had turned his head away, refusing to look upon what his force was unable to take. Great Britain seven centuries later had been at war for going on three years, with little to show for it save the loss of hundreds of thousands of men, including General Allenby's only son, dead on the Western Front when not yet twenty-one. The Great War had turned sour, gray, deadly, interminable. If Jerusalem could be taken, with after hundreds of years under Islam's rule the flag of a Christian nation rising above its spires and minarets, the Western Allies could perceive a measure of justification for all their sacrifices and a resultant rise in morale fallen grievously low.

Allenby began to study Palestine, the cockpit for armies for thousands of years, "with the diligence of a student working for a doctorate as much as of a general about to conquer the land," wrote his biographer Brian Gardner. He read geographical studies, ancient histories of Thutmose, Ramses, Sennacherib, Alexander, and others, read Herodotus and daily the Bible—not for religious inspiration but for information. He discussed with medical officers why five Crusades had failed of their objective, and found that Richard had advanced at a time of year when malaria was always prevalent. Napoléon's men, he learned, suffered through an epidemic of ophthalmia, causing blindness. He had in a fly expert from the British Museum, and naturalists to speak of the flora and fauna of the region. In the days to come he used his cavalry in both a heavy hit-home capacity and a deceptive manner, creating fifteen thousand horse dummies from tent poles and brown army blankets to place before a position he did not intend to assault, with riders put to dragging sleds about so that raised dust would deceive the enemy into thinking the dummies were real.

He could not extend the reach of his water pipelines, and so sent eight thousand horsemen to take Beersheba, south of Jerusalem. There were wells there, dug by Abraham some thirty-seven centuries gone. They were susceptible to destruction, he knew—the Philistines had thought to fill them with sand. From Colonel Lawrence, who maintained networks of Arab spies, he learned that the wells were mined and could be blown in a moment. If they were, Allenby's men and horses would be doomed to perish of thirst. On the last day of October 1917, four months after Allenby came to Cairo, the Desert Mounted Corps moved upon Beersheba. It had in its ranks British regiments, Australians, Ghurkas, Sikhs. Some of the horses traveled without water for as many as eighty-four hours. The Dorset Yeomanry went sixty miles in fifty-four hours without a drop. Everything depended upon getting control of the wells before the enemy blew them up, and a sword-swinging, straight-ahead charge was demanded of the fagged horses. Allenby's men rode over and past Turkish artillerymen and machine gunners and came into Beersheba, their sabres used on anyone in the streets, and secured the wells.

His troopers and horses were exhausted, but he forced them on toward Jerusalem as the enemy fled. Allenby came to the Judean hills, from time immemorial an almost impenetrable defense for the city. It began to rain, and the camels, his only means of transporting supplies of any kind, found it hard going to get up the slippery pathways of the rocky heights. The Bull displayed not an iota of lack of confidence and ignored any personal physical discomfort; tall, massive, he radiated tremendous resolution and steely discipline. He stood on the spot where Richard had, the commanding height of Nebi Samwil, and unlike the king, gazed down at the Holy City's spires and domes and minarets. Godefroi de Bouillon had led the sole successful Crusade, the First, and now newspapers in the Allied countries proclaimed the leader of the Egyptian Expeditionary Force as his like in triumphing with the Seventh. It was December 9, 1917. The mayor came out under a white flag with the keys to the city and approached two British sergeants. They did not feel themselves adequate to participate in what would soon be trumpeted in the papers as one of the most important occurrences of world history, and sent for a major, who had the same viewpoint. A lieutenant colonel came, who also declined the surrender offer, and then a brigadier general, who did likewise. "No one felt he was quite the man for such an historic event," the biographer Gardner wrote. Finally a major general did what was called for.

Allenby entered Jerusalem on foot, indicating that he did not ride as a sign of respect, with "no sign of emotion whatsoever; aloof, apparently unmoved and without dawdling." In England the great bell of Westminster Cathedral rang for the first time in three years, the bells of every church in Rome sounded for an hour, and in Paris a special service was held in Notre-Dame to celebrate the Christian return to Jerusalem after 730 years. When some 20 years later its conqueror died, the *New York Times* said: "In the history of the human race his name will be permanently written as Allenby, the deliverer of the Holy Land. It is likely that no name among those who held high command will be so long remembered." He himself was skeptical about that. "In fifty years," he told Colonel Lawrence, "your name will be a household word; to find out about Allenby they will have to go to the War Museum." (He was not off by much. In 1962 the film *Lawrence of Arabia* scored a worldwide triumph, Peter O'Toole playing the lead and with Jack Hawkins as Allenby in a minor role.)

The British paused for a time to look from Jerusalem's bell tower on the summit of the Mount of Olives down on the Garden of the Gethsemane, the Dead Sea, and the Jordan Valley, and to put into good repair the aqueduct built by Pilate in Herod's reign. Then they kept going. Allenby had Lawrence's people spread word that a great race meet was to be held in Gaza, the purported event existing only in the Bull's imagination, but the enemy accepted the idea and was found unready for an attack. Allenby sent nine thousand horsemen north along the coast, where after ten miles of travel they split, with half of them crossing the flat, dusty, waterless Plain of Sharon and making for the Aruna Pass and Megiddo, where thirty-five hundred years earlier Pharoah Thutmose went through with his thousand chariots to win the first clearly described battle in history. General Allenby's New Zealand Mounted Rifles, Australian Light Horse, and Royal Deccan Horse and Bengal Lancers and the others would in this Arabian Nights setting sweep all before them in what has come to be seen as the most polished display of horsed warfare known to history, even as the light of that military arm appeared to be going dim before blinking out. Allenby the student was perfectly aware of what horsemen long before him had done where now he campaigned, remarking that Alexander aboard Bucephalus had largely because of his cavalry overthrown the king of kings, Darius, at Issus near the modern Iskanderum—Alexandretta—where now a couple of days' march away his forces were smashing to bits the Ottoman Empire. In London, Prime Minister David Lloyd George, who detested Haig and many other Western Front generals for their "ridiculous cavalry obsession," paid tribute to Allenby's horses, who had come from all over the Empire to save the day and were "as unbeatable as their riders."

The Egyptian Expeditionary Force of horse, foot, and guns began its final drive in September 1918. "None were keener than the cavalry," wrote Major Vivian Gilbert, "for Allenby's plans would give them the opportunity for which they had been waiting—of proving to the world that they were as much needed in modern warfare as they had been in wars of the past. The advance in Palestine saved the cavalry from utter extinction, placing them back in their rightful position as indispensable in open fighting and a war of movement." The horsed columns shot forward, infantry and artillery following. In two days they captured twenty thousand Ottoman Empire soldiers. At Haifa, the Jodhpore Lancers went full pelt into quicksand, which cost them their leading horses and men, but they kept going, and speared the city's contingent of Turkish soldiers. The Desert Mounted Corps took Aleppo and Damascus, and came to Turkey's southern border. In six weeks the British front advanced 350 miles. Sherman's March to the Sea covered a distance half that; the German tank advance through France twenty-two years later, modeled on what Sherman and more particularly Allenby had accomplished, was 225 miles. Enemy casualties of killed, wounded, missing, and captured were calculated in scores and even hundreds of thousands; British losses were 5,666 with all but 650 cavalrymen. Turkey sued for peace, with, as had been anticipated, Bulgaria and Austria-Hungary following, and, in less than two months, Germany. For two decades and more the world's cavalry enthusiasts celebrated. America's *The Cavalry Journal*, organ of the United States Cavalry Association founded by Wesley Merritt in 1887, ran article after article about the dramatic and romantic horsed triumphs of the great Holy Land campaign.

The victor there in the withering deserts and the barren high ranges went home to England and a reception far greater than that accorded Haig. "The Bull Returns," a newspaper headlined. Eleven Allied nations decorated him, he was George V's guest at Balmoral, and was given at a glittering Guildhall banquet the Freedom of the City of London. Promotion to the highest rank his army knew came, and a viscountcy, so that he became Field Marshal Lord Allenby of Felixstowe and Megiddo. The first designation was for the home of his mother, to whom he had always been devoted, writing her daily for years, and the second for the site of the fighting that followed his riders' cramped traversing of the thin Aruna Pass even as once upon a time did the chariots of Pharoah Thutmose II. Lord

Allenby retired from the army to travel widely for plant and animal study and when at home spent hours each day in his aviary, which had artificial light and heating and where he kept rare birds from all over the world. He died in 1936 and was cremated, with his ashes placed in Westminster Abbey on May 19 of that year, coincidentally the first anniversary of Lawrence of Arabia's death in a motorcycle accident.

They had gone home, the soldiers. London decreed that their horses must stay. They were put up for sale, twenty thousand who had carried riders or pulled guns or wagons, at Cairo auctions for purchase by whomever, there in the sun, with the flies, the ever-lacking sources of good water and of good feed, in a culture of poverty where horses were tools harshly used. Officers of means offered to pay for transport of the mounts upon whose backs they had done so much to home in Australia or to England's green meadows. Indeed they begged. Policy refused their pleas, and some took to a remote spot those who might, one could say, be called their dear friends, and there with service revolvers put them down to rest forever in the sands. It was always different in the cavalry of the United States. No horses were ever sold off for use as drays, or pulling plows, or even children's mounts. If an animal was found unfit for service, the farrier sergeant chalked a line down from between the ears and one between the eyes and put a bullet where the two lines crossed.

In 1930 Brigadier General Geoffrey Brooke was posted to Egypt, now under British mandate. His wife found Cairo very difficult to take—the poverty, beggars, malnutrition, dirt, noise, heat, and most particularly the look of the city's legions of horses. They were universally so thin and raddled and galled by crude equipment as to be painful to see, and their ill-tended hooves were shod poorly or not at all. There was never a shine to their dusty coats, and their eyes were dull. When they were given drink, which was but infrequently in a place of few sources, it was with water warm and usually muddy. The city had one veterinary clinic, the inside of which very few horses ever saw. Worse yet was the manner in which their owners drove, brutally using sticks or lashes to goad them into pulling overloaded carts or wagons. Cairo's transport system was largely based on battered old horse-drawn cabs whose drivers were merciless in laying on. Some of the cabs were drawn by two animals, Mrs. Brooke saw, and very often a limping and obviously unsound one was coupled with one relatively fit, at least by Cairo standards. A driver plied his whip on the better one and put him into a fast trot, which the poor half-crippled harnessed mate had to keep up with for fear of falling to be dragged along. Cairo stables, or what passed for stables, had no bedding. The horses, for what rest they were given, stood or lay on cement or hard ground, from which their body wastes were rarely removed. Feed was of the slightest amount and the poorest quality. This was the East, poor and desperate and struggling, and with no concept of kindness to, nor concern for, animals.

The dreadful horse conditions were deplored by England's officers and merchants and administrators and their wives, and once Mrs. Brooke saw one of her compatriots drag a particularly cruel cabman off his vehicle to give him a thrashing. But what, she asked herself, did that accomplish? After the brute dusted himself off, he would likely take it out on his horse. She saw what she called a "half-starved wreck, an old crock," she remembered, and to her horror recognized by the brand on its quarters that she was viewing a horse that twelve years earlier had gained for Lord Allenby his fame and done so much to win the war for the Allies. She put up a few pounds to purchase the poor thing, whom she named Old Bill. But, she found, Egypt had thousands of Old Bills, those who yet lived from the twenty thousand sold off after the war. She could hardly purchase each one. And even if she could, what then? They were so battered, so trodden down, crippled, diseased, many half blind, beyond reclamation after so many desperate years. They were so tired. She was one woman, alone. She wrote a letter to *The Morning Post* back in London saying that England owed these who had done so much a final gift. Floods of money came in; and so she sat in a courtyard with volunteers, mostly serving British officers, administering what became her Old War Horse Fund as Egyptians dragged and whipped their property forward, each applicant averring he was presenting to the English lady an animal who had served her country well and whom now she must buy.

It was a dreadful business to see the dregs of Cairo's horses dragooned in by their shouting owners fighting for a place in line, yanking and kicking at their animals and at one another. The men could break one another's heads for all she cared, she thought, even as she acknowledged to herself that it was need, not inborn brutishness, that made them so repellent, but she secured constant police attendance to tamp down the chaos. To view hundreds upon hundreds of pitiful horses one after the other, day after day, an endless terrible testing, was hard and more than hard on her volunteers. They would ask for a respite of a day or two away. She never was absent from her post. In the worst condition of all coming before her were the poor creatures who labored in the mines outside the city, dragging carts through a dark waterless hell of noxious fumes and no sunlight. She had to look at such, and at the others, and with her volunteers determine one by one which horse actually had been of the noble gathering that Lord Allenby victoriously led to uphold the glory of five thousand years of the cavalry, and which horse had not. These last she must turn away to send back to perdition. She had no choice. Her mandate was to haggle with the men owning those once of the Egyptian Expeditionary Force, come to a price, put out the money, and transport the new property of the Old War Horse Fund to what, if only for a little while, must have seemed to each a sudden earthly paradise.

The grooms Dorothy Brooke hired laid down in the stables she created deep, gentle bedding. She used to walk through to hear the soft sounds the fund's new possessions emitted as for the first time in years they sank down to put their "poor old bones," she wrote, on a surface neither hard nor harshly wet and foul. There was abundant cool water for each horse, and she saw what that meant to them, how they put into the water and for long sweet moments kept there what she called "their poor old noses." There were so many horses to purchase, five thousand. She made arrangements for the minuscule number who survived the twelve years after the war in something approaching decent condition to be shipped home to England to live out their days there. (Her first, Old Bill, coddled and medically attended to and fed, brought back with expenditures of time and money and effort to at least an approximation of what a gallant aged charger should look like, appeared to great acclamation at British horse shows.) The Old War Horse Fund had just so much stable space. Yet at least for a few days, she felt, she and the others who worked with her could offer each of the horses who served Lord Allenby, and England, and the Empire, a brief time of quiet and peace—and love. That was what her book was called: *For the Love of Horses*. Then they must die so that others of the terrible unending stream could take their places. At least they would do so painlessly, she wrote, and with the sound of quiet English voices attending their passing.

She wrote of one who was granted an extra day. Horses long used together become enormously attached to each other. Egypt's conditions, she saw, produced pairs even more inseparable than animals of happier circumstance. In the lives they had lived since the war, she knew, they had had so little. All they had was each other. One time a group was led from in-line stalls out to where swiftly induced long sleep awaited. A horse whose day had not yet come—it would on the morrow—became terribly agitated. He had one eye missing and was frantically twisting around to use his good one to see where the others had gone. She understood. Perhaps he had served with the horse in the next stall when the great advance took Beersheba, or Jerusalem, or Aleppo. Then, she speculated, perhaps the two had been yoked together to draw a wagon or a cab. They could not be parted now at the last.

Mrs. Brooke went out to the waiting line and asked her people which of the wretched poor hulks had been next to the one-eyed horse. No one knew for sure. All looked the same, battered, hopeless. She had the one-eyed horse brought out to be walked in front of them. He went along and then stopped. His joy, and that of the wreck he greeted and was greeted by, told her what she needed to know. "He had found his pal." She had his pal put back in the adjoining stall to the one-eyed horse, and they had together one more day, and then went on. When Great Britain entered World War II, Mrs. Brooke exacted from the War Office a promise that whatever happened, no horse would ever again be left on foreign soil.

16

"It was a bit of a façade, wasn't it?"

It is an oft-told story that when the Great War's Armistice Day finally came after more than four years of warfare, a British officer cried, "Thank God that's over, and now we can get back to real soldiering!"

"Real soldiering" in the victors' armies particularly centered upon cavalry. The war had been from first to last largely a misery of muddy and pointless slaughter from whose beastliness soldiers turned away, averring that the Western Front was an anomaly that would never reoccur. The only bright spot of the whole wretched business had been the glorious horsed showing that carried the day in Egypt and Palestine, and it was far more uplifting to look back upon that and hope for more of the same than to dwell upon deadly trench warfare. That France's military horse feed costs for twenty years after 1918 greatly exceeded those for petroleum, the ratio in 1937 being four to one, tells much of that country's viewpoint. No doubt there were new helpful devices the cavalry could adopt, Lord Allenby wrote in 1921, but "nevertheless it must not lose faith in its old and tried weapons, the sword and the lance." In the United States, the First Cavalry Division was regarded as by far the best unit of the country's army, and indeed said to be the finest division in the world. It had six thousand horses, geldings of from fifteen to seventeen hands high and of not less than nine hundred or more than twelve hundred pounds, head and ears small, forehead broad, shoulders long and sloping back, forelegs straight and standing well under, and barrel large, mostly sired by thoroughbred or trotter stallions whose services the army made available without charge to anyone owning a mare, the thinking being that the resulting "get" might if necessary someday be impressed into military duty. The First Cav had by the time of Pearl Harbor 17 combat cars, 178 scout cars, and 187 trucks whose presence was almost lost in the masses of the six thousand horses.

The division's home was Fort Bliss, Texas, where at reviews thousands of sabres flashed as they pointed skyward in front of troopers' faces, red and white guidons fluttered along with national and regimental standards, bugles sounded as the bands played, and at the order "Pass in review!" the horses ceased their tossing of heads (with attendant rattling and jingling of bits and curb chains) to go forward at a trot before wheeling back to take up a gallop amid swirling dust. There was no formal basic training for new recruits. Men were individually instructed by corporals of their assigned troops, who generally served ten years before attaining that rank. The most stringent requirements were adhered to regarding the care of the shining horses and the glistening gear, and the policing of the trimmed-lawn post area, the cleanliness of the stables and barracks regularly checked by noncoms wearing white gloves that had better not show the slightest smudge after being rubbed over any surface. The horses were fed the finest hay obtainable, mostly timothy and clover, and the men's uniforms were inspected down to the tiniest detail, such as making sure that the rear side of brass buttons were as highly polished as the front. Beginning riders were lambasted as looking like tailors or fiddlers for the way they kept their elbows out, screamed at to sit up straight and not crouch like a monkey, to keep their knees down and their hands six inches apart, to feel the horse's mouth lightly.

Nothing in the enlisted man's way of life, which had most likely commenced in a Boston slum, or a Louisiana canebrake log cabin, or a far western prairie sod hut, could have been more different from that of his officer. The latter-day version of the medieval knight, in order to hold a hope of professional advancement, had to show well on the post tennis courts and golf course and dance floor; capably play bridge or poker, winning or losing with aplomb; know how to hold his liquor; tell a story or a joke with flair; and be flawlessly immaculate in his well-cut breeches, high-collared blouse with glistening Sam Browne belt, and Peal or Maxwell boots glitteringly shined by his orderly. His polo and horse-show jump riding and steeplechasing was of course of the highest order, reaching in many cases international standards, with Olympic equestrian events dominated by serving officers. It was best if he had a good singing voice—young officers growing up in the cavalry did a lot of singing in the evening; it worked to bind them together, as did a love of horses and polo, and pride in the regiment—and be able to hold up his end in amateur theatricals. Addressed by enlisted personnel in the third person ("Will the captain initial the status report?"), he must sedulously keep the lawn before his Officers' Row house free of weeds or children's toys, and have a wife active in post book clubs, sewing circles, charity doings and appropriately decorous women's sports events, a hostess of charm and taste. He must be a gentleman, unfazed by anything, courtly, having about him, wrote Major Malcolm Wheeler-Nicholson in his 1922 *Modern Cavalry*, "a knightly presence, knightly sense." Lucian K. Truscott III remembered how his officer-father of the same name paid great attention to his fingernails. "Well-cared-for hands were the mark of a gentleman."

Being one, however, was not to obscure the meaning of a horsed soldier's life. The elder Truscott got his boy into polo at a very young age, and spared him not at all, regularly banging him off his horse. There was a meaning to polo, the father explained. It taught how to react quickly, to be aggressive, to learn what the cavalry was all about—and it offered the lesson that beneath the velvet glove was an iron fist:

"Listen, Son, goddamnit. Let me tell you something, and don't ever forget it. You play games to win, not lose. And you fight wars to win! That's spelled W-I-N! And every good player in a game, and every good commander in a war, and I mean really *good* player or *good* commander, every damn one of them, has to have some sonofabitch in him. If he doesn't, he isn't a good player or commander.

"Polo games and wars aren't won by gentlemen. They're won by men who can be first-class sonsofbitches when they have to be. It's as simple as that. No sonofabitch, no commander." When years later General Truscott wrote his memoirs after World War II, his performance in handling massive all-arms forces marked by Dwight D. Eisenhower as second only to that of George Patton, he signed the preface L. K. Truscott, Jr., Cavalryman.

Officers assigned to the First Cavalry Division after graduating from West Point went to Kansas for specialized training in what was variously called the Cavalry School and the Mounted Service School. Informally, Mrs. Riley's School for Boys. It was said of Fort Riley that if a horse walked into your quarters you offered it the best chair in the house. There were places marked "This area is sacred to the horse," with signs saying that no motorized vehicle was ever authorized entry unless to save a man's or a mount's life. Students were issued four horses—an untrained remount, a green jumper, a green polo pony, and an experienced old jumper. One shoed them, sat for classroom map exercises, rode in terrain exercises, studied horse feeds and equine diseases and first aid, and learned liaison and logistic duties, staff functions, the proper packing of supply wagons, rail movements for horses, and how best to prevent dislocation of machine-gun rounds from belts carried in bouncing mule-drawn carts—at the end of a journey many always almost had to be reset. One learned in the sardonically termed Life of Riley horsed water crossing procedures; took courses in troop leadership, tactics, communications, and supply; spent days in the riding hall, on the cross-country and point-to-point courses, and in the dressage ring; was instructed not only by American experts but also those from the cavalries of France, Italy, and Poland. The future Lieutenant General W. H. S. Wright never forgot the "diadem, glory, and joy in those halcyon days." Many years after, it would all "flood back in glorious memory."

Fort Riley students working on scouting and patrolling slid their mounts down steep gullies and then swam them across the Republican River and put them over hurdles in endurance rides, and, until 1934, when the weapon was retired, slashed away with sabres at dummies of straw-filled gunnysacks while galloping over a winding course of post-and-rail, log, ditch, and brush jumps, to repeat the process with a pistol. The talk was all of horses, with rigid cavalry form prevailing as to customs, ceremonies, tradition, calls, dress, and leaving of cards. Besides polo there were weekly hunts with hounds. In 1909 the War Department had decreed that each horsed regiment should be encouraged to maintain a pack, and along with the dogs gathered at Forts Oglethorpe in Georgia; Ethan Allen in Vermont; Des Moines in Iowa; D. A. Russell, Bliss, and Brown in Texas; Meade in South Dakota; Leavenworth in Kansas; and Sheridan in Illinois; and at the Presidio in California and at West Point in New York came officer designations as whippers-in and Master, with the Cavalry School Hunt master wearing a red coat with a gold collar and a vest with gold buttons embroidered with C. S. H.

The country's premier cavalry post was Fort Myer, Virginia, just outside Washington. The colonel commanding must of necessity have access to very substantial private funds, for in an atmosphere of pomp, ceremony, drama, color, and supreme spit and polish, he must personally finance a ten-week series of mounted spectacles termed the Society Circus, which raised money for army charities and athletic activities while being major events of Washington's winter social season. Very likely his father-in-law had to meet the high expenses involved, for it is not infrequent that American officers take rich girls for their brides: Robert E. Lee wed the heiress of George Washington's fortune; that was the largest the country then knew; John J. Pershing married the daughter of Wyoming's richest man; the first Mrs. Douglas MacArthur possessed $150 million; Mrs. George S. Patton's monies, added to her husband's lesser holdings, enabled him never in his career to do other with his salary than donate it to army charities; Mamie Doud Eisenhower had a couple of million; and Mrs. Mark Clark as a junior officer's wife incurred the ire of senior's wives by driving an expensive car. During the Society Circus, Fort Myer's cavalry troopers, appropriately attired, replicated the Charge of the Light Brigade and Custer's Last Stand. They wore togas and laurel wreaths to show what Rome's chariot races must have been like, played mounted basketball, performed acrobatics (such as standing upright in their saddles at a gallop before leaning down to pick handkerchiefs off the ground with their teeth), jumped through flaming hoops, held races between six-horse teams pulling three-inch guns, which at the end fired off blanks to fill an indoor arena with dramatic thunder and smoke. Soldiers dressed as Crusaders, with debutantes in medieval costume recruited to ride in tandem. They participated in pageant, fair, and parade while wearing uniforms replicating those from the Revolution to the Great War and Depression Era's puttees and soup-bowl helmets. Fort Myer was the only post where "blues," mess jackets of that color with gold braid and shoulder knots and epaulets, were required, and officers were expected to join nearby hunt clubs in Virginia or Maryland, whose doings commenced in the morning with an elaborate hunt breakfast and concluded at night with a full-dress ball. They were called upon to serve as escorts, ushers, and aides at White House receptions and dinners and as tennis and bridge partners. They were in demand for officialdom's cocktail and dinner parties.

It was all very glamorous, but in Congress and in the War Department the very existence of the mounted cavalry was being called into question. For the clanking of what was called "the bullet proof horse" and "the mechanical cavalry" was heard in the distance. Tanks had been used in the Great War with varying success. In the last stages of the fighting, they had sent the Germans flying. But they were notoriously unreliable, horsemen never failed to point out, prone to breakdowns, likely to run out of gas or get themselves hung up on tree stumps or stuck in shell holes. While a horsed column could move at night with the hope of not being detected by an enemy, a group of tanks with roaring motors and plumes of exhaust smoke could not. Riders could enter a forest and remain unobserved by a foe's reconnaissance aircraft, but tanks smashed down trees and vegetation and left telltale tracks. Horses did not run out of fuel. Tanks did, and trucks bringing gasoline required at least halfway decent road networks and bridges, which were lacking in the trackless areas of most of the world. War flows over all sorts of terrain, much of it unsuitable for wheeled or tracked vehicles, while horses and pack trains can go anywhere. Yet the clanking grew louder.

It was all the fault of the Roaring Twenties' burgeoning auto-mobile industry, horsemen said, that with their admittedly improved suspension and transmission systems and engine design, tanks came to be seen by some as the logical replacement to the horse. Detroit profitably made tractors as well as cars, and if it had its way, cavalry-men declared, the horse would be banished from the farm as well as the army. Tanks and their replacement parts were monstrously expensive to produce, and of course that could mean great finan-cial gains for the motor moguls. And then there was the traditional envy held by the foot soldier for the mounted one, "forever jealous of the cavalryman riding up there tall in the saddle, kicking dust in the doughboy's face, playing polo, jump riding, wearing Peal boots instead of leggings and rolling along with nonchalant sang-froid." A "campaign of ridicule was launched," charged Major General John K. Herr, the army's last chief of cavalry, and "the cavalry was accused of living in the days of King Arthur—in a dream world learning practices which had died with General Custer. Cavalrymen on the march were often greeted with 'Where are your bows and arrows?' or 'Hiya, Sir Galahad' or 'What's good for the daily double tomorrow?' " By the early 1930s the cavalry was very much on the defensive. Army chief of staff Douglas MacArthur remarked that the horse "had no greater degree of mobility than a thousand years ago," and must be "replaced or assisted or else pass into the limbo of discarded military formations." The assistance, it was theorized, might come in the form of trucks taking horses to where they could be unloaded for performance of cross-country missions, but the idea never went very far.

That the horse who had "stood the acid test of war" not give way to the "untried machine" was Major General Herr's fervent hope, but even some of the stalwarts of his branch of the service were beginning to have their doubts. Cavalry training with its feats of harmless derring-do was fun, reflected Lucian Truscott, "great sport," but for what did it prepare? "The cavalry charge, that's what, and that maneuver, however exciting in practice, did not prom-ise to decide the outcome of the next war." In early 1933 the first American mechanized cavalry organization came into being, at Fort Knox in Kentucky. For some ten or twelve years after the 1918 armistice it was considered very risky for a cavalry officer's career to display an interest in tanks, but now a good many deserted the horses to apply for posting to Fort Knox. It was a matter of deepest concern to General Herr. "He was especially distressed that among these were many of the best horsemen and polo players." Even George Patton was among the apostates, a member in West Point days of a cadet crew known as "the cavalry fanatics," later Master of the Sword at Riley, and author of a Government Printing Office publication on his specialty. In it he attached great importance to keeping the left hand still while coming to "Point to The Right Rear and Point to The Left Front"—"Care must be taken not to move the bridle hand, do not derange the bridle hand." At Charge, sabre legs must remain in place and not go backward. Patton never lost his love for and involvement with horses, and in later years personally arranged the escape of the mounts of Vienna's Spanish Riding School from oncoming Soviet forces into areas held by the armies of the Western allies, but his fame is based on war without horses.

Generals always prepare to fight the last war, it has famously been said, and that was true for England's officers of the years following 1918. The Empire expanded its sway at the expense of Ottoman loss, and in Egypt and Palestine and elsewhere His Majesty's Forces taking possession of new areas particularly emphasized cavalry, as they did in India. Large-scale set-piece battles involving infantry and artillery were not expected to be in the cards. Any native uprisings were best suppressed by mounted columns.

The troopers who upon enlistment as teenagers took the King's Shilling lived a splendid life out there "abroad," as they called it. They had begun their cavalry careers with contact with horses entirely lacking, although they dressed in breeches and wore spurs. The instructor at the swords flung a piece of bamboo, which if not parried correctly got you in the nose. They were on the go from six in the morning, always hungry. Breakfast was bacon, beans, and porridge; at midday there was stew or meat pie, at tea bread and jam and perhaps a bit of fish, and in the evening soup or cocoa. But the portions were rather meager, considering that Great Britain was then seen as the richest country in the world. Their officers were uniformly bluebloods, talking as if, men said, they had plums in their mouths. After learning how to muck out and groom, soldiers were issued horses to lead into a mirrored riding hall, with walls that sloped down so that when eventually you got on board you wouldn't get your knees mashed. First the sergeant major instructor displayed how to put on a bit, saying one must always leave the chain loose enough to get a finger under. It was like the brakes on a car, and must be carefully employed. The girth and surcingle must never pinch. The saddle must shine, and also the bit and the saddle irons, polished with a steel chain of little links after being tossed in a sack filled with bran so that after burnishing they would fetch up bright. Once on a horse, men worked on how to hold the reins, and to have contact only with the upper thigh, none below the knee except for the heel. If your puttees were perfectly clean when you got off, and your heel soiled, you knew you were doing the right thing.

The enlisted men, the other ranks, rode with double reins, only officers permitted to do so on the snaffle. Orders were never shouted, always sung out—"*Riiiiight turn*"—and the older horses knew them as well as the riders. One practiced trotting without stirrups, which were slung up and tied in front of the saddle, and always carried a hoof pick, for a flint needing removal could get in at any time. After a time the riding hall was departed for the *meidaan*, an Indian word meaning a large expanse of land, always used in the British cavalry even by boys still not acquainted with any post save Somerset Barracks. Sometimes you'd see a horse out there say to himself, "I've got a mug up; back to the stables," and the lad would get himself quite a ride. If he fell off he'd have to get back on immediately, otherwise his nerve might fail him completely. Now and then you'd have someone simply refuse. Transfer to the artillery or the infantry followed.

After two or three months, men were put to jumping barriers around eighteen inches high, ten feet apart, two dozen in a row, with no stirrups, the object being to teach good balance and use of the thigh muscles. Being banged about, remembered Derek Howard Douglas, late sergeant major of H.M. First Royal Dragoons, made you sit tight. Ceremonial drills followed. If you wanted to smarten your horse's performance, you'd put a sharp point on your spur rowels, at the risk of being in trouble if you were found out. Officers had private horses, polo ponies, hunters, thoroughbreds. Troop horses for the other ranks were almost all Australian Whalers, the types regularly employed by Lord Allenby, who were like good heavy hunters. For shipment out to Egypt, Douglas remembered, you led your horse into the bowels of a vessel—the heat and the smell of ammonia enough to knock you out. The horses had to be walked around down there between the hay and corn and grain so they wouldn't die of colic. Then it was on to the old Ottoman barracks in Cairo, which were bloody awful, rife with bugs you got rid of by using fire on every nook and cranny of the iron bedsteads. It was better for the horses; their stables were huge and airy. A cavalry other rank started at a shilling a day while the fellaheen, peasants, made a shilling a month. That meant that even as a private Derek Douglas could pay to have his horse's stable mucked out. "You could even have your saddle done, but it was a terrible risk because the natives never did it right and you'd pay the consequences, which were no passes, no chance to go to the cinema or anything. You could go kick the bloke around, but so what?"

Soldiers did have to do stable guard duty for the horses, who were kept under eye twenty-four hours a day. "I remember a drum horse from the regimental band, a vicious beggar," Douglas said, looking back, "who used to get loose and chase you up and down. He'd unhook himself quietly and come at you with his bloody mouth open. He was a huge skewbald. Most of the horses were bays or livers. I can't recall a gray, and there was no such thing as a white. Our horses began with the regiment at about four or five and remained for about ten years." But looking back on it now"—in 1977—"it was a bit of a façade, wasn't it? When England should have mechanized her regiments she was dying on her feet, showing the flag instead. Those cavalry colonels, Colonel Blimps, the socialites, they weren't going to let their horse regiments go. They loved the cavalry, the bluebloods. They certainly weren't going to go off and be infantry. *Infantry?*"

The regiment went to India from Cairo. "Ghastly bloody place, awful. Horrible skin diseases, terrible poverty." That was not the way the Indian Army Viceroy's Commissioned Officer Freddie Guest esteemed the subcontinent. He remembered the spectacular dress uniforms of the officers of the grandly named cavalry regiments: the

Governor General's Bodyguard, 3rd Skinner's Horse, 7th Hariana Lancers, 9th Hodson's Horse, Hyderabad Lancers, 29th Deccan Horse, 38th Central India Horse. They outshone women's bright frocks and almost approached in splendor the apparel of a maharajah whose turban sparkling with diamonds and rubies Captain Guest never forgot. Receptions were held in enormous ballrooms with chandeliers of a hundred lights, and outside in illuminated gardens under a gaily colored and decorated marquee. There would be a magnificent champagne buffet. Guest saw a memorial erected in 1807 to one of his predecessors as a cavalry officer, who on a dare or perhaps a bet attempted a daring jump that killed both him and his horse. It was an act that while of unfortunate result was of an entirely familiar and recognizable nature, for sports were a main preoccupation in Guest's time in India. One took part in sculling at regattas and afterward sat in long chairs in the cool of the evening with a tall drink, and "chaps were keen as mustard" about pig sticking out in the countryside where native beaters had corralled prey. Superb horsemanship and good work with a lance were necessary to do in a hog as it jinked left and right, the activity improving one's riding and one's polo. After the event, orderlies and the *sowars* who tended to the mess camels served dinner, with a tablecloth and crockery placed on the ground and the *kitmaghar* offering whiskey and soda.

Actual work began with drill at 5:45 A.M., before the heat became too intense, with schooling of horses who needed it, and contingents moving in echelon and then wheeling into line, sometimes the entire squadron forming one grand straight line. Before noon it was over, with animal management and language classes concluded, grain and fodder inspected, equipment checked, sick or thin horses sorted out and attended to, remounts worked into their duties. Such were brought from Australia in masses, wild and uncouth creatures, hair and coats long and often caked with mud. The long sea voyage had not improved them. Selecting several for the regiment to put in training was the duty of three or four officers, including a very junior one. "It was a wonderful opportunity for a young officer to gain firsthand experience in trying to pick out good horses," Guest wrote. Sometimes one of the Indian Army's

few native officers was permitted to offer an opinion "if he was considered by long service and great experience to be a good judge of
horses." A regiment maintained a number of its own broodmares
of English stock, who when crossed with Australian Whalers produced acceptable animals. Breeding with India-breds, however,
never worked out: the foals lacked bone and were too excitable.

It was a duty, Guest remembered, to be correctly attired when
appearing in the officers' mess or at the Club. Each regiment had
different facings for full dress. The *lungi*—turban—could be worn,
with shoulder chains and a colored cummerbund, which had to be
tight to look smart. White melton breeches tapered down to black
knee boots with two-inch glittering spurs. A gramophone might
play in the ballroom, where the ladies of the regiment sat chat-
ting away as the gentlemen drank a *chota peg*. At polo tournaments
there were colorful tents, and grooms covering ponies with dust
sheets showing the colors of a participant's regiment; at race meets
officers competing against professional jockeys were listed in the
program as Gentlemen Riders, GRs. Englishwomen among the
spectators carried parasols, and Indian ones wore wonderfully decorated saris. As Indian Army officers of horse were forbidden to
marry before turning twenty-eight, they were steered clear of by
girls coming out from England. Many married older men, which led,
Guest punned, to an interesting "state of affairs." There were many
intrigues and scandals. Junior officers made five shillings and sixpence a day and customarily ran up debts that they planned to pay
off when they attained higher rank and income. (They spent half
their career in debt and the other half getting out of it, just in time
to retire. But then, the reason they were in the Indian Army and
not the British one was for lack of family money to meet the latter's
far greater financial obligations.)

When Derek Douglas was posted to Armnaga, in Kashmir, for
training as a riding instructor, his daily pay by contrast was one and
sixpence—although there was a threepence fine for anyone who
dropped his whip or got thrown. The course was eighteen months.
Students were issued three horses apiece, and rode with snaffle
bits in the manner of officers. There was no grooming or mucking
out; Indian servants did that. For months the students never were

permitted stirrups—"no saddles, nothing, just a stirrup leather around the horse's neck to hang on to." At the end of training, the men who passed were promoted to corporal and awarded a patch shaped like a spur to wear on their left shoulders. Back with the regiment, Douglas was issued an oddly gaited horse, Tiptoe, who walked in front and trotted behind. For a thirty-mile march calling for an hour of trotting alternated with twenty minutes of walking, Tiptoe's hind legs were always at the trot—and the corporal's legs, he remembered, were red raw. In 1935 he went to the peak of intersquadron jumping and all-arms competition with sabre and lance and revolver—a figure-of-eight course with parallel bars to stretch out the horse, other jumps, targets of balloons, dummies, doughnut-size rings—and won India's top meet, with a prize of five pounds and a silver cup. That year the regiment returned to England. As far as combat action when abroad, they had gone up against a group called the Red Shirts, who used to come down from the foothills of the Himalayas into Kashmir to burn villages and steal cattle. "We'd spot them in their shirts and charge, brandishing swords. Usually that was enough to drive them off."

There were three British cavalry regiments who did mounted duty on Horse Guards Parade in London, the Life Guards, the Horse Guards, and the Royal Dragoons. Selected men from the units sat for hour-and-forty-minute stints absolutely motionless in glorious headgear, huge shining boots to the top of the leg, glittering breastplate, gauntlets on the hands and sword at the shoulder, the horses under them trained not to move a muscle—"and they didn't, either." No tourist for decades failed to take a picture. In the years just before Great Britain went to war in 1939, Derek Douglas served on Horse Guards Parade. "Sometimes when you were sitting there women, tourists mostly, would come along and stick notes in your boot saying, 'Meet me in the So-and-so Pub,' and sometimes they'd even put money in." At the end of a shift, he remembered, you were paralyzed, literally paralyzed, and your mates had to lift you off the horse.

But while motionless soldiers on motionless mounts remain on Horse Guards Parade to this day, Britain in the year before the war came began mechanizing its cavalry regiments. (Even so, "the cavalry ethos remained dominant," with units seen as exclusive clubs "for scions of the landed elite." So late on as during the fighting in North Africa's Western desert, a mechanized cavalry officer refused the attachment to his unit of a regiment of the Royal Artillery. "We only accept support from the Royal *Horse* Artillery"— which although of course motorized yet bore the old designation.) Derek Douglas remembered how he and his mates drank to their horses when in 1938 several hundred Royal Dragoons mounts were sold off to Belgians who wanted them for meat. Others followed. By the end of the year the horses had almost faded from use, and Douglas was sent off to learn motor repair and maintenance. "When I got back the last of the horses were gone. The war was coming and we had tanks—large, impersonal lumps of metal. Put your hands on them and they are stone cold. They don't nuzzle you, they don't whinny. I miss the horses; I miss the cavalry."

17
The Last Cavalry Charge

Europe went to war; and in 1940 the United States Army, knowing it must inevitably get in, held the largest all-branches maneuvers the country ever saw. Much of Louisiana was given over to the exercise. Thousands of horses participated, and the leaders of the units in which they served felt happy about their performance. One regiment marched forty-four miles in twenty hours to make a Sabine River crossing and a simulated attack on opposing force communications, and another did seventy-one miles in thirty-five hours to cross the swollen Sabine and establish a bridgehead capable of being profitably exploited. The cavalry was saved, horsemen told one another. But it was not. Had they been permitted really to display their prowess, they said, "they would have wreaked such havoc as to silence forever the foes of the horse." But "it was felt by many, and with considerable bitterness, that these maneuvers were rigged to limit the activities of the cavalry, for the pressure was on from certain quarters to eliminate the mounted service," said Major General John K. Herr, the last chief of cavalry. The brilliantly successful German assaults on Poland and Western Europe were based on the tank, which had good radio communications, supported by the airplane, and in that equation the horse had no place. Three months after Pearl Harbor, when the First Cavalry Division shipped out for the Pacific, they took no horses. George Patton would say that if America had had one mounted division with pack artillery in Tunisia and Sicily, not a German would have escaped destruction for the horse's ability to get through mountainous country and block any flight until the tanks and infantry came up—but he was speaking in a purely theoretical manner about what never happened. Horses and mules were used in the Italian campaign, but purely for transport purposes. In August 1942, eight months into America's war, *The Cavalry Journal* eliminated from its cover the Frederic Remington depiction of a mounted trooper that had been there since 1903. Even as tankers served in units termed armored cavalry, those of Britain calling themselves hussars, lancers, and dragoons, the American ones with designations directly descended from the old horsed regiments, the magazine changed its name to *The Armored Cavalry Journal*, and then, in time, *Armor*.

On the war's first day, September 1, 1939, there came into being one of the conflict's great myths: that Poland's horse soldiers defending against Germany's blitzkrieg regularly did so by attacking tanks with lances. Poland did in fact have masses of cavalrymen, by some accounts as many as seventy thousand. Conversely, as a poor and backward country it had little in the way of mechanical equipment, with the total number of the nation's automobiles not exceeding twenty-five thousand. It is true that upon occasion during the brief conflict, Polish cavalry combating German infantry did find themselves dealing with tanks following the foot soldiers, with the results what might be expected. Poles knew how to die, a German general said, meaning the words as a compliment. Their easy-target horses were shot to pieces—bloodied riderless ones, their entrails dragging on the ground, loose stirrups and reins flapping, ran or limped through the walls of sand, dust, flame, and iron thrown up by the panzers. But even the Poles, although wedded to romanticized legends of their cavalry prowess through the ages, knew better than to use spears against metal monsters. General Heinz Guderian, World War II Germany's foremost leader of armor, remembered getting his men out of their machines—"dismounted" them was the leftover term from horse days—after one action. Like virtually all the war's tank generals, he was a former horse cavalryman; and as such he ordered the Poles' wounded mounts put out of their misery by use of his soldiers' sidearms.

Guderian's place in military history is secured by his tank advance through France, modeled on what Jeb Stuart and Edmund

Allenby had done, and he was imbued with what was called "the true cavalry spirit," which meant dash and swagger. But for the actual horse cavalry going up against modernity's weapons, there was hardly anything but disaster. A 1941 charge upon a German-held position by three thousand riders of Russia's 44th Mongolian Cavalry Division found but thirty horsemen reaching the objective, to perish there from the machine-gun fire that earlier slew the rest of the unit.

By then, 1941, the horsed forces of the United States consisted of one regiment, the 26th Cavalry, Philippine Scouts. One of its officers, all of whom were white, was in 1938 Lieutenant Hamilton H. Howze. He was of Old Army and old cavalry background, his father having fought the Sioux in the late 1880s as a member of the 6th Cavalry before becoming commandant of cadets at West Point, and his father-in-law Guy V. Henry Jr., who was an instructor of horsemanship at the Cavalry School and later captain of the U.S. equestrian team at the 1912 Olympics. Like Lieutenant Howze's father, he too served as commandant of cadets. (His father, Guy V. Henry Sr., is remembered for his comment when an Indian bullet took out one eye and several teeth in a fight along the Rosebud Creek as Custer headed for the Little Big Horn, the earlier quoted "It is nothing. For

The 26th United States Cavalry Regiment, Philippine Scouts, launched the last horsed charge of American history.

this are we soldiers.") Lieutenant Howze enjoyed his time with the 26th at Fort Stotsenberg, in the Philippines. Breaking remounts was "a great job, filled with action and all kinds of incidents, some of them delightfully funny," and he was captain of the regiment's polo team. He got $173 a month as a first lieutenant, plus $40 in allowances, which enabled him to have a cook, a houseboy, a washerwoman, and an orderly to care for his horses. Before Pearl Harbor he was ordered to Fort Riley and duty with a mechanized cavalry outfit that fought in North Africa and Italy. For his work after the war he is remembered as Father of the Helicopters. He always likened the machines to cavalry mounts. An airplane, he wrote, is stable and wants to stay upright and fly properly, but a helicopter can go bottom up "and is much like a fractious horse—it does silly things, like shying at blowing newspapers." All airborne troops, he felt, resembled horsed cavalry, retaining the spirit of mobility and the traditions, down to keeping boots at a high shine. "So, many years ago, did the old horse soldiers." In the old days, he wrote, a commander had a horse delivered to the front door of his quarters every workday morning, and as head of America's helicopter force, he had one of his whirlybirds similarly landed for him. The four officers who rode for the 26th's polo team ended with twelve stars among them, four of them his, and when General Howze came to write his autobiography—by then the old First Cav was the Airmobile—he gave it the nostalgic title A Cavalryman's Story.

Another officer of Island days, what soldiers and civil officials from the time of the Spanish-American War to Pearl Harbor called the Days of the Empire, was Jonathan Mayhew Wainwright IV. No one was ever more the cavalryman. His father had been one, killed in action in 1902 during the Philippine Insurrection, when the boy was fifteen. Ever after, and in fact even before, he wanted to be a horse officer. Family members called him Mayhew, while to everybody else all his life he was Skinny. (It is said that the only person to address him as Jonathan was Douglas MacArthur.) At West Point he was, along with George Patton, a member of the group of cadets known as "the cavalry fanatics." But while Georgie eventually went to the tanks, Skinny stayed with the horses, rising to the command of the First Cav. To him, wrote his niece-biographer, cavalry was "a veritable religion, because the U.S. Cavalry was Skinny's *life*, to which he was born and bred, and to which he was whole heartedly devoted to the end of his days." Wainwright could remark of a woman that she had "good-looking hocks" or that it was evident that she was "foaling."

Pre–World War II military life in the tropics was notable for its élan and elegance, with Manila's Army-Navy Club possessing a gracious formality of crystal chandeliers, cut-glass punch bowls, silver goblets, silk brocade curtains, and parquet floors, with officers in white with gold braid and their ladies in light frocks. General Wainwright always arrived at balls in a horse-drawn carriage, not an auto. His wife said it was silly, but he told her that the horse had been on earth before motorcars. He had three, his favorite being Joseph Conrad, a black thoroughbred jumper stallion he called Little Joe or Little Boy. Together they had won many ribbons. When in 1941 the Japanese came ashore in force in Northern Luzon, Wainwright took Joseph Conrad with him as he went to meet them, wearing twill breeches flaring over the tops of his English handmade cavalry boots, an old-style campaign hat on his head with its strap secured under his lower lip and an old Colt revolver on his hip. The field commander of some twenty-two thousand American and Filipino troops, his position was second only to that of MacArthur, the overall commander of the entire Pacific area. He faced some hundred thousand Japanese soldiers supported by naval units in the Lingayen Gulf unleashing on-shore bombardments. The enemy had overwhelming air superiority, for most of the American Air Corps planes in the Islands had been destroyed on the ground by Japanese bombers.

That he might have to deal with such a situation did not come as a surprise to Wainwright save for the loss of the planes, which could not have been anticipated during the twenty years America's military spent considering what might occur if Tokyo decided on a war. What was called the Orange Plan called for a showing on the landing beaches followed by a slow withdrawal south along the Bataan Peninsula and a holing-down there and in the giant island fortress of Corregidor. Then the Fleet would come with reinforcements and the ability to interdict Japanese waterborne supply lines, and so the invaders would starve on the vine and be done with.

But on the morning of December 7, 1941, half of America's ships in the Pacific sank under the waters of Pearl Harbor or sat burning at their anchorages. There would be no aid from anyone for the troops in the Philippines, in Northern Luzon and to the south. They were on their own. But it is not the part of a combat commander to dwell on unfortunate events of the past and perhaps the future, and Wainwright, in calmest fashion, oversaw in his area of operations a slow fighting retreat. He was always up front with his men, often boosting a wounded soldier onto Joseph Conrad to lead the horse on foot to where medical aid could be obtained. His tough American infantrymen, the Regulars, the Regs, stuck things out to give as good as they got as best they could. The same could not be said for the Filipinos comprising the bulk of his force. Neither well trained nor well equipped, they ran from the enemy.

Save for one outfit, the 26th Cavalry, Philippine Scouts. They endured air attacks and automatic weapons fire while ducking in and out in dispersed and spread-out order to minimize casualties. They suddenly showed themselves to advancing Japanese units and then galloped off, leaving the enemy to deploy from march into attack formation, the delay permitting endangered Americans to get away. "Here was true cavalry delaying action, fit to make a man's heart sing," Skinny Wainwright wrote later. Whenever the situation permitted, an aide remembered, he sat down with the 26th's commander, Colonel Clinton Pierce, also a longtime cavalryman, to "swap yarns about faraway places and times and the fine horses they used to ride." Once he ran into an officer who had served under him at Fort Myer. Japanese batteries were raining down shells, but the general sat to offer chitchat about jumpers he and the other man had trained, including Joseph Conrad, who stood by. When Wainwright got up to stretch his legs, enemy fire or not, "You'd have thought he was walking to the club for a Scotch."

On one occasion, in accordance with still-functioning army bureaucratic procedure, he took a report on medical matters, which were awful in their detailing of wounds, diseases, exhaustion. "That's the finest damn record I've ever seen," he said. His staff was flabbergasted. The general explained that the report indicated that in the entire corps only one case of venereal disease was noted for a month. "I wonder how that joker found himself a woman out here in the jungle. I bet you he was a cavalryman."

The Japanese came on. Wainwright's men had no food as they backed up to make for a measured retreat down the Bataan Peninsula. They ate what they could—monkeys, lizards, snakes, water buffalo, and iguanas, roots and leaves. Ammunition ran low. Once on Bataan, they felt, they would find some respite from Japanese pressure, for the peninsula's slimness would preclude massive full-front and flanking assaults. And Corregidor, "the Rock," had vast supplies of all types. They began filtering onto Bataan. Behind them came the thrusting enemy.

There was a coastal village on the Culo River of the highest strategic importance, Morong. If the Japanese took it, a floodgate for their troops would be opened. On January 16, 1942, Wainwright personally ordered Lieutenant Edwin P. Ramsey of the 26th Cavalry to hold Morong. Ramsey was up on Bryn Awryn, a chestnut gelding with a small white blaze on his forehead. Five straight days of uninterrupted fighting had cost the 26th more than a quarter of its officers and men and half its horses. Ramsey had three platoons. He entered Morong to see Japanese infantry by the hundreds coming across the Culo. It came to him that only the element of surprise could scatter the enemy. "A charge would be our only hope to break up the body of Japanese troops and to survive against their superior numbers.

"I brought up my arm and yelled to my men to charge. Bent nearly prone across the horses' necks, we flung ourselves at the Japanese advance, pistols firing full into their startled faces. A few returned our fire, but most fled in confusion, some wading back into the river, others running madly for the swamps. To them we must have seemed a vision from another century, wild-eyed horses pounding headlong; cheering, whooping men firing from the saddles."

The Japanese paused, and the American and Filipino forces got onto Bataan. Absent "this gallant little band of horsemen," Wainwright wrote, "I doubt if I could have successfully made that withdrawal." It was the last charge of the United States Cavalry.

Within a few weeks, the horses were gone. They could not be deployed in Bataan's almost impenetrable jungle, and so were taken down to be corralled near the Rock. But fodder ran out. A quartermaster officer went to Wainwright to say they were beginning to show signs of malnutrition. The general said, "Captain, you will begin killing the horses at once. Joseph Conrad is the horse you will kill first." His eyes filled up with tears. Soldiers ate slivers of noble flesh mixed with rice. In a short time, General Wainwright, left in overall Islands command in place of MacArthur, who was ordered to Australia by President Roosevelt, gave up a hopeless fight. After years in prisoner-of-war camps, he stood with MacArthur on the deck of the battleship *Missouri* when the Japanese turn for surrender came, and with it the end of World War's. He died in 1953, and was given a state funeral at Arlington, the caisson bearing his body drawn by six horses, three with soldiers aboard who held reins only in white-gloved left hand, the right kept at the side. Behind followed a jet-black horse, saddle and trappings of black and with boots reversed in the stirrups and sabre hanging, a soldier leading. Within a couple of years the last horses of the army were gone, save for twenty used for other funerals at Arlington.

In the early days of the war in Afghanistan, an odd event was seen on television news programs. Viewers were briefly shown American Special Forces soldiers riding horses they must have obtained locally up into the hills. No illuminating commentary was offered. It is hard to believe the men fought from their saddles. Perhaps they got off to do so in the manner of what used to be called mounted infantry. They were onscreen for but a few seconds, and then vanished before the commercial.

Bibliography

Books

Alberts, Don Edward. "General Wesley Merritt." PhD diss., University of New Mexico, 1975.

Ashley, Maurice. *The Greatness of Oliver Cromwell*. New York: Macmillan, 1958.

Baker, Alan. *The Knight*. Hoboken, N.J.: John Wiley and Sons, 2003.

Beamish, North Ludlow. *On the Uses and Application of Cavalry in War*. London: T. & W. Boone, 1855.

Belloc, Hilaire. *Cromwell*. Philadelphia: J. B. Lippincott, 1934.

Bennett, Matthew, et al. *Fighting Techniques of the Medieval World*. New York: St. Martin's Press, 2005.

Black, Robert W. *Cavalry Raids of the Civil War*. Mechanicsburg, Pa.: Stackpole Books, 2004.

Blackford, W. W. *War Years with Jeb Stuart*. New York: Charles Scribner's Sons, 1945.

Borcke, Heros von. *Memoirs of the Confederate War for Independence*. New York: Peter Smith, 1938.

Bourke, John G. *Mackenzie's Last Fight with the Cheyennes*. New York: Argonaut Press, 1966.

———. *On the Border with Crook*. New York: Charles Scribner's Sons, 1891.

Boyd, Mrs. Orsemus Bronson. *Cavalry Life in Tent and Field*. Lincoln: University of Nebraska Press, 1982.

Boyd, Thomas. *Light-Horse Harry Lee*. New York: Charles Scribner's Sons, 1931.

Brereton, J. M. *The Horse in War*. New York: Arco Publishing Company, 1976.

Buchan, John. *Oliver Cromwell*. Boston: Houghton Mifflin, 1934.

Bundy, Carol. *The Nature of Sacrifice*. New York: Farrar, Straus and Giroux, 2005.

Carr, Captain Camillus. *A Cavalryman in Indian Country*. Ashland, Ore.: Lewis Osborne, 1974.

Carter, Captain R. G. *On the Border with Mackenzie*. New York: Antiquarian Press, 1961.

Chamberlin, J. Edward. *Horse*. New York: Blue Bridge, 2006.

Chandler, David, ed. *The Dictionary of Battles*. New York: Henry Holt, 1987.

Churchill, Winston S. *A Roving Commission*. New York: Charles Scribner's Sons, 1930.

Connell, Evan S. *Son of the Morning Star*. New York: Harper & Row, 1984.

Cooke, John Esten. *The Wearing of the Gray*. Bloomington: Indiana University Press, 1959.

Cotterel, A. *The Chariot*. Woodstock and New York: The Overlook Press, 2005.

Cottrell, Sue. *Hoofbeats North and South*. New York: Exposition Press, 1975.

Cox, Jacob D. *The March to the Sea*. New York: Charles Scribner's Sons, 1882.

Craig, Captain Malin. *The Cavalry on the Offensive*. Fort Riley, Kans.: U.S. Infantry and Cavalry School, 1904–05.

Cruso, John. *Militarie Instructions for the Cavall'rie, 1632*. New York: Roundwood Press facsimile, 1975.

Custer, Elizabeth B. *Following the Guidon*. Norman: University of Oklahoma Press, 1966.

Dary, David A. *Comanche*. Lawrence: University of Kansas Press, 1976.

Davis, Burke. *Jeb Stuart*. New York: Rinehart, 1957.

Denison, Col. G. T. *A History of Cavalry from the Earliest Times*. London: Macmillan, 1913.

Devereux, Frederick L. *The Cavalry Manual of Horse Management*. Cranbury, N.J.: A. S. Barnes, 1979.

Dodge, Theodore Ayrault. *Gustavus Adolfphus*. Boston: Houghton Mifflin, 1896.

Downey, Fairfax. *Indian-Fighting Army*. New York: Charles Scribner's Sons, 1941.

Duffy, Christopher. *The Army of Frederick the Great*. New York: Hippocrene Books, 1974.

———. *The Military Life of Frederick the Great*. New York: Atheneum, 1986.

Duncan, Bingham, ed. *Letters of General J. E. B. Stuart to His Wife*. Atlanta: Emory University, 1943.

Dupuy, Trevor N. *The Evolution of Weapons and Warfare*. Indianapolis and New York: Bobbs-Merrill, 1980.

Eckert, Edward K., and Nicholas J. Amato, eds. *Ten Years in the Saddle: The Menoir of William Woods Averell*. San Rafael, Calif.: Presidio Press, 1978

Eggleston, George Cary. *A Rebel's Recollections*. Bloomington: University of Indiana Press, 1959.

Emerson, Edward W. *The Life and Letters of Charles Russell Lowell*. Boston: Houghton Mifflin, 1907.

Ergang, Robert. *Potsdam Führer*. New York: Columbia University Press, 1941.

Eschenbach, Wolfram Von. *Parzival*. Translated by Helen Mustard and Charles Passage. New York: Vintage Books, 1961.

Evans, David. *Sherman's Horsemen*. Bloomington: Indiana University Press, 1996.

Falls, Cyril. *Great Military Battles*. London: Hamlyn Publishing, 1969.

Forsyth, George A. *Thrilling Days in Army Life*. New York: Harper & Brothers, 1900.

Fraser, Antonia. *Cromwell*. New York: Alfred A. Knopf, 1973.

Gardner, Brian. *Allenby of Arabia*. New York: Coward-McCann, 1965.

Gerson, Noel B. *Light-Horse Harry*. Garden City, N.Y.: Doubleday, 1966.

Gibson, John M. *Those 163 Days*. New York: Coward-McCann, 1961.

Gilbert, Major Vivian. *The Romance of the Last Crusade*. New York: William B. Feakins, 1923.

Goldsworthy, Adrian. *The Complete Roman Army*. London: Thames & Hudson, 2003.

Goodenough, Simon. *Tactical Genius in Battle*. London: Phaidon Press, 1979.

Grant, R. G. *Battle*. New York: DK Publishing, 2005.

Greiner, H. C. *General Phil Sheridan As I Knew Him*. Chicago: J. S. Hyland, 1908.

Guest, Captain Freddie. *Indian Cavalryman*. London: Jarrolds, 1959.

Hatch, Thom. *Clashes of Cavalry*. Mechanicsburg, Pa.: Stackpole Books, 2001.

Herzog, Chaim, and Mordechai Gichon. *Battles of the Bible*. London: Greenhill, 1997.

Herr, Major General John K., and Edward S. Wallace. *The Story of the U.S. Cavalry*. Boston: Little, Brown, 1953.

Hollister, C. Warren. *Medieval Europe*. New York: Alfred A. Knopf, 1982.

Howard, M. *War in European History*. New York: Oxford University Press, 1976.

Howze, Hamilton H. *A Cavalryman's Story*. Washington, D.C.: Smithsonian Institution Press, 1996.

Ingelfingen, Prince Kraft zu Hohenlohe. *Letters on Cavalry*. Leavenworth: George A. Spooner, 1892.

Johnson, James Ralph, and Alfred Hoyt Bill. *Horsemen Blue and Gray*. New York: Oxford University Press, 1960.

Jones, Virgil Carrington. *Eight Hours before Richmond*. New York: Henry Holt, 1957.

Kaeuper, Richard W. *Chivalry and Violence in Medieval Europe*. London: Oxford University Press, 1999.

Keegan, John. *A History of Warfare*. London: Hutchinson, 1993.

Keen, Maurice. *Chivalry*. New Haven: Yale University Press, 1984.

Keim, D. B. Randolph. *Sheridan's Troopers on the Borders*. Philadelphia: David McKay, 1985.

Kidd, James H. *Personal Recollections of a Cavalryman*. Ionia, Mich.: Sentinel Press, 1908.

Kirshner, Ralph. *The Class of 1861*. Carbondale: Southern Illinois University Press, 1999.

Laffin, John. *Tommy Atkins*. London: Cassell, 1966.

Lane, Lydia Spencer. *I Married a Soldier*. Philadelphia: J. B. Lippincott, 1892.

Lawley, Robert Neville. *General Seydlitz*. London: W. Clowes & Sons, 1852.

Lewis, Thomas A. *The Guns of Cedar Creek*. New York: Harper & Row, 1988.

Littauer, Vladimir S. *Russian Hussar*. London: J. A. Allen, 1965.

Longacre, Edward G. *The Cavalry at Gettysburg*. Lincoln: University of Nebraska Press, 1986.

Luce, Edward Smith. *Keogh, Comanche, and Custer*. St. Louis: John S. Swift, 1939.

Martin, Samuel J. *Kill Cavalry*. Mechanicsburg, Pa.: Stackpole Books, 2000.

McClellan, H. B. *The Life and Campaigns of Major General J. E. B. Stuart*. Bloomington: Indiana University Press, 1958.

Mears, Betty Wainwright. Unpublished manuscript on Jonathan Wainwright, Special Collections, United States Military Academy at West Point.

Moore, James. *Kilpatrick and Our Cavalry*. New York: W. J. Widdleton, 1865.

Morris, Roy Jr. *Sheridan: The Life and Wars of General Phil Sheridan*. New York: Crown, 1992.

Nelson, Walter Henry. *The Soldier Kings*. New York. G. P. Putnam's Sons, 1970.

Newhall, Lt. Col. Frederick. *With Sheridan in the Final Campaign against Lee*. Baton Rouge: Louisiana State University Press, 2002.

Nolan, Captain L. E. *Cavalry: Its History and Tactics*. London: Bosworth, 1854.

Osborn, William M. *The Wild Frontier*. New York: Random House, 2001.

Parker, James. *The Old Army*. Philadelphia: Dorrance, 1929.

Patton, George S. Jr. *Saber Exercise*. Washington: Government Printing Office, 1914.

Pierce, Michael D. *The Most Promising Young Officer*. Norman: University of Oklahoma Press, 1993.

Porter, Lieutenant Colonel David L. *Colonel Ranald S. Mackenzie and the Remolino Raid*. Carlisle Barracks, Pa.: U.S. Army War College.

Pratt, Fletcher. *Eleven Generals*. New York: William Sloane, 1949.

Rickey, Don Jr. *Forty Miles a Day on Beans and Hay*. Norman: University of Oklahoma Press, 1983.

Robinson, Charles M. III. *Bad Hand*. Austin, TX: State House Press, 1993.

Roemer, J. *Cavalry, Its History, Management, and Uses in War*. New York: D. Van Nostrand, 1863.

Royster, Charles. *Light-Horse Harry Lee*. New York: Alfred A. Knopf, 1981.

Schultz, Duane. *Hero of Bataan*. New York: St. Martin's Press, 1981.

Scott, William Forse. *The Story of a Cavalry Regiment*. New York: G. P. Putnam's Sons, 1893.

Sergent, Mary Elizabeth. *They Lie Forgotten*. Middleton, N.Y.: Prior King Press, 1986.

Smith, Sherry L. *Sagebrush Soldier*. Norman: University of Oklahoma Press, 1989.

Stubbs, Mary Lee, and Stanley Russell Connor Stubbs. *Armor-Cavalry*. Washington, D.C.: Office of the Chief of Military History, 1969.

Summerhayes, Martha. *Vanished Arizona*. Philadelphia: J. B. Lippincott, 1908.

Thomas, Emory M. *Bold Dragoon*. Mechanicsburg, Pa.: Stackpole Books, 1993.

Thomason, John W. Jr. *Jeb Stuart*. New York: Charles Scribner's Sons, 1930.

Truscott, Lucian K. *The Twilight of the U. S. Cavalry*. Lawrence: University Press of Kansas, 1989.

Vale, Malcolm. *War and Chivalry*. Athens: University of Georgia Press, 1981.

Vogel, Victor. *Soldiers of the Old Army*. College Station: Texas A&M University Press, 1990.

Wavell, General Sir Archibald. *Allenby, a Study in Greatness*. New York: Oxford University Press, 1941.

Wheeler-Nicholson, Major Malcolm. *Modern Cavalry*. New York: Macmillan, 1922.

Wittenberg, Eric J. *Little Phil*. Washington, D.C.: Potomac Books, 2003.

Wood, General Sir Evelyn. *Achievements of Cavalry*. London: George Bell & Sons, 1897.

Woodham-Smith, Cecil. *The Reason Why*. New York: McGraw-Hill, 1954.

Xenophon. *Minor Works*. Translated by Rev. J. S. Watson. London: Bell and Daldy, 1869.

Periodicals and Papers

American Heritage, Southwestern Historical Quarterly, Civil War Times, The Century Magazine, Harper's New Monthly, The Confederate Veteran, The Journal of the United States Cavalry Association, North American Review, Southern Historical Society Papers, New Mexico Historical Review, Army and Navy Life, Army, American Historical Review, The Pointer, Papers of the Military History Society of Massachusetts.

Index